DATE DUE			

WEST CAMPUS

ADVANCE PRAISE FOR *THE SECULAR CONSCIENCE*

"With intellectual vigor and moral confidence, Austin Dacey demonstrates the self-defeating fallacies of efforts to privatize individual conscience and belief. Secularists and nontheists should heed his call to join public debates about fundamental ethical values, instead of questioning the impulse to conduct them."

—Wendy Kaminer, lawyer and author of *Free for All*

"*The Secular Conscience* breathes new life into an old topic. Dacey thinks outside the box. His argument for allowing believers back into the 'public square'—and then subjecting them to a forceful critique—is fresh and convincing, as is his surprising critique of the reasoning in *Roe v. Wade*. And his chapters on secular ethics are superb."

—Peter Singer, Ira W. DeCamp Professor of Bioethics, Princeton University

"There is much here for a religious believer to applaud. Dacey's insistence on conscience as a corrigible moral guide, on a public square informed by the vigorous discursive pursuit of first principles, and on their defense in reason are extremely positive. At a certain point a believer must part company, but for much of the way we can walk and work together."

—Alan Mittleman, director of the Louis Finkelstein Institute for Religious and Social Studies, Jewish Theological Seminary

The
Secular
Conscience

The
Secular
Conscience

Why Belief Belongs in Public Life

Austin
Dacey

Prometheus Books

59 John Glenn Drive
Amherst, New York 14228–2119

Published 2008 by Prometheus Books

Inquiries should be addressed to
Prometheus Books
59 John Glenn Drive
Amherst, New York 14228–2119
VOICE: 716–691–0133, ext. 210
FAX: 716–691–0137
WWW.PROMETHEUSBOOKS.COM

12 11 10 09 08   5 4 3 2 1

Library of Congress Cataloging-in-Publication Data

Dacey, Austin, 1972–
    The secular conscience : why belief belongs in public life / by Austin Dacey.
      p. cm.
    Includes bibliographical references and index.
    ISBN 978–1–59102–604–4
    1. Secularism. 2. Religion and ethics. 3. Religion and politics. I. Title.
BL2747.8.D23 2008
211'.6—dc22

2007051797

Printed in the United States of America on acid-free paper

For my mother, the creator of my conscience.

Contents

Introduction

INCANTATION

Human reason is beautiful and invincible.
No bars, no barbed wire, no pulping of books,
No sentence of banishment can prevail against it.
It establishes the universal ideas in language,
And guides our hand so we write Truth and Justice
With capital letters, lie and oppression with small.
It puts what should be above things as they are,
It is an enemy of despair and a friend of hope.
It does not know Jew from Greek or slave from master,
Giving us the estate of the world to manage.
It saves austere and transparent phrases
From the filthy discord of tortured words.
It says that everything is new under the sun,
Opens the congealed fist of the past.
Beautiful and very young are Philo-Sophia
And poetry, her ally in the service of the good.
As late as yesterday Nature celebrated their birth,
The news was brought to the mountains by a unicorn and an echo,
Their friendship will be glorious, their time has no limit,
Their enemies have delivered themselves to destruction.
　　　　—Czeslaw Milosz, translated by Robert Pinsky and the author

On the streets of London, the placards scream, "FREE SPEECH, GO TO HELL," an unintentional masterpiece of British irony. In Beirut, twenty thousand amass at the Danish embassy with signs reading, "Damn your beliefs and your liberty." In Damascus, the embassy is burned. In Pakistan, the national parliament unanimously passes a resolution of condemnation, and President Pervez Musharraf comments, "I have been hurt, grieved and I am angry." In the Palestinian Territories, the Hamas party, fresh from its victory in parliamentary elections, organizes a rally of fifty thousand people. Danish goods are burnt, and the crowd chants: "Let the hands that drew be severed!" In Iran, President Mahmoud Ahmadinejad proposes a Holocaust cartoon contest, while pastry shops rename Danish pastries "Roses of the Prophet Muhammad."[1]

Several months earlier, the small Danish newspaper *Jyllands-Posten* had published twelve cartoons depicting the Prophet Muhammad in hopes of raising questions about the limits of free expression in Denmark. As the editor Carsten Juste later told *Der Spiegel*, "We wanted to show how deeply entrenched self-censorship has already become."[2] After the images were distributed around the world (along with some pornographic additions by a group of Danish imams intent on fomenting a reaction), *Jyllands-Posten* gets their answer.

The experiment succeeds beyond all expectations, not for its violent outcome but in demonstrating the refusal on all sides to engage in critical debate about Islam. The Danish prime minister, Anders Fogh Rasmussen, apologizes on behalf of the nation on Arabic satellite television; British foreign secretary Jack Straw calls the publications "insensitive," "disrespectful," and "wrong." The US State Department issues a statement saying, "Anti-Muslim images are as unacceptable as anti-Semitic images, as anti-Christian images, or any other religious belief."[3] Some newspapers in Germany, Italy, France, Spain, Belgium, and the Netherlands reprint selected images as a defense of free expression, and *Die Welt* asserts a "right to blaspheme" as crucial to the European cultural heritage.[4] Yet astonishingly, British and America media refuse to exercise this right. CNN, NBC, the *New York Times*, *Washington Post*, *Wall Street Journal*, and all but a handful of major daily newspapers in the United States somehow see fit to run stories on the controversy without running what the controversy is about—the cartoons themselves. The managing editor of the *Chicago Tribune* expresses his magical belief that "we can communicate to our readers what this is about without running it."[5] When the secular humanist journal *Free Inquiry* becomes the first American magazine of note to reprint the images, leading booksellers refuse to carry the issue.[6] In effect, Western governments and media concur with the chilling comment from the Vatican: "Freedom of thought or expression . . . cannot imply a right to offend the religious sentiments of believers."[7]

Freedom of thought means nothing unless it implies the right to blaspheme, for blasphemy is a victimless crime. Why are so many Western liberals unwilling to say so? How is it that they are unable to distinguish between religious traditions that should be revered or tolerated and those—like capital punishment for apostasy and blasphemy—that must be denounced and reformed? Faced with the greatest threat to its core values since Stalin, the open society had turned the other cheek.

On his way to becoming Pope Benedict XVI, Cardinal Joseph Ratzinger argued that the West has lost its way and is suffering from dangerous moral disorientation:

> The small boat of thought of many Christians has often been tossed about by these waves—thrown from one extreme to the other: from Marxism to liberalism, even to libertinism; from collectivism to radical individualism; from atheism to a vague religious mysticism; from agnosticism to syncretism, and so forth. . . . Having a clear faith, based on the Creed of the Church, is often labeled today as a fundamentalism. Whereas, relativism, which is letting oneself be tossed and "swept along by every wind of teaching," looks like the only attitude (acceptable) to today's standards. We are moving towards a dictatorship of relativism which does not recognize anything as for certain and which has as its highest goal one's own ego and one's own desires.[8]

What, in the pope's view, has precipitated this civilizational crisis? Secularism: "Secularism and de-Christianization continue to advance. The influence of Catholic ethics and morals is in constant decline. Many people abandon the Church or, if they remain, they accept only a part of Catholic teaching. . . . Many of the ideas put forward by modern society have led nowhere, and many young people have ended up mired in alcohol and drugs or in the clutches of extremist groups."[9]

The secularism of the West has loosed civilization from its moral moorings, leaving us adrift in a universe without absolutes where nothing really matters except self-gratification. Now we are caught between secular amorality and fundamentalism; only a return to the Christian vision of the good society can deliver us.

Some of Europe's leading intellectuals agree. Jürgen Habermas, the reigning philosophical champion of the European establishment, has conceded that "Christianity, and nothing else, is the ultimate foundation of liberty, conscience, human rights, and democracy . . ."[10] Marcello Pera, an atheist philosopher and former president of the Italian Senate, agreed with then-cardinal Ratzinger in a coauthored book that only a return to Christian tradition could save Western civilization from the twin perils of multiculturalist relativism and ascendant Islamic illiberalism.

Secular liberals may recoil from Dr. Ratzinger's prescription but find it hard to shake the lingering feeling that there is something to his diagnosis. Something disquieting has been happening to the Western mind over the last half century. One philosophy professor reports that while none of his students are Holocaust deniers, a disturbingly rising number are worse: "They acknowledge the fact, even deplore it, but cannot bring themselves to condemn it morally. 'Of course I dislike the Nazis,' one student comments, 'but who is to say they are morally wrong.' They make similar observations about apartheid, slavery, and ethnic cleansing." For these young people, to pass judgment, "they fear, is to be moral 'absolutist,' and having been taught that there are no absolutes, they now see any [judgment] as arbitrary, intolerant, and authoritarian."[11] Cultural critics trace creeping moral relativism to the permissive, antiauthoritarian ideology of the 1960s. Observers across the political spectrum agree that the relativistic shift has been correlated with lamentable social trends, for example, a dramatic rise in crime and social dysfunction in the United States and the United Kingdom in the decades following the 1960s. But the ideology of the '60s can be seen as an outgrowth of the more fundamental liberal notions of autonomy, freedom of choice, and freedom of conscience. Britain's chief rabbi, Jonathan Sacks, describes the liberal aversion to all "external authority over the one sovereign territory that is truly our own: our choices." The liberal ideal, on this view, is an "autonomous being, a person who accepts no other authority than the self. By the 1960s this was beginning to gain hold as an educational orthodoxy. The task of education is not to hand on tradition but to enhance the consciousness of choice."[12]

In the United States, *secular* and *liberal* have become dirty words. The irreligiousness of the Democrats, claim the pundits, cost them the 2004 presidential election. Secular government based on reason and fact, say many elected officials, is no longer adequate to provide for citizens; we need "faith-based" services. Best sellers allege that liberalism is a dogmatic faith, a critique popularized by evangelical leaders in the 1980s who began arguing that secular humanism is the state-sponsored religion of America's public schools (its tenets include atheism, Darwinism, sex education, and global socialism).

When a rare few secularists push back against religious belief in print, they are branded—often by fellow seculars and liberal religionists—"dogmatic," "evangelical," "militant," and "fundamentalist" atheists.[13] Their scandalous premise is that religion is an urgent topic of conversation and therefore subject to the intellectual and moral standards of all serious conversation. There are dogmatists of every stripe, but God knows what an atheist fundamentalist would look like. If the mantra of religious fundamentalism is "I'm right, you're wrong, go to hell," the atheist creedo seems to be "I'm right, you're wrong, let's talk about it some more."

Secular liberalism is not a religion. It is an intellectual and political movement that puts the freedom of the individual first, before God or government. Here a secularist is not necessarily an atheist, but someone who seeks sources of meaning, morality, and community outside of organized religion. A liberal is not the opposite of a conservative, but anyone who asserts the priority of individual liberty. Secular liberalism cannot be confined to a character in the Punch and Judy show of contemporary American two-party politics. It has a proud and rich tradition stretching back to the founding of the country, to the European Enlightenment, and far beyond. Yet most secular liberals today seem to be incapable of standing up for their values in public debate.

In the summer of 2003, the Vatican finally speaks out against violence against children. It is not referring to the Church's child sexual abuse scandal then raging but instead to gay adoption. In a document titled *Considerations regarding Proposals to Give Legal Recognition to Unions between Homosexual Persons*, the Congregation for the Doctrine of the Faith asserts, "Those who would move from tolerance to the legitimization of specific rights for cohabiting homosexual persons need to be reminded that approval or legalization of evil is something far different from the toleration of evil."[14] Permitting children to be adopted by gay couples, the congregation continues, "would actually mean doing violence to these children, in the sense that their condition of dependency would be used to place them in an environment that is not conducive to their full human development." The language got the attention of liberals around the world. But precious few could bring themselves to publicly disagree with Rome's claim that same-sex coupling is "evil." Most objected along the same lines as editors of the *Boston Globe*, who opined, "The greatness of America is its pluralism, and neither president nor pope can impose his religious beliefs on the public realm."[15] Apparently, there is no mistake in thinking that same-sex couples who adopt are perpetrating violence against children; the mistake lies in mentioning it in public. As the influential American philosopher Richard Rorty put it, "Religion is unobjectionable as long as it is privatized."[16]

Faith-based notions of sexuality are a significant vector of sexually transmitted disease and misery. One would expect secular liberals to make this a major political cause. A *New York Times* columnist writes of the "dismal consequences of this increasing religious influence," namely, "policies that are likely to lead to more people dying of AIDS at home and abroad, not to mention more pregnancies and abortions."[17] Then he goes on to chastise fellow secularists: "Liberal critiques sometimes seem not just filled with outrage at evangelical-backed policies, which is fair, but also to have a sneering tone about conservative Christianity itself. Such mockery of religious faith is inexcusable." Secular liberals are being asked to perform an act of cognitive contortionism, to object to the "consequences" of conservative religion without objecting to the moral precepts that cause them. What could be more appropriate than to evaluate a system of beliefs on the basis of its consequences for individual and social behavior? If causing more people to die pointlessly is not an objection to a system of beliefs, what would be?

Everywhere secular values are under assault, and almost nowhere are they being defended. On questions of religion, ethics, and values, secular liberals are strangely silent. At the moment their perspective is most needed, they have lost their moral identity, self-confidence, and voice in public affairs.

Politics abhors a vacuum. And so the space in public discourse left unoccupied by secular liberals has been filled by religious conservatives, along with a new arrival: the Religious Left. Religious lefties, like their counterparts on the Right, quote the Bible to buttress their policy proposals, but they differ on their favorite verses. Whereas Pat Robertson likes Leviticus, Jim Wallis, an evangelical antipoverty activist, likes Micah ("Do justice, love kindness, and walk humbly with your God"). Wallis distinguishes between two uses of religion in American public life: "The first way—God on our side—leads inevitably to triumphalism, self-righteousness, bad theology, and often, dangerous foreign policy. The second way—asking if we are on God's side—leads to much healthier things, namely, penitence and even repentance, humility, reflection, and even accountability."[18] In practice, Wallis seems every bit as confident as Robertson that God is on his side (Wallis's best-selling book laying out his politics is called *God's Politics*); it's just that they serve different gods. Wallis contends that what American politics needs is not less religion but more of the right kind of religion; namely, a progressive or "prophetic" Christianity that concentrates on social justice, peacemaking, and the poor.

Meanwhile, Rabbi Michael Lerner, editor of the progressive Jewish magazine *Tikkun*, has put forward "The Left Hand of God" as an alternative to The Right. The Left Hand of God is about "kindness, generosity, nonviolence, humility, inner and outer peace, love, and wonder at the grandeur of creation"; The Right Hand of God represents "the hand of power and domination."[19] He says that the Democratic Party must choose between serving one or the other, and he proposes a "network of Spiritual Progressives to take Washington and change the world."[20] The Religious Left has every right to exist, but what ever happened to the Secular Left? Where did secular liberalism go wrong?

It has been undone by its own ideas. The first idea is that matters of conscience—religion, ethics, and values—are private matters. The privatizing of conscience started with two important principles: religion should be separated from the state and people should not be forced to believe one way or the other. But it went further to say that belief has no place in the public sphere. Conscience belongs in homes and houses of worship, not in the marketplace. By making conscience private, secular liberals had hoped to prevent believers from introducing sectarian beliefs into politics. But of course they couldn't, since freedom of belief means believers are free to speak their minds in public.

Instead, secularism imposed a gag order on itself. Because "private" is equated with "personal" and "subjective," questions of conscience were placed out of bounds of serious critical evaluation. Subjective phenomena—like the thrill of skydiving or the taste for spicy food—are determined by the attitudes and thoughts of the subject experiencing them. How can I evaluate your experiences? It seems I must simply accept them for what they are. If conscience is beyond criticism, however, liberals cannot subject religion to due public scrutiny when it encroaches on society. The result: in public discourse it is acceptable to say that addicts should give up heroin for Jesus, but not to ask obvious policy questions such as whether faith-based social programs are actually proven more effective than secular alternatives (it turns out there's no good empirical evidence that they are). Worse still, since secularists want belief to be left at home and not "imposed" on others, they are unable to unabashedly defend their own positive moral vision in politics. No wonder they are accused of having lost their moral moorings.

Call this liberal confusion the Privacy Fallacy. The Privacy Fallacy consists in assuming that because matters of conscience are private in the sense of nongovernmental, they are private in the sense of personal preference. A related confusion comes from the idea of freedom of conscience. This confusion begins in the core liberal principle that conscience must be left free from coercion. The mistake lies in thinking that because conscience is free from coercion, it must be free from criticism, reason, truth, or independent, objective standards of right and wrong. The indispensable principle of freedom of belief has mutated into an unthinking assumption that matters of belief are immune to critical public inquiry and shared evaluative norms. This is the Liberty Fallacy.

Fortunately, there is another way to conceive of secular liberalism, and it comes from understanding what can be called the *openness of conscience*. The basic idea of the open conscience (open as in *the open society*) can be illustrated by the example of the press. In a free society, the press is to be protected from autocratic control by the state and other power-wielding institutions. We want wherever possible to allow it to pursue its own course autonomously. But we don't say that therefore it is "private." The press is protected, left free and open, not so that it may be private but so that it may perform a vital function in the public sphere. In the same way, conscience is protected in order that it may pursue—in dialogue with others—its vital questions of meaning, identity, value, and truth.

The press may say what it wants, but we don't say that therefore it is subjective or arbitrary. The press is free, but not a free-for-all. It is liberated so that it may be constrained, freed to abide by the standards that define its distinctive nature. These are the standards of journalistic objectivity, transparency, truth, and service to the public interest. In the same way, conscience is free so that it may respond only to the standards that define its nature, the standards of reason, impartiality, and concern for others. Conscience is open to the public. The press and conscience are open in another way, in that their answers are open-ended. They perform their unique roles by working through, and sometimes revising, their questions and conclusions over time and under conditions of liberty. The press is free so that it can be free to follow, free to follow the story where the story goes. Conscience is free to follow the argument wherever it leads.

According to this alternative understanding of secular liberalism, then, conscience is open in the sense of being socially protected from coercive power, open to public evaluation and discussion on the basis of shared standards, and open to future development, change, and revision. In other words, it is characterized by liberty, objectivity, and revisability. Secularism does not privatize conscience. It keeps conscience open; it protects conscience from autocratic control so that it may freely pursue its public, open-ended inquiry.

The Privacy Fallacy and Liberty Fallacy are not historically inevitable. In fact, they are relative newcomers in the West's intellectual and political life. In some forms, these confusions have only been with us since the latter half of the twentieth century. The secular liberal tradition did not always understand itself this way. The great promise of America, and of Western liberalism itself, was the promise of a moral foundation for society that could transcend religious differences. That moral foundation, which seventeenth- and eighteenth-century liberal thinkers described in terms of natural rights evident to a universal moral sense, would support a new kind of government, a secular civil order secured against sectarian persecution and war. The public values of this civil order would be those enunciated in the preamble to the US Constitution: justice, tranquility, common defense, general welfare, and liberty.

For the architects of the secular liberal tradition, like Spinoza, Adam Smith, John Locke, James Madison, and John Stuart Mill, the aim was not to ignore the moral and spiritual dimensions of human life. Less still did they want to deny all dimensions but the economic, reducing all value to market value and all interests to self-interest. Rather, the point was to move matters of belief from the governmental arena of law and coercion into the arena of conscience and conversation. The West has achieved their dream of an open society but forsaken the public ethics that it needs to defend itself and endure. Justice, welfare, and liberty have become husks of words whose moral substance has decayed away. The sphere of conscience has collapsed into the private sphere. Secularism has lost its soul.

Secularism is not dead. Those of us who identify with the secular liberal tradition can reclaim the language of ethics and values. We can relearn to speak with the voice of conscience and make it our own. This means rejecting the Privacy Fallacy. It does not mean commingling conscience with government, making it a subject for coercive law or decision by majority vote. Between the private sphere—of personal property, preferences, and relationships—and the civil sphere—of state power and institutions—there is a public sphere. This is the social space in which citizens carry on debate about their shared life in newspaper editorials, letters to the editor, blogs, houses of worship, local government forums, office break rooms; it is the argumentarium, the agora, the marketplace where we weigh and exchange each other's reasons for what we think and do. The public sphere is the proper domain of conscience.

Secular liberals must lift the gag order on ethics, values, and religion in public debate. We can no longer insist on precluding controversial moral and religious claims from public conversation. Let believers and unbelievers speak their minds and let honest debate ensue. This is not to say anything goes in public discourse. Claims of conscience in politics should be held to the same standards as other serious public proposals: honesty, consistency, rationality, evidential support, feasibility, legality, morality, and revisability.

This means understanding and avoiding the Liberty Fallacy. Susceptibility to public criticism is the price of admission to public debate. Religious conscience does not get in free. Many secular liberals have convinced themselves that freedom of belief entails respect for all religions, and that respect means refraining from criticism. But that is not respect; it's just blanket acceptance, even disregard.[21] Understood correctly, respect is not just compatible with criticism—respect entails criticism. To respect someone we must take him seriously, and taking someone seriously sometimes means finding fault with him.

Finally, secular liberals must rediscover and defend the ideal of the secular moral conscience against the old shibboleth that secularism equals amorality. Secularists are constantly accused of believing in nothing greater than themselves. However, if you look carefully at the connection between religion and morality, it turns out that the relationship is in fact exactly the other way around.

The story of Abraham and Isaac—foundational to Judaism, Christianity, and Islam—is usually presented as a paradigm of religious faith in which ethical obligation flows from obedience to religious authority. And yet, Abraham is always free to obey or disobey. If his act of faith is to be genuine, it must flow from his own reflective judgment about what he has most reason to do. All normal people naturally have capacities of reason and empathy—the ability to feel and understand what it would be like to be in another person's situation—and with these faculties we can form judgments about what makes most sense to believe or do, taking into consideration all the relevant interests and reasons. This is conscience.

When you think for yourself about what you have most reason to do or believe about a matter of central human concern, you are exercising your conscience. Reasons are universal. To say that some course of action is best is to say that you have a reason to pursue it, and that anyone in a relevantly similar situation would have a reason to do the same. The exercise of conscience takes shape inside a social context of people giving reasons to each other. In this way, although conscience issues reasons to an individual, its exercise is inherently public. Like goods in a marketplace, it can be appraised by others. We can inspect the reasons of others and assess their strength, weakness, and relevance. Moreover, we share our reasons with others. It is by citing our reasons that we explain our behavior to each other. From a scientific perspective, it should not be surprising that reasons are by their very nature shareable, since they probably arose in our evolutionary past to enable complex social interactions among our ancestors.

Conscience answers when reasons of a special kind are called for, when a person's assessment of what is best stands in need of justification. We wouldn't say that algebra is a matter for conscience because there is no important disagreement about the quadratic equation. And while people differ over which brand of toothpaste they prefer, these differences don't make a difference to anything that matters. In neither case do we call on each other to justify our views. But when it comes to matters of central human concern on which there is important disagreement, we speak of conscience. Conscience is what stakes a claim on contested territory. Prisoners of conscience are prisoners because someone wants their ideas locked away, and politicians are said to "vote their conscience" when there are other forces—like politics—pulling them elsewhere.

The conventional view that genuine conscience requires religion has it precisely wrong: genuine religion requires conscience. If one's practice of a religion is to be authentic, it must be based on one's own honest assessment of what makes sense. The difference between believers and unbelievers, then, is not that the latter lack a conscience but rather that their conscience inclines them away from belief. That same conscience, however, can guide them in living ethically, without religious reference points. In this way, the secular conscience stands prior to and independent of all religions and points toward a shared vocabulary for public debate in a pluralistic society.

The secular moral conscience has a rich history in the West (as it does in Persian, South Asian, and Chinese cultures as well). Advocates of the Religious Left like to point to the abolitionist and civil rights movements as models of prophetic politics. Abolitionism was unquestionably a Christian phenomenon (although so, too, was the white supremacy that resisted it). The story of civil rights has further complexities. Religionists naturally emphasize the pivotal role of Martin Luther King Jr. and the black church. But one need not look far to find the socialist W. E. B. Du Bois, the labor leader A. Philip Randolph, and the highly unorthodox Baird Rustin, without whose organizational ingenuity the March on Washington would have never gotten anywhere. Marcus Garvey's philosophy of black pride and self-sufficiency arguably influenced Malcolm X's thought more than Muhammad, and Andrew Goodman and Michael Schwerner—both secular Jews—died alongside James Chaney in Freedom Summer.[22]

And what of the other great liberation movements of the last one hundred and fifty years? Where were the Hebrew prophets when Mary Wollstonecraft, Susan B. Anthony, Elizabeth Cady Stanton, and Matilda Joslyn Gage launched first-wave feminism? (Stanton didn't find the Bible too helpful to women, so she wrote her own.) Which scriptural witness spoke on behalf of gay rights and indigenous rights activists in the late twentieth century? Was it Christian stewards of Creation who sparked a worldwide animal rights movement or the secular ethicists Jeremy Bentham and Peter Singer?

Secularists have the moral high ground, if they will only claim it, and in so doing break the religious monopoly on the language of ethics and values. After all, they're the ones who don't have to be told by anyone to love their neighbors. Secularists believe in moral rights and wrongs, and it is in these terms that they must stake their public claims about secular government, freedom of expression, human rights, the integrity of science, as well as culture war issues like stem cell research, gay marriage, or the right to die. What makes these liberal values *moral* ideals, as opposed to mere personal tastes or prejudices? They are the ideals that have emerged from the historical exercise of conscience: they are the conclusions arrived at by thoughtful people who in deciding how to live have endeavored to take into consideration all the relevant interests and reasons of themselves and their neighbors and fellow beings.

Secular liberalism is in disarray. Abroad, the confrontation with Islamic totalitarianism shakes the complacency of the open society. At home, liberals are soul searching. This book attempts to show how they can reclaim the language of meaning, morality, and value in the culture wars at home and in the struggle for toleration abroad. They must remove the gag order on ethics, values, and religion in public debate; hold religious claims accountable to public criticism; rediscover the secular moral conscience; and advance a moral case for their values of personal autonomy, equality, toleration, self-criticism, and well-being.

By treating matters of conscience as open, secular liberals could engage in serious ethical debate and address religious intolerance without compromising the separation of religion from government. They could subject religion to due public scrutiny when it encroaches on politics. Just as important, they can advance their own positive moral vision in public affairs without fear of "imposing" their beliefs on others. By embracing the open, public role of conscience, secularists could rededicate themselves to the future of their tradition.

On July 5, 1852, in Rochester, New York, Frederick Douglass delivered perhaps the greatest speech of his life, "What to the Slave Is the Fourth of July?" Douglass, who taught himself to read and escaped slavery in Maryland to become a leading abolitionist, would go on personally to advise President Lincoln on the Civil War and the necessity of immediate, uncompensated emancipation of the slaves and full equality for African Americans. He insisted on speaking the day after the Fourth, a day he refused to celebrate until all Americans were free, and used the occasion to assail the hypocrisy of a slave-owning democracy and in particular the complicity of organized Christianity:

> The church of this country is not only indifferent to the wrongs of the slave, it actually takes sides with the oppressors. It has made itself the bulwark of American slavery, and the shield of American slave hunters. Many of its most eloquent Divines, who stand as the

very lights of the church, have shamelessly given the sanction of religion and the Bible to the whole slave system . . . and this horrible blasphemy is palmed off upon the world for Christianity! For my part, I would say, welcome infidelity! welcome atheism!

No polite accommodation of religion here, when moral progress is at stake: "In prosecuting the antislavery enterprise, we have been asked to spare the church, to spare the ministry; but how, we ask, could such a thing be done? We are met on the threshold of our efforts for the redemption of the slave, by the church and ministry of the country, in battle arrayed against us; and we are compelled to fight or flee."[23]

Ten years later, in 1862, God was of two minds. The Emancipation Proclamation was coming, and Lincoln was receiving the counsel of clergy both for and against the act. As he put it, "I am approached with the most opposite opinions and advice, and that by religious men, who are equally certain that they represent the Divine will." Consequently, as Lincoln pointed out to a group of such men who came calling to the White House in September of that year, he would have no choice but to make up his own mind: "I hope it will not be irreverent for me to say that if it is probable that God would reveal His will to others, on a point so connected with my duty, it might be supposed that He would reveal it directly to me. . . . These are not, however, the days of miracles and I suppose it will be granted that I am not to expect a direct revelation. . . . I must study the plain, physical facts of the case, ascertain what is possible, and learn what appears to be wise and right."[24]

With his talk of facts, practical wisdom, and moral right, Lincoln was using a vocabulary of public discourse that is secular in the most important sense—nonreligious, grounded in human reason, and oriented toward the human affairs of this world. God is always of many minds, and so thoughtful people must turn to their own minds for guidance. God's followers are of many names and tribes, and so citizens must appeal to a law higher than God's if they wish to coexist in peace. That higher law is the rule of conscience.

1.

How Secularism Lost Its Soul

Aristocracy links everybody, from peasant to king, in one long chain. Democracy breaks the chain and frees each link. As social equality spreads there are more and more people who, though neither rich nor powerful enough to have much hold over others, have gained or kept enough wealth and enough understanding to look out for their own needs. Such folk owe no man anything and hardly expect anything from anybody. They form the habit of thinking of themselves in isolation and imagine that their whole destiny is in their own hands. Thus, not only does democracy make men forget their ancestors, but also clouds their view of their descendants and isolates them from their contemporaries. Each man is forever thrown back on himself alone, and there is danger that he may be shut up in the solitude of his own heart.

—Alexis de Tocqueville

This is the story of a good idea gone bad. The good idea is that matters of conscience—religion, ethics, and values—are to be left to individuals to decide, free from interference or coercion by government. The idea helped make possible the open, secular society. Here's how it goes bad. Matters of conscience are up to us, so they can amount to no more than subjective preferences. As such, they cannot be critically discussed by others who do not share them. Conscience is personal, so politeness and civility forbid bringing it up in public. Call this the Privacy Fallacy. Conscience is free, so it must be liberated from shared objective standards of rightness and truth. Call this the Liberty Fallacy. The result of these misconceptions about privacy and freedom is a culture unwilling or unable to sustain a real public conversation about religion, ethics, and values. What culture can survive without that conversation? The bad news is that too many would-be defenders of the secular liberal society are unquestioning followers of the Privacy Fallacy and the Liberty Fallacy.

Schools and utilities markets may be another matter, but when it comes to religion, secular-minded people have embraced privatization with fervor. Their mantra: beliefs are fine in private, so long as you don't "impose" them on others. Prayer is vertical; piety is personal. Leading historians define the rise of Western liberalism itself in terms of the privatization of religion, its "removal from the public realm, and its transfer to the private world of individual freedom of conscience, belief, and practice."[1] It is one thing to privatize the institutions of religion, to remove them from state power or public subsidy. It is another thing to privatize conscience.

The privatization of conscience goes long and deep. Historian of philosophy Charles Taylor had documented what he calls the "inwardness" of the self in Christian culture. He begins his story with Augustine of Hippo. Augustine could be seen as the most self-absorbed of saints. He expended inordinate theological energies on explaining his inability to control his erections (God is not the only thing that moves in mysterious ways). Taylor points out that for Augustine, introspection was essential to religious wisdom:

> Augustine's proof of God is a proof from the first-person experience of knowing and reasoning. I am aware of my own sensing and thinking; and in reflecting on this, I am made aware of its depen-

dence on something beyond it, something common. But this turns out on further examination to include not just objects to be known but also the very standards which reason gives allegiance to. So I recognize that this activity which is mine is grounded on and presupposes something higher than I, something which I should look up to and revere. By going inward, I am drawn upward.[2]

Augustine finds God not just in the structure of the world but in the structure of his subjective experience itself, the "incorporeal light . . . by which our minds are somehow irradiated, so that we may judge rightly of all these things."[3]

The next watershed in the history of privacy was the Lutheran revolt, the Protestant Reformation. From a lecture hall at the University of Wittenberg, Martin Luther sparked a Copernican revolution in Christian thought. In the new Christianity he envisioned, the Church would be put out of the salvation business. No pope or bishop, no cathedral or reliquary, and no amount of prayer, sacrament, or indulgence would be enough to atone for sin. Nothing any human could do could make one worthy of redemption. Salvation would be a work of grace between God and a single believer, an act of a love gratuitous, lavished on the undeserving. All we are to do is receive it willingly and love God in return.

Luther is a folk hero of conscience. The climax of the popular history is his appearance in January 1521 before Emperor Charles V at the Diet of Worms. He was asked to recant his heresy. His statement has become the archetype of the triumph of the individual conscience, unbowed by authority and orthodoxy: "Unless I am proved wrong by the testimony of Scriptures or by evident reason I am bound in conscience and held fast to the Word of God . . . therefore I cannot and will not retract anything, for it is neither safe nor salutary to act against one's conscience. God help me. Amen."[4] The words still inspire, as they should. But if Luther is held up as a hero, it is because one already assents to the substance of his case against clerical hegemony. The conscience that bound Luther was private with a vengeance, impervious, he claimed, to everything outside itself. Against the skeptical Desiderius Erasmus, Luther declared, "The Holy Spirit is no Skeptic, and it is not doubts or mere opinions that he has written on our hearts, but assertions more sure and certain than life itself and all experience."[5] When a spirit takes one in a grip so firm that it can be moved by no doubt, opinion, or experience, we call it demonic.[6]

In the Protestant practice of faith, religious virtues, duties, and discourse are internalized and people's everyday lives are invested with new spiritual significance. Luther wrote, "For all Christians whatsoever really and truly belong to the religious class, and there is no difference among them except insofar as they do different work."[7] No less than bishops, priests, and monks, all ordinary Christians are called to serve God in their chosen vocation, and so their mundane and personal activities are given a place in the sacred order. The rejection of the monastic life by the Protestants was "an affirmation of ordinary life as more than profane, as itself hallowed and in no way second class. The institution of the monastic life was seen as a slur on the spiritual standing of productive [labor] and family life. . . . Luther marks their break in his own life by ceasing to be such a monk and by marrying a former nun."[8] This "priesthood of all believers" encouraged a special orientation toward the personal lives of believers and another inward turn of the Western self.

Protestant religious culture is also a culture of conversions and revelations. Luther himself reported having a road-to-Damascus experience while alone in his study, situated in a tower of the home of the Augustinian monks. This *Turmerlebnis*, or "tower experience," as he called it, was as much existential transport as intellectual realization: "I felt myself straightway born afresh and to have entered through the open gates into paradise itself."[9] When later retelling the story of his awakening, Luther would connect it with a verse from St. Paul's letter to the Romans that had sown the theological seed of his rebirth: "For therein is the righteousness of God revealed from faith to faith: as it is written, The just live by faith."[10] Centuries later, in 1738, while Luther's *Preface to St. Paul's Epistle to the Romans* was read aloud in a London chapel, John Wesley's "heart was strangely warmed." And so scales have been dropping from eyes and hearts warming among Protestants right up through the evangelicals, for whom being "born-again" is a birthright. It is easy to imagine that in this religious universe, a soul-defining event can take place in a moment, with a single person, in perfect silence and stillness. Protestant belief is an inside job.

With the rise of modern science, the ascendant worldview of Western civilization became the empirical, naturalistic worldview, in which the universe is understood as a system of natural processes, unhaunted by occult or spiritual forces. The world doesn't get to cheat and bring things about by magic but rather always by some causal mechanism. This is the outlook presupposed by all of the biology, psychology, and history with which we understand ourselves and our place in nature, as well as the physics, chemistry, medicine, and engineering by which we have transformed ourselves and our places.

Although it claimed fewer lives than the Protestant revolution, the scientific revolution precipitated no less of a metaphysical and epistemological crisis in European thought. For some early modern thinkers, the disenchantment of the world signaled that the human soul and moral conscience—if they are to have any real existence at all—must be a part of nature and therefore open to objective, public inquiry. Thomas Hobbes wrote: "For what is the heart, but a spring; and the nerves, but so many strings; and the joints, but so many wheels, giving motion to the whole body, such as was intended by the Artificer?"[11] Other thinkers lowered their brows and dug deeper into the conventional metaphysical moat between physical and spiritual, matter and mattering. René Descartes reasoned that the mind must be made of a special nonphysical, insensible substance. He threw open the gates of the body to quantitative, mechanistic science, banishing consciousness and free will into hiding—the mind-body dualism. As empiricism came to rule the external world, what escaped the empiricist's net would become inner, subjective, and private, a ghost trapped the tower of the body.

The European rediscovery of classical literature and pre-Christian naturalism had brought with it a revival of classical skepticism about knowledge. The new methods of science appeared especially vulnerable to old arguments of the Greek and Roman skeptics. Following the experimental spirit of Galileo, natural scientists sought to rebuild human knowledge on human observation. But how could they know that these methods reliably track the truth? Why should they accept the scientific criterion for what counts as knowledge, without first knowing whether that criterion is true (and to know that, they would need another criterion for knowledge, about which the same question could be raised)? After all, it seemed to some, the observing mind can have contact only with its own sensations and perceptions; a veil of perception separates the mind from the world as it really is, from the things in themselves. Galileo's empiricists are but veil gazers, leaving what lies beyond unseen, unknown.

Descartes proposed an Augustinian solution to this epistemological crisis of modernity. After checking to make sure he existed (which was not a problem so long as he was checking), Descartes would look into his own mind for an idea of God, a sign of perfection that could only have been imparted to him by an actually existing perfect being. Since God exists and is not a deceiver, Descartes argued, we can be confident that we are not systematically deceived about what lies beyond the veil.

European philosophy was still exploring about and between the poles of Hobbes's empiricism and Descartes' rationalism when Immanuel Kant began a Copernican revolution of his own. Startled from a "dogmatic slumber" in his fifties by what he saw as empiricism's corrosive effect on traditional concepts of knowledge, morality, and personhood (personified by the naturalistic skeptic David Hume), Kant turned inward, as had Descartes, to find unshakeable foundations for knowledge. Kant's innovation was to attribute knowledge to the necessary structure or categories of the mind itself. Our perceptual experience is intelligible to us, we are not always baffled by what we see and hear, and this is only possible if we presuppose certain ideas—

like cause and effect. Upon such ideas our claims about the world can rest. Kant's argument is called a transcendental deduction, but it was Augustine and Descartes whose cognitive spelunking ultimately led them to the inner light of the transcendent. For Kant and after Kant, the mind finds itself alone within the contours of its own logic.

As the Kantian direction in philosophy played out on the Continent, it led to a crescendo of increasingly radical conclusions. Whereas for Kant the mind is a kind of legislator of knowledge, for neo-Kantian idealists like Fichte the mind became a creator of knowledge and, at the limit, a creator of reality itself. Nietzsche, not keen on epistemology, and preoccupied by the spiritual degradation of the West, heralded the death of God and the self-creation of values. Nietzsche was a raging atheist, but he had a vision of the good life, with its joyful "seriousness of the child at play" and manly virtues of an idealized pre-Christian civilization. By the time of the twentieth-century existentialists, with European society staggering in the wreckage of the wars, that, too, was gone. Sartre believed that with God died human nature, for it was only under God's gaze that our nature was fixed. Now not even the categories of the mind could guide choice. There was choice alone.

Kant's great idea was that choices are free and authentic to the extent that they are constrained only by the rule of reason, since reason is the expression of our distinctive nature as persons. Kantian freedom, or autonomy, is the freedom of one ruled by himself or herself, the self-legislator, the democratic citizen. For the modern existentialists, the individual has no nature, so even the rule of reason is alien, and choices are free and authentic only when constrained by *nothing*—not even reason or value. The only freedom is absolute freedom, the only authentic act the *acte gratuit*.[12] The Kantian conscience is free in order that it may follow norms—of logic and morality—that are publicly available, examinable, shareable; it is free for public standards. On the existentialist outlook that came to color so much of European life, conscience is free from public standards.

❈ ❈ ❈

The forces unleashed by the Reformation would ultimately—tortuously—lead to the triumph of religious toleration in European and American societies. Reformation created a proliferation of dissident Protestant sects that would struggle for freedom of conscience against the persecuting majority faiths. In the process, they produced some of the most influential arguments for freedom of belief. Reformation also plunged Europe into a century of brutal religious war. The tourniquets that stopped the bloodletting were the treaties and rulings such as the Edict of Nantes, which preserved official state religions while providing for a measure of toleration of minority faiths. The revulsion at the carnage of the religious wars eventually led to expanded toleration and religious liberties. Then with the European Enlightenment came wholesale skepticisms about traditional, institutionalized religion and a rising confidence in the ability of ordinary human beings working through nonreligious institutions to meet the needs and challenges of society. The upshot was a modern, secular view of the state as a mechanism designed to secure individual rights and well-being, not to inculcate religious virtue or advance the interests of any sect.

Sociologists of religion sometimes distinguish between secularism, secularity, and secularization. Secularism is the political arrangement that separates civil and ecclesiastical power and, typically, affords robust freedom of conscience to citizens. Secularity is the nonreligiosity or religious indifference of the citizens. Here a secular person is not necessarily an agnostic or atheist but one for whom organized religion holds little significance. Secularization is the process (still the subject of dispute among scholars) in which societies tend to increase in both secularity and secularism as they modernize and urbanize.[13]

The word *secular* (from the Latin *saecularis*, "of the age" or "of the era") can be traced back to a distinction in the medieval Christian Church between those clergy who were a part of a monastic order and those who lived outside the cloister among ordinary believers.

Someone could argue therefore that "secularism" carries with it some unwanted theological freight. This argument is vulnerable to a general difficulty: etymology is not destiny. That is, word origins do not permanently color present-day meanings like the stain of original sin—they matter only insofar as they are responsible for changes in the behavior of actual current language users. Clearly in this case no such influence remains from the Church origins. Only a relatively small number of people even know about the word's origins. But not even they *use* the word that way. In modern usage, *secularism* has no more connection to Jesuits and Dominicans than *lunacy* has to the moon.

The modern usage owes more to George Jacob Holyoake, a lecturer and campaigner against British blasphemy laws, whose 1846 book, *English Secularism*, popularized the term in English.

> Secularism is a code of duty pertaining to this life, founded on considerations purely human, and intended mainly for those who find theology indefinite or inadequate, unreliable or unbelievable. Its essential principles are three: (1) The improvement of this life by material means. (2) That science is the available Providence of man. (3) That it is good to do good. Whether there be other good or not, the good of the present life is good, and it is good to seek that good.[14]

By secularism Holyoake meant "a form of opinion which concerns itself only with questions, the issues of which can be tested by the experience of this life." Secularism is not atheism. There is a perfectly ordinary contemporary usage in English that just denotes matters independent of religion. For instance, when the famous Lemon Test for violations of the Establishment Clause refers to a law's "secular purpose," it does not mean "atheist purpose"; when journalists speak of a political party in Iraq or Palestine as a "secular party," they are not talking about a party composed of non-Muslims.

There is no question that Western Europe, Australia, New Zealand, Canada, the United States (and, in different ways, Japan, South Korea, India, and Israel) have undergone secularization in one form or another. Generally speaking, they have followed three different paths. In the

Western European model, the state would protect freedom of conscience (the last execution for heresy by the Spanish Inquisition took place in 1826, stirring outcry across the Continent), while at the same time maintaining a special formal relationship to a church. In many cases, the established church would receive public support (or, in Germany's case, any of several churches of citizens' choosing). Simultaneously, their role was gradually reduced to mere ceremony, with little to no authority in running matters of state. Then for reasons that have yet to be fully explained, beginning in the 1960s, Western Europeans stopped going to church. As a representative case, 80 percent of the Danish today say that religion is unimportant to their lives. This mirrors the rate of the unchurched in Western Europe generally at the turn of the twenty-first century. Anyone who has visited a European cathedral lately can appreciate Nietzsche's exclamation that they are "crypts and tombs of God," lifeless but for art-ogling tourists. Atheism increased but did not directly track the rise in secularity. At least 45 percent of Danes do not believe in the Christian God. And yet, many European states retained their formal religious establishments. The Danish People's Church, or Folkekirke, is supported by tax revenue and could claim over 80 percent of the citizenry as members in 2006.

In the European experience of secularization, matters of religious conscience became private in the same sense that intimate details about one's love life are private. They are just not something that you talk about. When asked by an interviewer about the importance of religion to British prime minister Tony Blair's relationship with US president George W. Bush, Blair's advisor, Alastair Campbell, replied, "We don't do God." The attitude toward religion in public life is like the old-fashioned attitude toward children: best seen but not heard.[15]

The exceptions to the European rule, as they will be happy to tell you, were the French. A strong anticlerical sentiment fueled the French Revolution, especially in its Jacobin phase. In the Napoleonic Concordat of 1801, religious liberty was affirmed while at the same time designating the Catholic Church as the majority religion. But anticlericalists and republicans believed that a modern democratic

France could not emerge until the authority of the Church had been crushed. Their struggle with traditionalists in the nineteenth century pitted two visions of the country against each other: a Catholic France, "eldest daughter of the Church," versus a republican France, the daughter of the Revolution.

The winning vision was institutionalized with the passage of a 1905 law on the separation of church and state, which established the peculiarly French system of *läicité*. "Läicité refers to an institutional system informed by a secular worldview that determines a civic and moral ideal, unifies the community, and legitimates sovereignty."[16] The word, coined in the 1870s, comes from the Greek word *laos*, for the "unity of a population." "The laic [layman] is a man of the people, whom no prerogative distinguishes or elevates above the others. . . . He can be the faithful member of a particular religious group, but also someone with an atheistic worldview, the founding conviction of which is distinct from that which inspires religion."[17] While the rest of Europe would later slouch toward secularity, lapsing into religious apathy under the unwatchful eyes of the established state churches, laicization in France abolished the state church and deliberately set about divesting religion of social power. Läicité is today regarded by most French as a cherished achievement that is crucial to their national identity. The French model of secularism combines not only strict separation of the church and state and explicit defense of läicité but also massive irreligiousness of the population. In 2003, only 8 percent attended religious services weekly.

The contrast in practice between the French and European models of secularism was highlighted in debates surrounding the subculture of the country's large Muslim immigrant population. With the ban on the headscarf in schools and the establishment of a state-approved French Council on the Islamic Faith, public officials showed a willingness to speak publicly and critically about religious matters whenever this was seen as necessary to preserving the culture of läicité.

Whereas the European model combines a formally religious government with a secular populous, and the French a secular government and a secular populous, the American model is a secular government and a religious populous. The state would stay out of the religion business in order that religious sects could compete in a free market. As Adam Smith observed in his *Wealth of Nations*: "sects . . . sufficiently numerous, and each of them consequently too small to disturb public tranquility, the excessive zeal of each for its particular tenets could not well be productive of any very harmful effects, but, on the contrary, of several good ones: if the government was perfectly decided to let them all alone, and to oblige them all to let alone one another."[18]

In the American religious bazaar, the individualism of Protestantism was exacerbated by the Great Awakenings, charismatic movements in the 1730s to 1740s and 1820s to 1830s that placed a premium on personal conversion experiences. The Awakenings produced a schisming of Christianity into increasingly competitive and individualistic strains. By the middle of the twentieth century, the free market in religion was tending to produce theologies catering to personal worldly needs at the expense of eternal verities and narratives of sin, redemption, and duty. Belief systems sought to outdo each other in offering a diverse buffet of beliefs from which browsers could pick and choose the timeless wisdom best suited to their immediate interests.

Evangelical Protestants in particular have excelled at adapting the methods of commercial culture in both the content and the conduct of their ministries. Churchgoers are seen as consumers to be lured away from competitors with offers of superior childcare, health and counseling services, as well as more entertaining and affecting worship. Rick Warren became a captain of the industry in 2002 with the publication of *The Purpose Driven Life*, a Christian advice book that sold over twenty-four million copies. The pastor of a "seeker-sensitive church" in Orange County, California, Warren and his organizations have trained over one hundred thousand pastors in marketing techniques and real estate–based business models. In Houston, the nation's largest church bought the Compaq Center sports arena, where the Houston Rockets once played, to house its services drawing up to sixteen thousand people. The pastor, Joel Osteen, keeps the message positive: "To come on the weekend and get some practical advice from the Bible is a real lift."[19]

Sociologist of religion Alan Wolfe has documented the transformation of American religion by commercial culture:

> Democratic in their political instincts, geographically and economically mobile, attracted to popular culture more than to the written word, Americans from the earliest time have shaped religion to account for their personal needs. . . . In every aspect of the religious life, American faith has met American culture—and American culture has triumphed. . . . Talk of hell, damnation, and even sin has been replaced by a nonjudgmental language of understanding and empathy. . . . More Americans than ever proclaim themselves born again in Christ, but the lord to whom they turn rarely gets angry and frequently strengthens self-esteem. Traditional forms of worship, from reliance on organ music to the mysteries of the liturgy, have given way to audience participation and contemporary tastes.[20]

Under entrepreneurial Protestantism, spiritual goods are another kind of consumer good. In a market-oriented society, social space tends to be bifurcated into the public (governmental, regulatory, bureaucratic) and the private (property, family, personal taste). Since values, ethics, and religion are among the things that the state ought not to interfere in, they tend to be lumped in with private possessions and market choices. Americans now talk about belief using the language of private property: "I have a *right* to my belief"; "You can't take it away from me"; "You're *entitled* to your opinion."

Alongside the religious landscape, independent developments in twentieth-century American law and political philosophy led secular liberals to gravitate toward the concept of privacy in thinking about freedom of conscience. The right to privacy in the United States first emerged in tort law, where it concerned such things as publication of gossip in society newspapers and the use of a person's image in advertising without authorization.[21] The Supreme Court first explicitly recognized the right to privacy in the 1965 case *Griswold v. Connecticut*, which overturned the state's ban on contraceptives. The privacy at stake, wrote the justices, was the right of citizens to keep certain personal or intimate matters to themselves. Privacy so conceived would be imperiled by attempts to enforce the Connecticut law: "Would we allow the police to search the sacred precincts of marital bedrooms for telltale signs of the use of contraceptives? The very idea is repulsive to the notions of privacy surrounding the marriage relationship."

This early use of privacy by the Court was not a commitment to the Privacy Fallacy, the view that matters of conscience are beyond the scope of public debate. Rather, it was predicated on the moral importance of the marital relationship. As Michael Sandel has shown, the important shift in the meaning of privacy came seven years later in *Eisenstadt v. Baird*, which concerned a law prohibiting the distribution of contraceptives. Because it regulated distribution and not use of contraceptives, this law could be enforced without intruding on privacy in the traditional sense. Despite this, the Court struck down the law:

> Rather than conceiving privacy as freedom from surveillance or disclosure of intimate affairs, the Court found that the right to privacy now protected the freedom to engage in certain activities without governmental restriction. Although privacy in *Griswold* prevented intrusion into "the sacred precincts of marital bedrooms," privacy in *Eisenstadt* prevented intrusion into decisions of certain kinds. . . . The Court protected privacy in *Eisenstadt* not for the social practices it promoted but for the individual choice it secured. "If the right of privacy means anything, it is the right of the individual, married or single to be free from unwarranted government intrusion into matters so fundamentally affecting a person as the decision whether to bear or beget a child."[22]

In its written decision in *Roe v. Wade*, the Supreme Court acknowledged that at stake in the case of abortion was a grave moral question: whether the developing fetus deserves full moral consideration as a human person: "Texas urges that . . . life begins at conception and is present throughout pregnancy, and that, therefore, the State has a compelling interest in protecting that life from and after conception."

Famously, the Court ruled that the life of the early fetus does not deserve protection. Astonishingly, the Court did this not by endeavoring to show that Texas was mistaken about the beginning of life or that the interests of the fetus are negligible as compared to the interests of the mother. It maintained that the case could be resolved without addressing these matters at all: "We need not resolve the difficult question of when life begins. When those trained in the respective disciplines of medicine, philosophy, and theology are unable to arrive at any consensus, the judiciary . . . is not in a position to speculate as to the answer."[23] The Court's problem with the Texas antiabortion statute was not that it was wrong about the moral worth of early fetal life but rather that it adopted a "theory of life" at all: "In view of all this, we do not agree that, by adopting one theory of life, Texas may override the rights of the pregnant woman that are at stake."[24]

Whatever one thinks about the jurisprudence of the case, the strategy of bracketing the moral issue just doesn't make sense upon reflection. For "whether it is reasonable to bracket, for political purposes, the moral and religious doctrines at stake depends largely on which of those doctrines is true."[25] If the Catholic Church "is right about the moral status of the fetus, if abortion is morally tantamount to murder," then the liberal defense of abortion on grounds of toleration and women's autonomy must become "an instance of just-war theory; he or she would have to show why these values should prevail even at the cost of some 1.5 million civilian deaths each year."

To appreciate the force of this point, try bracketing some other moral issue you care about; capital punishment, perhaps. Staunch abolitionists say that the practice is immoral because state power ought not to be used to take a citizen's life unless doing so would be necessary to protect another citizen's life. We may agree or disagree, or we may attempt to decide the legality of capital punishment by bracketing the question of its morality. After all, there is intense, widespread, earnest moral disagreement on this point. It is not the role of our public institutions to enter into the private domain of conscience. Therefore the state may not adopt one "theory of mercy" favored by abolitionists to override the compelling state interest in deterring crime and providing restitution to victims. Because public institutions aren't in a place to say whether a practice is immoral, they are justified in acting as though it is not.

That argument should not satisfy the abolitionist who believes that the practice is immoral. If, as the abolitionist sincerely believes, punitive killing by the state is always a grievous moral wrong, then public institutions are not justified in acting as though it is not. But for the same reason, bracketing does not satisfy the antiabortionist. Neither should it satisfy the secular liberal who seeks an intellectually coherent and socially enduring case for the permissibility of abortion. Abortion is permissible because of a problem with the doctrine of early fetal personhood. The problem with the doctrine is not that it is private but that it is false. Early fetuses have no interests to be protected.

The Bracketing Strategy is one offshoot of the Privacy Fallacy that has done quite well for itself. It has convinced generations of secular liberals that the way to deal with moral problems in our shared life is not to deal with them. However, the benefits of this move are dubious. Abortion rights in the United States, for example, remain in constant peril. *Roe v. Wade* is roundly criticized on all sides for having circumvented a broader public debate on the moral issues that might have produced a more stable national consensus. At the same time, the costs of the Bracketing Strategy are clear. Secular liberals have in large measure abandoned the field of public moral debate over the beginning of life, forfeiting a great deal of social influence and exposing themselves to the charge that they have lost their moral compass. For there is no noticeable difference between believing that the moral dignity of the fetus or the barbarity of state execution can be bracketed and believing that they are not worth worrying about at all.

The irony is that the Privacy Fallacy and the Bracketing Strategy constitute a betrayal of the traditions of secular liberalism. The intellectual ancestors of contemporary liberalism did not attempt to bracket moral issues. They did not treat conscience as a private matter. They assumed that conscience is open, that we can reason together about ethics and values, and they advanced their case for a liberal society in explicitly moral terms.

With *Roe v. Wade*, the right of privacy famously came to include a woman's decision whether or not to terminate her pregnancy. After *Roe*, it continued to expand, amorphously, until the much-debated 1989 *Casey v. Planned Parenthood* passage: "At the heart of liberty is the right to define one's own concept of existence, of the universe, and of the mystery of human life. Beliefs about these matters could not define the attributes of personhood were they found under the compulsion of the state."

In the public consciousness, the post-*Roe* meaning of privacy in US jurisprudence lends credence to the secular liberal doctrine that matters of conscience are private in the sense of being immune from public inquiry. In one sense it is undoubtedly right (whether it is constitutionally mandated is another question) that the state may not use coercive measures to make you give up your own "concept of existence." It does not follow that your concept is beyond criticism or that fellow citizens and even public officials may not affirm or deny it in public debate.

In the latter half of the twentieth century, English-speaking political theory began to use the themes of privacy and neutrality to explicate the nature of a secular, liberal society. The arguments typically start with the fact of pluralism, or "reasonable pluralism," as it is sometimes called. Reasonable pluralism is the undeniable fact that the citizens of modern democratic societies hold a variety of incompatible yet reasonable religious, philosophical, and moral doctrines: Orthodox Judaism, liberal Protestantism, Marxist materialism, New Age spiritualism, secular humanism, ad infinitum. In the terms used in political theory, pluralistic societies are home to many "conceptions of the good," "ideals of the good life," or "comprehensive doctrines" about which sincere, well-meaning, and rational people disagree.

How should we respond to the fact of reasonable pluralism? One answer is to restrict politics to just those areas on which all reasonable people agree. Since the reasons that are endorsed by one person or community may not be endorsed by another, discourse in a pluralistic society ought to be public: participants may introduce only those reasons that can be endorsed by all. In a deeply diverse society, citizens must set aside their "private" convictions when seeking a secure grounding for the political order.

In liberal political theory, the privacy argument can be traced at least to the beginning of an intellectual era inaugurated by the late John Rawls in 1971. His monumental *Theory of Justice* articulated the view, which had been emerging in American jurisprudence since the 1940s, that the state should remain "neutral" on all contested conceptions of the good life.[26] Rawls's equally influential *Political Liberalism* went further, defending an "ideal of public reason" according to which discussion of fundamental political questions should appeal only to beliefs and values that are acceptable to all reasonable citizens.[27] Under the influence of Rawls's later work, secular liberalism came to be linked to this supposed contrast between public reasons and private conscience. The task of liberal political theory, as it was practiced in the late 1980s and 1990s, was to provide a "public justification" for the structure of the state.

Rawlsian public reason can be traced back to the philosophy of Immanuel Kant. Kant's famous answer to his famous question, "what is enlightenment?" was "man's emergence from his self-incurred immaturity."[28] Immaturity is one's inability, owing to lack of conviction and courage, to "use one's own understanding without the guidance of another." Kant says that in order to emerge from immaturity, everyone must enjoy "the freedom to make public use of one's reason in all matters."[29] He characterizes a public use of reason as "that use which anyone may make of it as a man of learning addressing the entire reading public,"[30] or "the world at large." A private use of reason is that which is directed toward a more limited audience: "A clergyman is bound to instruct his pupils and his congregation in accordance with the doctrines of the church he serves, for he was employed by it on that condition. But as a scholar, he is completely free as well as obliged to impart to the public all his carefully considered, well-intentioned thoughts on the mistaken aspects of those doctrines, and to offer suggestions for a better arrangement of religious and ecclesiastical affairs."[31] When the clergyman addresses his congregation, his use of reason is "purely private."

When the word *private* emerged in English in the mid-fourteenth century (as *pryvat*), it had two primary meanings. One meaning concerned what is distinctive or set apart. It owed to a borrowing from the Latin *privatus*: apart from the public life, deprived of office. A second meaning, that of something secret or in solitude, developed from a borrowing of the Old French word *privaute*. *Privatus* and *privaute* both in turn derive from the Latin *privus*: one's own, single, individual.

What emerges from the religious, legal, philosophical culture of the West is a very slippery concept of privacy, which slides back and forth between several main meanings. It is entirely reasonable and good to say that conscience is private in the sense of being set apart from government or civil affairs. The mischief arises when this meaning of privacy slips imperceptibly into another—*privatus* to *privaute*—so that conscience also comes to be seen as personal, subjective, and closed to the critical scrutiny of others.

Secularism was not always about stopping conversations. It used to be about sparking them. Spinoza was in exile from the Jewish community of Amsterdam for heresy when he wrote his masterpiece, the *Theological-Political Treatise*. He hoped its argument for freedom of expression would persuade European governments to permit unfettered discussion of his revolutionary theological ideas, and thus allow him and others like him to return to public life. The point of Kant's call for enlightenment was to grant free rein to the public use of reason, with which we address the world at large and submit our thoughts to the critical scrutiny of others. John Stuart Mill favored the open society since only its members would enjoy the autonomy to conduct "experiments in living" and share their results with each other, with the goal of discovering those forms of human life that are most excellent and worth living.

There is no doubt one sense in which it is correct to say that religion is a private affair. The apparatus of state power should not be placed under clerical control or used to favor any religion (or religion over irreligion). That is, religion ought to be a nongovernmental affair. If that is what secularists mean by *private*, they would do well to simply say what they mean and retire the troublesome concept of privacy.

2.

Why Belief Belongs in Public Life

(And Unbelievers Should Be Glad)

If the time should ever come—and I do not concede any conflict to be remotely possible—when my office would require me to either violate my conscience or violate the national interest, then I would resign the office.

—John F. Kennedy

A majority of Americans believe it is appropriate in general for public officials to rely on their faith when thinking about policy decisions, according to polling data. Yet, curiously, the polls also show that when confronted with actual religious statements by politicians, many Americans feel uncomfortable. What could this mean? Do Americans like deeply held beliefs so long as they carry no political implications? If so, how deep could they be? Or do they prefer deeply held beliefs whose political implications are dissimulated in public? Hardly a basis for public dialogue in a democracy.

Welcome to secularism in America, where this strange tension in attitudes is not just a statistical oddity; it's a political philosophy. Secularism per se is not to blame. America's strict separation of religion and state and freedom of belief remain among its greatest achievements—and its most precious ideological exports. Rather, the confusion stems from a particular interpretation of secularism, now the dominant view, which equates it with the idea that conscience is a "private matter."

Unfortunately, this interpretation of secularism gets the politics of conscience almost entirely wrong. What's more, liberals and secularists should be the first to give it up, since it confounds their own best efforts to check the cultural influence of conservative religion. "Privacy" gets conflated with personal preference and subjectivity, and subjectivity implies immunity to criticism. If, as the old joke goes, a liberal is one who won't take his or her own side in an argument, today's secularists are those who can't. This is the Privacy Fallacy.

Ironically, America could never have escaped theocracy if its church-state fathers had believed that religious claims are "private reasons." Instead, John Locke, Roger Williams, Thomas Jefferson, and James Madison held that religious claims, like all claims of conscience, are open to examination and discussion by the public. The inheritors of the secular liberal tradition would do well to do likewise. This is not only a matter of simple intellectual clarity and honesty. It is also the only way to do justice to the significance of conscience and its proper place in the public discourse of a pluralistic society.

What started as the confirmation hearing for the federal court appointee William Pryor in July 2003 soon turned into a holy war of words. When Democrats pressed Judge Pryor, an ardent Catholic, on his conservative judicial record, his Republican allies accused them of anti-Catholic bias. It was plain that the committee members had cause to be concerned about Pryor's religious beliefs. After all, here was a man who declared before a Ten Commandments rally in Montgomery, Alabama, that "God has chosen, through his son Jesus Christ, this time, this place for all Christians—Protestants, Catholics and Orthodox—to save our country and save our courts."[1] Pryor's opponents were concerned about the ways in which beliefs like this might or might not affect the nominee's actions as a federal judge. Why should such questions be off limits? In a letter to the *New York Times*, the chairman of the Senate Republican Conference condemned the judicial committee's treatment of Pryor by describing any questions regarding "deeply held beliefs inspired by religious convictions" as "dangerous."[2] Secular liberals would be forced to agree, if they insist that religion is a private matter.[3] One key meaning of *private* is "personal," and personal matters are just those to which we may deny others access.

A family meal at home is private because not everyone is invited. The family may deny others participation in the meal or even information about it without their consent. Most ethicists point out that personal matters have moral importance not just because they give people power over each other, for well or for woe (as in blackmail and or identity theft). The additional moral value, they argue, is people's autonomy, or self-direction and self-determination. By invading someone's privacy we fail to respect that person's autonomy.[4] One argument for the link between privacy and autonomy is that it is hard to be yourself when you are being watched. You will feel some level of pressure to alter your behavior in light of the judgment of others. This invasion of privacy diminishes the self-direction of your action.[5] A shield of personal privacy makes possible an environment in which one can explore and experiment with one's motives, fears, and weaknesses without being inhibited by the risk of public failure or censure. This kind of self-experimentation is an important contributor to personal autonomy.[6]

The ethical analysis accords with common sense. It is out of bounds to drag another's personal life into public view (without some compelling reason, such as national security). If conscience in general and religion in particular are private (personal), then they fall into this same sensitive sphere. As one American jurist wrote, "We of this country made it an article of organic law that the relations between man and his Maker were a private concern, into which other men have no right to intrude."[7]

At the same time, in a free society everyone has a right to access information *about religion*, as your local librarian can tell you. So, that can't be what people mean by the privacy of conscience. Perhaps what they mean is that you can't bring information about *my religiosity* into view without my consent. But suppose I put it there in the first place. When President Bush tells *Ladies Home Journal* that he takes great comfort from reading Charles Stanley devotionals every morning, he has effectively invited the public in for a look around the interior of his worldview. Whenever citizens or politicians voluntarily present their own religious beliefs in politics, it makes no sense for secularists to object on grounds of personal autonomy.

Consider this analogy. It could be that being gay is a private matter, in the sense that this information may justifiably be withheld from others. However, this does nothing whatever to show that homosexuality cannot be discussed in politics. It may be an invasion of a person's privacy to disclose his homosexuality, but it is not therefore an invasion of his privacy to engage in political debate or action concerning homosexuality. By making homosexuality a political issue, we are not thereby disclosing any private information about him without his consent.[8]

Even when it is motivated by a spirit of toleration, the idea that conscience is personal can actually hinder the possibility of respectful critical dialogue on religiously charged political issues. Thus, when *Newsweek* magazine should have been scrutinizing Bush's faith, it ended up commenting on his character. Religion scholar Martin Marty accused Bush of arrogance for thinking that he is doing God's will. It may be easier for secularists to label a belief in infallibility a personality flaw rather than a flawed theology, but it is certainly no more respectful or helpful. They have no choice so long as questioning someone's religious beliefs is tantamount to meddling in his personal business.

Why should private conscience be precluded from politics, even when it produces disagreement? After all, when we encounter disagreements in everyday life, our first impulse is usually to get to the bottom of them; to seek resolution, to figure out which alternative view is best. Why should we treat disagreements in the public sphere so differently? The most common answer is based on a fundamental liberal principle about the legitimacy of government, itself thought to flow from the basic commitment to respect for all citizens as free and equal. Respect for citizens as free and equal requires that no citizen may be subjected to state action unless there is some reason for this action that makes sense to him or her. Government actions are legitimate to the extent that they can be *justified* to those who will be subject to them. From these fundamentals, many liberals draw the conclusion that political decisions must be made on the basis of public reasons. As the influential liberal philosopher John Rawls put it: "[S]ince the exercise of political power itself must be legitimate, the ideal of citizenship imposes a moral, not a legal, duty . . . to be able to explain to one another on those fundamental questions how the principles and policies they advocate and vote for can be supported by the political values of public reason."[9] According to this line of thought, appeals to conscience constitute an illegitimate use of political power and therefore are inappropriate.[10]

This argument is fine except that it doesn't work. Logically, you can't get from the idea that government decisions must be legitimate to the idea that political reasons must be public. The principle of legitimacy demands that each citizen accepts some reason for the political decision at hand. It does not follow that there must be a single reason that every citizen accepts. Different reasons might justify the decision to different citizens. A policy can be justified when it is favored by a *convergence* of citizens' varying reasons, without there being any *consensus* on those reasons themselves. And there is no reason why the claims of conscience can't be a part of such a convergence. For example, you might favor the creation of a federal wildlife preserve because you believe it will be good for the tourist economy, while I might favor it because I believe God made people stewards of the environment. So long as our reasons converge, the decision is justified to each of us and the ideal of legitimacy is preserved. There is nothing necessarily illegitimate about conscience.

But even if the argument from legitimacy succeeded, there would still be a strong case against precluding conscience from politics. First, liberals often use it to cry foul when religion is invoked on behalf of a cause they oppose, but not otherwise. You don't hear anyone protesting about the privacy of conscience when the pope calls for world peace, or Episcopal ministers cite scripture in defense of gay marriage. This invites the charge of hypocrisy. It also suggests that what liberals actually find objectionable is the *content* of certain claims of conscience, not their source. Why not identify these objections for what they are and let honest debate ensue?

A number of commentators have also observed that a rule of public reason would unduly restrict the liberty of religious citizens by requiring them to refrain from acting on their beliefs in public.[11] Freedom of conscience means nothing if it does not include the freedom to speak and act socially and politically as conscience compels, even when its conclusions are not universally shared.

Another serious problem with restricting debate to public reasons that everyone agrees on is that not everyone agrees on what counts as a public reason. This problem is illustrated by the debate in the United States over the teaching of evolution and "intelligent design theory" in public school science classes. The intelligent design movement, or ID, was swiftly attacked as religion masquerading as science, "creationism in a lab coat." The IDers attempted to rebut this charge, claiming that a dispassionate examination of the evidence led them to conclude that certain biological structures are too complex to have evolved through Darwinian natural selection. The resulting public debates ranged over sensitive philosophical and theological subjects such as the role of God in natural history and the relationship of science to religion. Some might wonder whether such subjects are fit for political discussion at all. However, this debate could not have been circumvented by a filter on so-called private reasons, because the disagreement itself was to a great extent about whether the ID arguments were religious or scientific; whether they were an exercise in private, theological reasoning or public, scientific reasoning.

Another major public issue is the regulation of agricultural biotechnology such as chemical pesticides and genetically modified foods. Suspicion and opposition to agricultural biotech is especially pronounced in Europe. The European Union has adopted tight restrictions on the trade of genetically modified organisms. The national constitution of Switzerland requires respect for the "integrity" and "dignity" of living things and for "living nature as a whole." These attitudes have real costs. In 2002, the government of Zambia refused donations of American corn for famine relief because the corn had been genetically modified, citing antibiotech arguments. Western nations' ban on the pesticide DDT for decades effectively blocked its use in Africa to combat mosquito-borne malaria, which kills on the order of five thousand children each day.

Is the opposition to antibiotech religious? It is not easy to say. Critics claim that it springs from a quasi-spiritual, nondoctrinal mélange of environmentalist politics, Mother Earth worship, Romantic idealization of nature, and the voodoolike farming techniques of Rudolph Steiner.[12] Activists on the other side prefer to think, instead, that their views are based in objective factual assumptions and concern for public health. Here again, the secular liberal rule of public reason is of no use. Antibiotech is a complex mix of factual reasons and nontraditional, post-Christian spirituality, and the parties to the debate disagree on where one ends and the other begins. A better approach is to forget about what kind of arguments they are and concentrate on whether they are any good.

Finally, the strictures of public reason would not only cut against the religious conscience. A filter fine enough to keep religious ideals and values out of political debate will also keep out fundamental *moral* convictions, such as the ideals of freedom, fairness, or benevolence. Matters of morality, as much as matters of faith, are subject to disagreements among sincere and sensible people. Therefore it would be arbitrary to single out one but not the other for political exile. Yet to exile both would leave citizens with next to nothing to discuss. Some would reply that religious differences should be singled out because they are inevitably more divisive than differences of other kinds. But this reply is empirically dubious. The bitter disputes surrounding globalization, race relations, global warming, tax policy, or the war on terrorism, for example, are not theological in nature but ethical, social, and factual. There is no nonarbitrary way to bar religious conscience alone from politics. Either bar no claims of conscience, or bar them all. Unless liberals are ready to abandon moral discourse altogether, the choice is plain.

Many would reply that the distinctive trouble with religious conscience is that it is "subjective"—it is beyond debate. As philosopher Thomas Nagel put it, when "part of the source of your conviction is personal faith or revelation," political debate becomes a mere "clash between irreconcilable subjective convictions" rather than a disagreement in "the common, public domain." Instead, our political reasoning must meet a certain level of "higher-order impartiality" or objectivity. One must be prepared "to submit one's reasons to the criticism of others, and to find that the exercise of a common critical rationality and consideration of evidence that can be shared will reveal that one is mistaken."[13] This is the Argument from Subjectivity. Let's look more closely at the supposed subjectivity of conscience.

American Airlines flight 1304 was scheduled to leave Southwest Florida International Airport for Dallas, Texas, one afternoon in March 2004 when the Transportation Security Administration received a call that there might be a bomb onboard. The caller was a self-professed psychic who had apparently received this information via extrasensory powers. The TSA and Port Authority police investigated, delaying and consequently canceling the flight, but nothing was found. A local TSA administrator commented, "We can't ignore anything. We want to take the appropriate measures."[14] Ask yourself how the authorities should have dealt with the caller, given that the emergency turned out to be entirely unreal.

The Department of Justice's *Criminal Behavior Manual* section on Prosecutive Policy for Imparting or Conveying False Information— Bomb Hoax, details the legal repercussions of making airline bomb threats that turn out to be false: "civil and criminal felony provisions for the conveyance of false information regarding attempts or alleged attempts to destroy, damage, or disable aircraft, aircraft related facilities or motor vehicles and their related facilities." The penalties are attached to "false information . . . resulting in delay of the flight or inconvenience to airport employees and passengers."[15] Does it make a difference that the source of the false information is supposed to be a mysterious intuition unknown to science? Or should the law apply to "psychic" bomb threats just as it does to teenage pranks?

The point of this story is not that psychics are a serious threat to air safety. Rather the story illustrates something important about subjectivity; namely, that the *source* of a belief in an intuitive or first-personal experience does nothing whatever to remove that belief from the realm of interpersonal scrutiny and accountability. Nagel's observation is an important one, but it must not be overstated. Just because you do not or could not share a conviction does not mean that it is beyond your comprehension and critical evaluation. My irrational fear of flying (rooted in a childhood experience, let's say) can be intelligible and open to critical evaluation by you (on the grounds, for example, that flying is by far the safest way to travel long distances), even though you lack it and the experience that produced it. The fact that a belief originates in a subjective experience does not inoculate it against interpersonal criticism. Would it change our moral condemnation of the three Rwandan Roman Catholic nuns convicted of aiding the slaughter of ethnic Tutsis to discover that they were impelled by secret spiritual visions?

So long as the reasons we introduce into public discourse—reasons of conscience included—are regarded by all as open to public scrutiny, then the challenge of subjectivity can be grappled with, if not totally eliminated. Ideally, conversation in politics abides by the norms of all reasoned conversation. Unless we are willing to present others with reasons for what we say that are open to analysis by them, we are engaging in monologue, not dialogue. A serious, earnest claim of conscience should be held to the same standards as any other: honesty, rationality, consistency, evidence, feasibility, legality, morality, and revisability.

Honesty means we typically say what we really think; rationality, that we take efficient means to our ends (at least); consistency, that we are prepared to accept the implications of our views as they apply in other instances; evidence, that it matters how our reasons link up with the real world (or don't); feasibility, that the proposal is realistic; legality and morality, that it is in accord with our laws and ethics; and revisability, that we are prepared to entertain objections, criticisms, and changes.

Honest religious believers have nothing to lose and much to gain by treating their faith as objective in this sense. Susceptibility to criticism is the price of admission to serious public life. But it is a price that they should be willing to pay, for convictions take their strength from surviving trials, not from avoiding them. Anything less would be a trivialization of religion, the notion that "religion is like building model airplanes, just another hobby: something quiet, something private, something trivial—and not really a fit activity for intelligent, public-spirited adults."[16] The Privacy Fallacy gets both faith and secularism wrong. If secularism is to fulfill its historical role in containing the illiberal encroachments of religion, it must give up privacy for the openness of conscience.

If religious and moral conscience is allowed into the democratic conversation, whither the separation of church and state?[17] Won't this put society on a slippery slope toward theocratic politics? On the contrary, as the following chapter shows, we can better secure the principles of separation of religion and state and the freedom of belief by including conscience in public debate than by precluding it.

Would a politics of the open conscience give a green light to the "imposition" of sectarian religious ethics on public life? The first thing to say is that if you are worried about the imposition of sectarian ethics on public life, the privacy of conscience is of no help. It won't prevent religious citizens from contributing to public life, as is their right in a free society. The Privacy Fallacy will only hamper the secular liberals who would otherwise be responding and defending their alternative moral views. This is precisely what has happened in the American debates over the rights of human embryos.

Embryonic stem cells have become the latest battle in the War of the Wombs. As scientists have learned, they hold the (as yet unproven) potential to revolutionize medicine and improve life, giving us new tools to deal with conditions such as Parkinson's and Alzheimer's disease, spinal cord injury, stroke, burns, heart disease, diabetes, arthritis, perhaps even HIV-AIDS. The best source of stem cells to date is cloned embryos, embryos derived from transferring the nucleus—the command center of the cell—from a bodily cell into an egg cell. Citing ethical and religious concerns, the Bush administration enacted a moratorium on federal funding for creating new lines of stem cells and later advocated a blanket ban at the United Nations.

Why? The argument favored by the President's Council on Bioethics, and its chairman, Leon Kass (an MD and the author of a book called *The Beginning of Wisdom: Reading Genesis*), was that techniques like cloning violate the "dignity of human procreation." Of course, since 1972 Dr. Kass had been making similar warnings about an emerging reproductive technology called in vitro fertilization, or IVF. On July 25, 1978, Louise Brown was born, the first IVF baby. Since then, more than a million births worldwide have confirmed that IVF and related assisted reproductive techniques, although not risk free, are largely safe. Has human life lost its humanness? Apparently it, and in particular, Ms. Brown's, has not.

There are real ethical concerns about the rights and status of the women whose eggs are used (in large quantities) for research involving nuclear transfer. Egg donation is an invasive surgical process that carries risks of liver damage, kidney failure, or stroke. There are also worries about the commodification of women's bodies. If one is concerned about the rights of egg donors, however, banning cloning is the worst remedy. When national governments wash their hands of embryonic research, they only encourage commercialization by leaving the research to private interests. This is what happened with the in vitro industry. Because of the opposition, the government withdrew, leaving assisted reproduction to a largely unregulated private industry with little oversight on disclosure of health risks, no limits on the number of implantations, and severe economic inequity in access to assisted reproduction. The most ethical and prudent response to these new biomedical practices is to publicly support them under a system of regulations designed to protect and promote important social values, such as health, safety, liberty, and respect for persons.

What explains this shameful failure to promote promising medical science while fully protecting the rights of research subjects? It is the belief that a fertilized egg cell is owed the same moral consideration as an adult human person, that blastocysts have rights (the "life begins at conception" formulation was made obsolete by nuclear transfer technology, which requires no sperm). This is the only argument that, if successful, could support an all-out ban on nuclear transfer research: no zygote left behind. If it is correct, then cloning for stem cells results in the murder of countless innocent people in order to increase the still uncertain chance of helping some other people. Without question, that would make it a great moral outrage that must be stopped.

The conviction that zygotes are not just biologically human tissue but full moral persons is indispensable to the stem cell and cloning debate in America. But it is an utter failure as an argument against the practices. Every reasonable ethical system draws a distinction between biological humanness and moral personhood (even the Catholic Church conceded in 1987 that personhood is a philosophical question that cannot be resolved simply by citing scripture). We accord persons moral consideration because they have sentience and interests, features totally absent from dot-sized clumps of cells. What's more, if week-old embryos are persons, then we should prohibit not only stem cell research but IVF as well, which also involves creation and destruction of excess embryos, hundreds of thousands of them. The only "compromise" in such a situation would be to stop the practice and conduct proper burials for the thousands of frozen embryos now stored in the nation's fertility clinics. In vitro ad absurdum. Suffice it to say that if any one of us were passing by an in vitro fertilization clinic in flames and we had the ability to save a five-year-old girl trapped inside, or save two or even ten thousand frozen embryos instead, no one would hesitate for even an instant.

What is most astonishing is that despite the utter failure of zygotic personhood as an argument, almost no notable critics of the administration's policy have addressed it. How can this be? One explanation is that the value of life, the theory of ensoulment, and the miracles of creation are private matters, according to the Privacy Fallacy. Therefore, they are not appropriate subjects for political conversation. This is the generalization of a lesson—mistakenly drawn from *Roe v. Wade*—that the politics of abortion could be settled by bracketing the question of the moral status of the fetus.

Unfortunately, it is impossible to seriously engage the opposition to stem cell research without taking on the question of the moral status of the embryo. This exchange from the debates in the US Congress is typical. An opponent of embryonic stem cell research invokes the sanctity of life: "I support stem cell research with only one exception—research that requires killing human life. Taxpayer-funded stem cell research must be carried out in an ethical manner in a way that respects the sanctity of human life."[18] A defender responds with anecdotes of medical miracles: "When I was injured in an accidental shooting almost twenty-six years ago, I was told I would never walk again. I always held out hope that someday that would change. Through the miracles of science and prayer, there would be a cure for spinal cord injuries. It is only today that that promise for a cure has become truly real."[19] Is the legislator advocating the state-sanctioned killing of a large number of people to benefit the health of one? That is what is at stake, unless zygotes are not persons.

In the American debates over stem cells, George W. Bush cited a higher medical authority ("life is a gift from God"). Ron Reagan Jr., a nonbeliever, sought a second opinion. Unlike most secularists, however, Reagan did more than just gripe that God doesn't belong in politics. Rather than throwing up his hands and seeing the disagreement as a "clash of irreconcilable subjective convictions," he defended the claims of his conscience against the claims of his opponents' conscience. In a letter to the *New York Times* on August 12, 2004, he wrote: "Those opposed to embryonic stem cell research are entitled to their beliefs. But those making a moral argument are obliged to be morally consistent. If destroying even an artificially created 'embryo' in a petri dish is equivalent to murder, then I would expect the White House to campaign vigorously against in vitro fertilization clinics that routinely dispose of unused early-stage embryos by the thousands." Reagan did not challenge the very right of religious moralists to make their assertions in public. Instead, he took their assertions for what they are: serious contributions to our collective life that merit critical scrutiny in light of public standards of conscience.

Secular liberals cannot tackle bioethical controversies like stem cell research without unflinchingly looking the moral and religious issues in the face. The same can be argued for political debates over genetic engineering, HIV-AIDS research and prevention in the developing world, sex education, gay marriage, abortion, euthanasia, and capital punishment. What's required is a little of the clarity and honesty of Louis Guenin of Harvard Medical School, who said, "We honor human life by probing our moral views to their foundations. There we find a common conclusion. It is virtuous to eliminate suffering in actual lives when we may do so at no cost in potential lives. In this work of mercy, scientists form the vanguard. They also respect human life who toil to relieve its afflictions."[20]

Over two decades ago, Richard John Neuhaus decried the "naked public square." As he saw it, religion was being driven out of public life by secularism taken too far. Today, politics is pious as never before, and it's the secularists who have lost their shirts. Secularism has reached an impasse. The project of "privatizing" conscience has become self-defeating. By relegating conscience to the world of the subjective and personal, the Privacy Fallacy insulates it from due public scrutiny and collapses questions about a person's beliefs into attacks on a person's identity. If they want to resist the social agenda of theological conservatism, secular liberals will have to do better than asking the devout to please refrain from speaking their minds.

While the politics of conscience sketched above is not entirely welcome to strict secularists who regard any introduction of religion into the public square as an illegitimate intrusion, neither is it comforting to those religious citizens who suppose that their faith can provide a voice of moral authority that issues from someplace "higher," above the rigors of politics or the conscience of their secular peers. At its best, the public square can be an attractive space, a place where signs of our dearest convictions may be exchanged under a canopy of civility and mutual respect. But by all rights it is also a place searched by the light of public scrutiny, a light which is often neither soft nor flattering. Those who wish to locate their religion there should not be surprised if it never looks the same again.

3.

Spinoza's Guide to Theocracy

We suffer constantly from a certain desire to make other people share our views; it is part of our calling, so to speak.
—Montesquieu, *The Persian Letters*

Theocrats are not idiots. John Calvin, the great Protestant theologian who had Michael Servetus executed in 1553 for denying that Jesus was his own father, earned a doctorate in law at the age of twenty-three. His correspondence fills eleven volumes. Among the first generation of the American Puritans, there was roughly one university-trained scholar, often from Cambridge or Oxford, for every forty or fifty families.[1] "Only six years after John Winthrop's arrival in Salem harbor, the people of Massachusetts took from their own treasury the fund from which to found a university."[2] Were any young minds to stray too far from the orthodoxy of the "Christian communion," however, they could face a death sentence for blasphemy under Massachusetts Bay Colony law. The Iranian revolution that would usher in a clerical tyranny under the Ayatollah Khomeini was embraced by the fashionable French structuralist thinker Michel Foucault, who said it represented the "perfectly unified collective will" of the people.[3]

Neither are theocrats crazies, as a matter of course. Think about it from their point of view. You are responsible for the broader community. Governments exist to shape and serve the community. Their roles are defined and constrained by a more fundamental moral order, which is discoverable through the ethics of the true religion (yours, naturally). One role of government is to secure the good of its members, the citizens. Part of securing the good of citizens is helping them to pursue lives of moral and religious virtue so far as this is possible.

In the *Laws*, Plato's "Athenian Stranger" discusses the best laws for the regime of a new city-state. Among them are a general prohibition of impiety and punishments for atheism ranging from admonition and temporary imprisonment to death. In the discussions of official delegations to sacrifice to gods in foreign nations and the invocation of gods during homicide trials, Plato also recommends what we would now regard as an extensive intermingling of religious and political life (the ancients didn't draw the same distinction).[4] The rationale for these practices is straightforward. The aim of good legislation is to make citizens as virtuous as possible. Piety is important for virtue. So the regime ought to use its power to encourage right religious conduct.[5]

None of these ideas is bonkers. Most of us believe that governments are legitimate to the extent that they accord with some more fundamental, prepolitical norms. We believe that murderers are punished because murder is wrong; not that murder is wrong because murderers are punished. If homosexuality were gravely immoral, why shouldn't this, too, be reflected in law in the same way? Most of us believe it is the responsibility of the state to protect certain things dear to its citizens. If protecting the good of citizens means protecting their life, health, and property, how much more important is it to protect the life everlasting, the health of the soul? Many of us believe that the state ought to have a hand in inculcating certain traits of character, necessary to self-government, such as trustworthiness and civility. But if fidelity to one's word is important, fidelity to one's God must be paramount.

If I disagree with your idea of a religious state, and I wish to disabuse you of it, I get nowhere by saying that God and morality are private matters, if by private matters I just mean things that the state should not mess with. For whether God and morality are things that the state should not mess with is precisely what is at issue in our disagreement. I can't start with the premise that theocracy is a mistake to justify the claim that theocracy is a mistake, at least not if I am trying to persuade someone who doesn't already reject theocracy. In philosophy, this error in reasoning is called begging the question, the fallacy of simply presupposing the rejection of an interlocutor's position when one should be giving him reasons to reject it. Compare: Every sentence in this book is true. What's my evidence, you ask? Please see the sentence before last. That does not settle the question of whether the sentence before last is true. In the same way, a bald appeal to privacy in an argument against a theocrat will only beg the question of whether matters of conscience are private.

The theocrats in the history of Christendom were not defeated by the idea that conscience is private. That idea could arise only after secularism had won the West for reasons of an entirely different sort. The original authors of the secular liberal tradition would not recognize themselves in their descendants of today. They never maintained that political discourse must be "neutral" on spiritual questions. In fact, most of their most influential flagship arguments against the establishment of religion depended on controversial theological claims. That is certainly true of Baruch Spinoza, the great progenitor of European Enlightenment. Here I follow Rebecca Goldstein's *Betraying Spinoza*.

Spinoza had a vision. A Jewish skeptic whose parents had fled Portugal to escape the Inquisition, he glimpsed modernity under lugubrious Dutch skies. This gentle philosopher, who earned a modest living grinding lenses, invented a new way of seeing religion, society, and conscience. His visionary ideas, published in the 1670 *Theological-Political Treatise*, were declared heresy, even in the exceptionally tolerant atmosphere that prevailed in the Dutch republic at the time. The West would never look at the Bible the same way again. The *Treatise* (like the posthumous *Ethics*) was banned but found its way onto the bookshelves of John Locke and, through him, influenced the founding of America. The European and American Enlightenments began in seventeenth-century Holland.

The *Treatise* is an extended argument for freedom of conscience and against state enforcement of traditional religious orthodoxy. It concludes that "every man may think as he pleases, and say what he thinks":

> The most tyrannical government will be one where the individual is denied the freedom to express and to communicate to others what he thinks, and a moderate government is one where this freedom is granted to every man. . . . It is not, I repeat, the purpose of the state to transform men from rational beings into beasts or puppets, but rather to enable them to develop their mental and physical faculties in safety, to use their reason without restraint. . . . Thus, the purpose of the state is, in reality, freedom.[6]

Spinoza carefully constructs two arguments for the secular, open society. One is an argument based on human nature and the nature of belief. But the bulk of the work is given to an elaborate religious argument, an Argument from Theology for secularism.

The theological argument is both utterly simple and fiendishly sophisticated—its moves bold and unanticipated. One might expect Spinoza to deny that the state has the right to enforce religion on its subjects. Instead, he argues that this is the responsibility of the state— to ensure obedience to the true, universal religion. The practice of the universal religion consists solely in acts of justice and charity toward one's neighbors. Therefore, when the state uses the force of law to compel citizens to be fair and good to one another, it is thereby legislating piety: "Wherever justice and charity have the force of law and ordinance, there is God's kingdom."

> I can now venture to enumerate the dogmas of the universal faith, the basic teachings which Scripture as a whole intends to convey. These must all be directed to this one end: that there is a Supreme

Being who loves justice and charity, whom all must obey in order to be saved, and must worship by practicing justice and charity to their neighbor.[7]

Spinoza documents his radical revision of Western religion by painstaking exegesis of the Old and New Testaments. In the first step of this exegesis, Spinoza attempts to show that the biblical prophets "possessed only an extraordinary power of imagination, not of intellect; and that God did not reveal to them any philosophic mysteries, but only things of a very simple nature, adapted to their preconceived beliefs." Second, "Scripture conveys and teaches its message in a way best suited to the comprehension of all men, and not resorting to a chain of deductive reasoning from axioms and definitions, but speaking quite simply." Third, "The difficulty in understanding Scripture lies only in its language, and not in the high level of its argumentation."[8]

There is universal agreement that Scripture was written and disseminated not just for the learned but for all men of every time and race, and this by itself justifies us in concluding that Scripture does not require us to believe anything beyond what is necessary for fulfilling of the said commandment.[9]

The realization that the aim of scripture is not to impart philosophical or scientific knowledge "leads obviously to the conclusion that Scripture demands nothing from men but obedience, and condemns not ignorance, but only obstinacy."[10] Even Moses was more lawyer than philosopher. He presented the Jews with a covenant, not an argument. Rather than attempting to persuade them of the truth of doctrine by reason, "He induced the people to obey the Law under threat of punishments, while exhorting them thereto by promise of rewards."[11]

So, the Bible teaches only those things needed for obedience to God. The final step of Spinoza's Bible study is the claim that "obedience to God consists solely in loving one's neighbor (for he who loves his neighbor in obedience to God's command has fulfilled the Law, as Paul says in Romans chapter 13 v. 8)."[12]

> The message of the Gospel is one of simple faith; that is, belief in God and reverence for God, or—which is the same thing—obedience to God. . . . Scripture itself tells us quite clearly over and over again what every man should do in order to serve God, declaring that the entire Law consists in this alone, to love one's neighbor.[13]

If the powers that be restrict themselves to promoting this simple faith, they will have no stake in divisive theological controversies over esoteric dogmas like unitarianism, transubstantiation, or infant baptism. These debates will be left to the free conscience. The universal religion should contain "only those dogmas which obedience to God absolutely demands, and without which such obedience is absolutely impossible. As for other dogmas, every man should embrace those that he, being the best judge of himself, feels will do most to strengthen him in love of justice. Acceptance of this principle would, I suggest, leave no occasion for controversy in the Church."[14]

In Spinoza's vision, it is under the institutions of the tolerant secular state that the reign of the true religion can come to earth. A state that respects conscience grants the widest possible space to human understanding and so frees us for the most noble activity of which we are capable. In contemplating our place in the workings of nature and its eternal, necessary laws, our minds meet the divine. This *amor intellectualis Dei*, the intellectual love of God (for Spinoza, something like the immutable laws of nature themselves), is the unsurpassed human good. In his political theology, the secular state is a sacred state.

Obviously, Spinozist spirituality will not satisfy the religious traditionalist who holds that there is more to the one true faith than loving one's neighbor. In this sense, Spinoza's Argument from Theology is radically skeptical about traditional religion. It succeeds only insofar as it convinces believers that the covenant with the Israelites, the resurrection of Christ, the revelation to Muhammad, and all other religious dogmas are in fact unimportant to a life of real holiness. The contemporary mood, "spiritual not religious," is only now catching up to Spinoza.

The Argument from Theology is meant to justify the use of state power to change citizens' behavior, bringing it under the sway of justice and charity. In a second argument running through the *Treatise*, Spinoza shows why attempts to use state power for anything more— to change citizens' minds—must end in self-defeat. Coercion of conscience is futile because human nature is such that belief answers only to evidence and not to command: "It would be vain to command a subject to hate one to whom he is indebted for some service, to love one who has done him harm, to refrain from taking offense at insults, from wanting to be free of fear, or from numerous similar things that necessarily follow from the laws of human nature."[15]

> Honesty and sincerity of heart is not imposed on man by legal command or by the state's authority. It is an absolute fact that nobody can be constrained to a state of blessedness by force or law; to this end one needs godly and brotherly exhortation, a good upbringing, and most of all, a judgment that is independent and free.
>
> Therefore, as the sovereign right to free opinion belongs to every man even in matters of religion, and it is inconceivable that any man can surrender his right, there also belongs to every man the sovereign right and supreme authority to judge freely with regard to religion, and consequently to explain it and interpret it for himself.[16]

Attempts to compel belief by force of law will fail, and worse, they will only provoke citizens to turn against the government. "Men in general are so constituted that their resentment is more aroused when beliefs which they think to be true are treated as criminal, and when that which motivates their pious conduct to God and man is accounted as wickedness. In consequence, they are emboldened to denounce the laws and go to all lengths to oppose the magistrate, considering it not a disgrace but honourable to stir up sedition and to resort to any outrageous action in this cause."[17] State promotion of piety is self-defeating and futile because it operates by coercion, while authentic belief springs from conscience according to its own laws. This is the Argument from Futility.

Both of Spinoza's arguments are for liberty of conscience; neither is for privacy of conscience, and neither holds that conscience is free from objective standards of truth and right. His case for secularism presupposes that conscience is open—that questions of religion and value can be discussed critically and openly on the basis of shared norms. Had he instead held that matters of conscience have no place in rational public discourse, the Argument from Theology would have been impossible to formulate. It is all about miracles, prophecy, and the intentions of God in history. The whole spirit of Spinoza's critical biblical exegesis—which aimed to bring biblical claims under objective, natural scientific scrutiny—is anathema to the Privacy Fallacy.

Spinoza's Argument from Futility is the antidote to the Liberty Fallacy, according to which conscience is free from norms because it is free from coercion. Spinoza's argument says that conscience cannot by its nature be forced. Even if we wanted to, we could not surrender our right to make up our own minds on religious questions. The problem with coercing belief in general is that belief is not simply up to voluntary choice. Belief tracks objective states of affairs, not our subjective attitudes. Even when we are left free to believe, we are not free to believe whatever we want. We are given the political and social space in which reason and evidence can take belief where they will.

If I have only gratitude and loyalty toward you, no one can command me to believe that you have wronged me. If I reflect on the matter, my conscience tells me the opposite, and I cannot tell it otherwise. I might reconsider the matter from another perspective or take into account new or revised information. I may even be persuaded to change my judgment. Yet even then the change would have been wrought by my conscience, not by my or anyone else's act of will. The coercion of conscience, then, is self-defeating because conscience is objective. This is the paradox of conscience; that in the same moment when he exercised the greatest freedom of conscience, Martin Luther could truthfully declare, "I cannot do otherwise."[18] Freedom of conscience is an overriding value in Spinoza's philosophy because conscience gives us truth. It is through the free interplay of thought and expression that we can understand our world, ourselves, and enter into the communion of the intellect with the eternal principles of nature, the intellectual love of God that is our *summom bonum.*

Spinoza's life, like his philosophy, was about conversation, about people seeking truth together: "I value, above all other things out of my control, the joining hands of friendship with men who are lovers of truth."[19] As a young man, Spinoza contracted the contagious skepticism of Descartes, who had spent his most productive years in Holland. It would undermine his faith. He concealed his doubts until after the death of his pious father, then voiced them to the Jewish community of Amsterdam, which excommunicated him while he was still in his twenties. Fellow Jews, including his relatives, refused to speak with him, and consequently he was forced to leave his position in his family's business. Living in The Hague, Spinoza occasionally attended church services so as to better join in the discussion of religious subjects with his Christian neighbors. He turned down a professorship at Heidelberg but devoted himself to correspondence with scientists and scholars from across Europe. Upon retirement, he went to live among dissident Christians.

The arguments that ultimately would win the day in favor of liberty of conscience and church-separation in Europe and America were versions of the Argument from Theology and the Argument from Futility. One of the earliest defenses of toleration in Europe, *Concerning Heretics and Those Who Burn Them*, came in 1524 from the Swiss Anabaptist Balthasar Hubmaier. It was an appeal to Christian principles, an Argument from Theology: "The law that condemns heretics to the fire builds up both Zion in blood and Jerusalem in wickedness. This is the will of Christ who said, 'Let both grow together till the harvest, lest while ye gather up the [weeds] ye root up also the wheat with them.' The inquisitors are the greatest heretics of all, since, against the doctrine and example of Christ, they condemn heretics to fire, and before the time of harvest root up the wheat with the [weeds]. For Christ did not come to butcher, destroy and burn, but that those that live might live more abundantly."[20] Hubmaier's fellow followers of Christ burned him four years later, but his argument lived on. Other dissenters fled the pyres of Europe for the New World. America was the project of heretics, but they were not secularists. The Massachusetts Puritans came not to escape theocracy but to escape someone else's theocracy. They soon set about erecting one they could call their own. The Puritan dissenters Roger Williams and Anne Hutchinson left to live more abundantly in Rhode Island. There they created what was the most secular government the world had ever seen.

Like Spinoza, Williams derived secularism from biblical theology.[21] He inferred from scriptural-historical evidence that no actual nations since Israel possessed or will possess its special status as God's nation. God no longer makes direct covenants with nations. Therefore, no existing government has the right to represent itself as favored by God. Government should avoid public funding of churches, religious tests for civil office, official prayers, and civil oaths that invoke the name of God. Above all, the state must not compel people to adopt the correct religious doctrines or forms of worship. Churches may be directed only by the righteous or "regenerate." Since the sovereignty of government resides in the people, and since most people are not among the regenerate, governments may not do the Church's work. In a metaphor that would later be picked up by Thomas Jefferson in his famous letter to the Danbury Baptists, Williams spoke of a wall separating the "garden" of the Church from the "wilderness" of the secular state.

Put on trial by the Massachusetts Bay Colony for convening "subversive" religious gatherings of women in her home, Anne Hutchinson told the court that God "hath left me to distinguish between the voice of my beloved and the voice of Moses, the voice of John the Baptist and the voice of antichrist, for all those voices are spoken of in scripture. Now if you do condemn me for speaking what in my conscience I know to be truth I must commit myself unto the Lord." Asked by the court how she knew which voice is the voice of the spirit, she replied, "How did Abraham know that it was God that bid him offer his son?"[22]

In the hands of secularists influenced by the European Enlightenment, the Argument from Theology would make use of highly unorthodox theology, as Spinoza had done. Benjamin Franklin, Thomas Jefferson, and James Madison were men of the Enlightenment. They had given up the God of Abraham for the more remote God of deism, an impersonal rational force (Tom Paine's "Almighty lecturer") now in retirement after thinking the world into being. But even the earnest Christian John Locke raised skeptical doubts in his famous 1689 *Letter concerning Toleration*. He aimed to afflict would-be persecutors with the question, What if we are wrong? "Princes, indeed, are born superior unto other men in power, but in nature equal. Neither the right nor the art of ruling does necessarily carry along with it the certain knowledge of other things, and least of all of true religion. For if it were so, how could it come to pass that the lords of the earth should differ so vastly as they do in religious matters?"[23] Locke assumes that those who would be responsible for establishing the state religion do not know which religion is true (or at least that others cannot know whether or not they know): "The one only narrow way which leads to Heaven is not better known to the Magistrate than to private Persons, and therefore I cannot safely take him for my Guide, who may probably be as ignorant of the way as my self." Locke's argument is based on a bold theological claim: no one can really be confident about which religion is true.[24]

The Argument from Futility has deep roots in the Christian tradition. Since the beginning, some Christians have always been persecuted, if not by someone else then by their coreligionists. And so they have invoked the Argument from Futility as a defense against persecution. In 1324, Marsilius of Padua wrote in his *Defensor Pacis* (Defender of the Peace) that "it would be useless . . . to coerce anyone to observe them [Christ's commandments], since the person who observed them under coercion would be helped not at all toward eternal salvation."[25] Or Erasmus: "That which is forced cannot be sincere, and that which is not voluntary cannot please Christ."[26] With the fracturing of Christendom in the sixteenth and seventeenth centuries, the dissident Protestant sects of the Baptists and Anabaptists would carry forward the cause of liberty of conscience. Leonard Busher, a member of the first Baptist congregation in England, declared in 1612: "[A]s kings and bishops cannot command the wind, so they cannot command faith. . . . You may force men to church against their consciences, but they will believe as they did afore."[27]

Locke's *Letter* makes much use of the voluntariness of belief:

> The care of souls cannot belong to the civil magistrate, because his power consists only in outward force; but true and saving religion consists in the inward persuasion of the mind, without which nothing can be acceptable to God. And such is the nature of the understanding, that it cannot be compelled to the belief of anything by outward force. Confiscation of estate, imprisonment, torments, nothing of that nature can have any such efficacy as to make men change the inward judgment that they have framed of things.[28]

Locke adds another layer to the argument, by claiming that even if coerced faith were possible, it would not be sufficient for salvation:

> All the life and power of true religion consist in the inward and full persuasion of the mind; and faith is not faith without believing. Whatever profession we make, to whatever outward worship we conform, if we are not fully satisfied in our own mind that the one is true and the other well pleasing unto God, such profession and such practice, far from being any furtherance, are indeed great obstacles to our salvation. For in this manner, instead of expiating other sins by the exercise of religion, I say, in offering thus unto God Almighty such a worship as we esteem to be displeasing unto Him, we add unto the number of our other sins those also of hypocrisy and contempt of His Divine Majesty.[29]

It is in this form that the argument came to America through the work of Jefferson and Madison. The American Revolution had led to the disestablishment of the Anglican Church, but some in Virginia sought public support for all recognized churches. Madison led the debate against Patrick Henry, whose proposed Virginia tax to support religious education provoked Madison's *Memorial and Remonstrance* in 1785:

> The Religion, then, of every man must be left to the conviction and conscience of every man; and it is the right of every man to exercise it as these may dictate. This right is in its nature an unalienable right. It is unalienable, because the opinions of men, depending only on the evidence contemplated in their own minds cannot follow the dictates of other men: It is unalienable also, because what is here a right towards men, is a duty towards the Creator.[30]

Henry stood by the ever-popular hypothesis that civil order cannot survive without a religious populace (as evidenced today by the lawless Denmark and Norway). Madison didn't challenge the hypothesis directly but instead took issue with the assumption that government is the best instrument for inculcating public religiosity. The debate largely came down to the proper way to promote piety.

Another argument from the *Memorial* is that the establishment of religion is bad for religion: "During almost fifteen centuries, has the legal establishment of Christianity been on trial. What have been its fruits? More or less in all places, pride and indolence in the Clergy, ignorance and servility in the laity, in both, superstition, bigotry and persecution."[31] By propping the Church on state support, establishment saps the vitality and self-sufficiency of the congregation. The effect is to "weaken in those who profess this Religion, a pious confidence in its innate excellence, and the patronage of its author; and to foster in those who still reject it a suspicion that its friends are too conscious of its fallacies to trust it to its own merits."[32] Again, Madison's case depends on a theological premise about the value of maintaining a particular kind of spiritual community.

The following year, Madison worked with Jefferson to pass a bill that Jefferson had drafted, the Virginia Statute for Religious Freedom, which would soon serve as a blueprint for the religion clauses of the First Amendment to the US Constitution. The Virginia Statute opens with these words: "Whereas Almighty God hath created the mind free; that all attempts to influence it by temporal punishments or burthens, or by civil incapacitations, tend only to beget habits of hypocrisy and meanness, and are a departure from the plan of the Holy author of our religion."[33]

Unlike their contemporary liberal descendants, the architects of American secularism did not insist that public debate should be purged of claims of religious and moral conscience. For them, like Spinoza, the aim of freedom was not to stifle but to further truth-seeking conversation on questions of conscience. As the Virginia Statute for Religious Freedom put it: "Truth is great and will prevail if left to herself . . . she is the proper and sufficient antagonist to error, and has nothing to fear from the conflict, unless by human interposition disarmed of her natural weapons, free argument and debate." Just after presenting his Argument from Futility, Locke goes on to explain that public figures may legitimately use means other than coercion to influence the consciences of others:

> It may indeed be alleged that the magistrate may make use of arguments, and, thereby; draw the heterodox into the way of truth, and procure their salvation. I grant it; but this is common to him with other men. In teaching, instructing, and redressing the erroneous by reason, he may certainly do what becomes any good man to do. Magistracy does not oblige him to put off either humanity or Christianity; . . . Every Man has Commission to admonish, exhort, convince another of Error, and, by reasoning, to draw him into Truth . . .[34]

Spinoza, Hutchinson, Williams, Locke, Jefferson, and Madison—none believed that claims of conscience, including theological claims, are private reasons having no place in politics. Instead, their arguments treated these reasons as open, open to rational examination and public debate. They envisioned a society in which people were free to share the insights of conscience and thereby draw each other into truth. They argued for the separation of religion and government. But they did not, and could not have advocated the separation of conscience and politics.

✣✣✣

What is the relevance of their views today? Why does it matter? It matters first because secular liberals should understand their own tradition. Even more critical, Western societies are now confronting and engaging at all levels with antisecular and antiliberal forces within Islam and Muslim cultures. Are there lessons to be had and resources to be found in the history of secularization in the West?

From its beginnings, Christian thought placed a wedge between the temporal order and the spiritual order: "Render unto Caesar what is Caesar's, and unto God what is God's." With the Christianization of the Roman Empire in the fourth century, God and Caesar found themselves sharing the same throne. Increasing interference by the empire in Church affairs spurred Christian leaders to define the civil and ecclesiastical roles more sharply. In the early fifth century, Augustine described Christians as dual citizens dwelling in the earthly City of Man but belonging to a heavenly City of God, the community of all saved souls. In 494, Pope Gelasius I wrote to the Emperor Anastasius:

> There are two powers, august Emperor, by which this world is chiefly ruled, namely, the sacred authority of the priests and the royal power. . . . If the ministers of religion, recognizing the supremacy granted you from heaven in matters affecting the public order, obey your laws, lest otherwise they might obstruct the course of secular affairs by irrelevant considerations, with what readiness should you not yield them obedience to whom is assigned the dispensing of the sacred mysteries of religion.[35]

This foundational Christian dualism has no analogue in Islamic civilization. Muslim life took its blueprint from the Quran and the sayings and deeds of the Prophet Muhammad and his companions, collected as the hadith. But the Quran and the hadith could not reasonably dictate every detail of life. So, they were developed into Islamic law, or sharia (literally, a path to a source of water) through interpretation and application by the four major Sunni schools of law. Sharia presents itself as a comprehensive path for living. It is a self-help manual, municipal code, and constitution combined, legislating everything

from personal hygiene and diet to the running of a judicial system—
Augustine's two cities merged, Gelasius's royal and priestly powers
fused into one hegemon. Muhammad was simultaneously the spiritual,
civil, and military leader, a tribal chief. Whereas the first Christians
kindled the light of their prophet in cellars, catacombs, and caves
hidden from the sword of earthly power, the first Muslims followed
their prophet into battle, conquering cities, then empires, for him.
Where they went, they would become the earthly power.

Today, confronted with global jihadism and Islamic theocracy in its
Sunni (Saudi Arabian) and Shia (Iranian) incarnations, some secular liberals call for a "reformation" of Islam that would make it a "personal,
private faith": "The restoration of religion to the sphere of the personal,
its depoliticization, is the nettle that all Muslim societies must grasp in
order to become modern."[36] Surely the depoliticization of Islam is a
great goal. But how to achieve it? Islam cannot simply be "restored" to
the personal sphere since, unlike Christianity, it was never there to begin
with. As practiced by the majority sects, Islam is essentially political.
How could the faith be privatized without being obliterated? Here it is
important to distinguish between so-called moderate Muslims and
reform-minded Muslims.[37] While moderates condemn violence and
repression but deny that Islam is in any way responsible, the reform-
minded take it as their religious duty to change their religion.

The Privacy Fallacy suggests a narrative of the West according to
which Europeans and Americans privatized Christianity while leaving
it doctrinally intact. In fact, Christianity was privatized through massive theological transformation, in some cases in the direction of the
Protestant model of salvation, and in others toward wholesale skepticism about the applicability of ancient scripture to society: the Argument from Futility and the Argument from Theology.

Do these arguments have analogues in the Islamic context? Just ask
Sayyid Iyad Jamaleddine, a reform-minded Iraqi Shiite cleric and one
of the true revolutionaries calling for absolute separation of mosque
and state in Iraq: "I am a Muslim. I am devoted to my religion. I want
to get it back from the state and that is why I want a secular state. . . .

When young people come to religion, not because the state orders them to but because they feel it themselves in their hearts, it actually increases religious devotion."[38] Madison couldn't have said it better.

Some secular liberals imagine that somehow Islam will reform itself without the bruising of anyone's theological opinions. Thankfully, Jamaleddine doesn't share their compunction. "Secularism is not blasphemy," he asserts. "The Koran is a book to be interpreted [by] each age. Each epoch should not be tied to interpretations from 1,000 years ago. We should be open to interpretations based on new and changing times." Jamaleddine's notion is not at all alien to Islamic tradition. In fact, it is deeply Quranic. Traditional thought makes room for a procedure known as *naskh* (literally "deletion") by which certain Quranic verses are modified or abrogated by others, a procedure sanctioned by the Quran itself. The towering figure of the Islamic Enlightenment, Ibn Rushd (known in the West as Averroës), believed that whenever scripture contradicts reason or knowledge, scripture must be reinterpreted allegorically to remove the conflict.

Another entry point for the theological transformation of Islam is the concept of revelation. The religion begins with the revelation to Muhammad. Yet according to some accounts, he could not read or write. The Quranic story of Joseph alone is 111 verses long. What does revelation mean in this context? That Muhammad had the story perfectly memorized (line by line or scene by scene)? And how does one verify that the companions of the Prophet understood his transmission of the story perfectly? The skeptical Muslim philosopher Ibn al-Rawandi observed in the ninth century that the Prophet himself admitted the fallibility of prophecy. Muhammad claimed that the Jews and Christians cling to many false beliefs that were revealed to them by their prophets.[39] The celebrated medieval medical pioneer, chemist, and philosopher Abu Bakr al-Razi argued that an all-wise deity would not give a special revelation to just one person, knowing that this would incite antagonism and disagreement. Instead, revelation would be given to all. Spinoza's strategy would be to open up the Muslim texts and their real origins to historical, scientific study.[40]

A tradition of so-called progressive revelation was developed by the Baha'is, who began in Iran in the 1840s as a dissident Muslim sect. Religious truth is revealed in installments, each one delivered by a different Manifestation of God (Krishna, Zoroaster, Buddha, Jesus, Muhammad, and Bahá'u'lláh) and targeted at a particular audience to match its present needs and level of understanding. Through successive revelations, and a series of religions founded thereupon, humanity receives increasing religious wisdom as it becomes ready to receive it. The latest revelation supersedes the previous (which may present the Baha'is with the unusual problem of having to explain why one shouldn't convert to Scientology).

The burning question is whether there exist Islamic analogues to the dissident Protestant sects that pioneered the freedom of conscience—minority Muslim communities that possess both the intellectual armamentarium and the institutional and demographic strength to start an enduring and affecting social movement of religious reform. The Baha'is, unlike the Puritans who rose up against the Crown in the English Civil War, are apolitical by creed. The Ahmadiyya Muslim Community, originating in South Asia, officially stands for peace and universal brotherhood, but its far-flung adherents lack the Islamic cultural authority reserved for Sunni Arabs.

Muslims like Jamaleddine contend that there can be no lasting democratic reform of Islamic societies without doctrinal reform of Islam so as to embrace reason, science, and free inquiry. As with Spinoza and Madison, these Islamic reformers can construct their cases for secularism only by operating outside of the confines of the Privacy Fallacy. The full defense of secularism inevitably involves substantive claims about religion. To the extent that secularism forbids public deliberation about such claims, it becomes self-undermining. Globally, religion is more important than ever before. Some sociologists of religion speak of the coming desecularization of the industrialized world. From a purely pragmatic standpoint, secularists should avail themselves of the arguments that reach the religious where they live—at the level of conscience.

The pragmatic approach convinced Thomas Farr, the first director of the Office of International Religious Freedom at the US Department of State: "American diplomats have got to abandon their disposition to treat religion as a private matter or something unfit for policy analysis. American diplomacy must accept that most religious communities by their nature seek to influence the rules and the norms under which they live."[41] The challenge, as he sees it, "in planning democracy, certainly in Muslim countries, is not one of privatizing religion—that's a fool's errand—but of enticing Muslim communities to embrace liberal norms as consistent with their own religious beliefs." This does not mean that diplomats need degrees in theology. But they need to be "realists when it comes to the issue of religion, addressing religion much as they do economics and politics—as a powerful, natural, human enterprise that influences how men, women and nations behave."

Another society interpenetrated by public religion is India. South Asia and East Asia are rich in secular and humanist heritage. While secular government may have come first in Western Europe and North America, secular values of pluralism and toleration go much further back in South Asia, from the world's oldest materialistic philosophical school, the Carvaka of the seventh century BCE, to the liberalism of the Mughal kings, and the humanism of Bengali literature and music, like that of Lalon Shah, the eighteenth-century troubadour, who wrote, "Oh when will we see a society that recognizes no racial distinctions between Muslim, Hindu, Christian, and Buddhist?"

India's relationship to secularism today is as complex as all things Indian. Thanks to the influence of Western-educated founders like Nehru, the constitution of the country is explicitly secular. Article 51a makes it a duty of every Indian citizen to cultivate a spirit of inquiry, humanism, and "scientific temper." Arguably, Nehru's concept of secularism was closest to the American concept: total separation of religion from government and freedom of conscience. However, the meaning of secularism in India is hotly contested. The Hindu Right, which remains a very powerful force, makes the perversely logical argument that Hinduism is inherently secular because of its pluralism and tolerance and therefore secularists should favor the establishment of Hinduism as an official state religion. Their slogan is "Hindu India, secular India." Others argue that Indian secularism requires equal promotion of all religions (*sarva dharma samanvay*) rather than neutrality. Such policies are extremely dangerous in a society constantly vulnerable to deadly Muslim-Hindu riots such as those in Gujarat.

The pragmatic path of religious diplomacy may be unavoidable, but it is perilous. The peril is that "addressing" faith will in practice come to compromising on matters of principle in pursuit of "stability" or short-term strategic interest. Secular liberals must be prepared to talk religion while insisting on certain nonnegotiable political values: freedom of conscience and secular government. A positive model of this strategy could be found in June 2007, when Iraqi clerics convened for a major interreligious conference in Baghdad.[42] They issued a document, also signed by a representative of the prime minister, calling on Iraqis to oppose the militias and to support reconciliation and democracy. The conference was organized, at the request of the clerics, by the US Department of Defense. Meanwhile, "enticing Muslim communities to embrace liberal norms" has proved equally treacherous in Afghanistan.

In 2002 the US-led coalition routed the Taliban from Afghanistan (or at least from Kabul) and worked with Afghans to create a new government, importing a law professor from New York University to advise them on the writing of the constitution. The Americans were overanxious not to offend religious sensibilities in the new Islamic Republic of Afghanistan. From the process emerged a regime that is subordinate to Islamic law and in principle at the mercy of mullahs' interpretation, so that, when an Afghan named Abdul Rahman converted from Islam to Christianity, he was sentenced, in early 2006, to beheading for apostasy. The constitution states in Article 3 that "no law can be contrary to the beliefs and provisions of the sacred religion of Islam." The judiciary interpreted this statement to mean that sharia law overrides the guarantee in Article 7 to abide by the Universal Declaration of Human Rights. International outcry eventually brought about Rahman's removal to safety in Italy. But this result came about in spite of the legal structure of the American-backed government, not because of it.

The case of Mr. Rahman should weigh heavy on the heart of every secular liberal and every decent human being. However, there are no solutions to be found in the Privacy Fallacy. The privacy of conscience has little to do with preventing the intermingling of the institutions of religion and government. On the one hand, sectarian arguments can be used for secularism, and on the other hand, public reasons can be marshaled against it.

Some of the most famous arguments for intermingling religion and government have been premised on the presumably public values of civil order and national self-interest. Jean-Jacques Rousseau argued that a "civil religion" is necessary to motivate citizens to follow the law and thus to maintain the social order.[43] The civil religion he advocated in *The Social Contract* is a "purely civil profession of faith, the articles of which it is the business of the Sovereign to arrange, not precisely as dogmas of religion, but as sentiments of sociability without which it is impossible to be either a good citizen or a faithful subject."[44] The articles of civil religion are the "existence of a powerful, wise, and benevolent Divinity, who foresees and provides the life to come, the happiness of the just, the punishment of the wicked, the sanctity of the social contract and the laws."[45] The sovereign is entitled to enforce this civil religion by expelling those who disbelieve its doctrines and by putting to death those who publicly profess belief but fail to act accordingly. Illiberal it may be, but the rationale for Rousseauian civil religion is a public one: the necessity to motivate citizens to follow the law and keep the peace.[46]

Consider temporary debates about the public funding of sectarian schools in England or faith-based community services in the United States. Defenders of state funding for sectarian schools typically appeal to public, nonsectarian reasons such as the value of equal opportunity to education: through no fault of their own, many children would be unable to receive high-quality education without the existence of programs that result in the channeling of public funds to religious organizations. Secularists can object to these arguments on the merits (for instance, that they will fuel social balkanization and inter-religious strife), but they cannot complain that they are private. There is no necessary link between the use of public reasons to support a policy and the secular character of that policy, nor between private reasons and antisecular policies.

Among the most successful arguments for secularism in the West historically were the Argument from Theology and the Argument from Futility. Both deployed controversial religious and theological assumptions in their critiques of theocracy. The Privacy Fallacy would have secular liberals avoid contested religious claims altogether, thus preventing them from openly criticizing the case for theocracy and helping themselves to any workable argument against it. Liberals should be busy upholding and popularizing the best arguments for secular government, not worrying over which arguments can pass through the screen of publicity.

Freedom of belief is central to secularism. Which ideal will better protect it—the private conscience or the open conscience? The first thing to note is that the Privacy Fallacy, when put into practice, will unduly curtail the freedom of religious believers and ethical secularists alike by making the public sphere a conscience-free zone. Freedom of conscience includes the freedom to speak publicly, as conscience compels us insofar as this is compatible with the same freedom of others. As guardians of the open society, secular liberals should be first to extend to religious citizens the opportunity to speak their minds in public (judges and elected officials are another matter, since they are bound to uphold the nonreligious nature of state institutions). At the same time, all citizens must insist that ethical and religious proposals in public conversation abide by the guiding norms of honesty, consistency, rationality, evidence, feasibility, legality, morality, and revisability. That is the point of the open conscience.

Why does freedom of conscience matter? Clearly, as Spinoza

warns, attempts by the state or community to control belief would be disruptive, harmful, and ultimately horribly inefficient. This militates against violations of conscience. But what can be said positively *in favor* of its free flourishing? There is nothing about unfettered thought as such that necessarily merits reverence; thought can be unfettered but insipid, stupid, or spiteful. I might lavish my powers of reasoning on a pointless project—counting blades of grass or organizing the items in my garbage by color. Rather, when we value the exercise of conscience it is because we believe it to be getting at something outside itself, something of great human concern: questions of meaning, identity, and value. Conscience takes a position on meaning, identity, value, and so points beyond itself, beyond subjectivity, toward some independent standard, contrary to the Liberty Fallacy.[47] It is not that conscience is worthwhile only when it gets the answers right. Rather, the questions hold objective importance, and therefore the endeavor to engage those questions is itself worthwhile. None of this makes sense if conscience is free from all standards.

In our steadfast protection of this freedom, we are affirming the equal worth of each citizen's exercise of conscience. But if conscience were radically private, what grounds would we have for attributing equal worth to the conscience of others? How could we know that their conscience is anything like ours? The judgment of equal worth is a substantive cross-personal judgment in itself, one that would be impossible if the Liberty Fallacy were valid. To equally honor the conscience of all is to acknowledge everyone's potential for engagement with questions of meaning, identity, and value. In this way, the ideal of ethical and religious liberty presupposes that conscience is open, not private.

In the political arena, freedom of conscience deserves protection as much as freedom of religion. The free world should not stand just for Abdul Rahman's right to convert to Christianity—what if instead he had gravitated toward Buddhism or atheism? The right at stake is the right to dissent from any and all creeds. It is not freedom to practice religion but freedom to exercise conscience that is fundamental.

Article 18 of the Universal Declaration of Human Rights states, "Everyone has the right to freedom of thought, conscience and religion; this right includes freedom to change his religion or belief, and freedom, either alone or in community with others and in public or private, to manifest his religion or belief in teaching, practice, worship and observance." The UN Council on Human Rights (then the Commission on Human Rights) has explicitly stated in clarification of Article 18 that it "protects theistic, non-theistic and atheistic beliefs, as well as the right not to profess any religion or belief."

In the case of blasphemy and apostasy penalties, often the people most in need of protection are secular dissenters. In 2001 a Pakistani professor named Younis Shaikh at a medical college in Islamabad was put on death row on charges of blasphemy. The blasphemy charge had been brought against him by some of his students after he remarked in class that that Prophet Muhammad could not have become Muslim until the age of forty, the age at which he received his first revelation, and that his parents were non-Muslims, since Muhammad had not yet founded Islam at the time of their deaths. Thanks in part to a public campaign led by humanist organizations along with Amnesty International, Dr. Shaikh is alive today. So is Pakistan's blasphemy law.

Finally, it is the commitment to freedom of conscience—not freedom of religion per se—that can help us distinguish between religious beliefs and practices that liberals should tolerate and accommodate and those that must be denounced and resisted. In the end, it is not religions that deserve our respect. A religion is a collection of metaphysical ideas and moral ideals. Ideas are believed or disbelieved; ideals are pursued or rejected. What deserves respect (or not) are people. We do not respect people by accepting whatever they think and do, but by holding them to the same intellectual, moral, and legal standards we apply to ourselves. The liberal position is clear. Religious practices face legal sanction if and only if they harm other people, including the dependent children of the religious. Religion faces intellectual and moral sanction whenever and wherever it undermines freedom of conscience.[48] This is crucial in global clashes of cultures, like the cartoon wars. Blasphemy and apostasy taboos must be opposed always because they are by their nature antithetical to the free exercise of individual judgment. Sometimes in order to respect religions' peoples, we must critique people's religion.

Secular liberalism needs the secular state and freedom of conscience, but it needs to jettison the Privacy Fallacy and the Liberty Fallacy. Conscience is not public, in the sense of civil or governmental. But conscience is not private. It is open. What then is to become of the core political principles of secular liberalism: freedom of belief and secular government? Each of these principles has been linked to the privacy model in popular understanding. Yet on closer examination, it turns out that the privacy of conscience is not needed to uphold freedom of conscience or secular government. In fact, these secular principles find firmer footing in the alternative model that sees conscience as open.

Freedom of belief means permitting claims of conscience in public debate and submitting them to the same standards as other political arguments. Freedom of belief is worth protecting because belief points beyond itself to questions of objective importance. Religion-state separation is not ensured by confining politics to "public reasons." Public arguments can be used to undermine secular government, and private reasons can be used to shore it up. Historically, the arguments that won the West for secularism rested on controversial assumptions about religion. Conscience is the soul of secularism.

4

Why There Are No Religions of the Book

I am a writer, and what I write is what I hear. I am a secretary of the invisible, one of many secretaries over the ages. That is my calling: dictation secretary. It is not for me to interrogate, to judge what is given me. I merely write down the words and then test them, test their soundness, to make sure I have heard right.

—J. M. Coetzee

In the beginning there were two. The beginning of religion, that is, takes two, at least. As practice and ritual, religion is essentially social. Practice needs practitioners. As an outlook, religion is always an encounter with another. For traditional faiths and new spiritualisms alike, the universe is a Thou, not an It (animistic faiths and Indian-born polytheisms may even face overpopulations of Thous). The belief in a personal deity—a being with whom the believer can have a relationship—is a denial of a private self. If there is such a being, then it knows us better than we know ourselves, and we are not alone (even when we might prefer to be).

The stuff religions are made out of is public stuff—written or oral traditions, social practices. The stuff religions are about is public stuff—the purpose of life, the biography of the cosmos, the nature of humanity, morality, the significance of death. But to fully understand the nature of religion and how it fits into society, we need to go beyond the private-public dichotomy. We need to recognize a third, distinct category of the open. Open matters are not public in the sense of being civil, governmental, or endorsed by all members of a given community. But they are open to objective inquiry, where an objective claim is either true or false, and its truth or falsity does not depend solely on the attitudes or belief of the individual making it. Lastly, religions are open to editing.

It is tempting to think of scripture as a direct line to the divine. The idea is that once scripture is available, anyone can engage with the Author in a private, individual relationship. In his 1659 defense of religious toleration, John Milton remarked that whereas the law of the Old Testament was "written on tables of stone, and to be performed according to the letter, willingly or unwillingly," the new covenant of the Gospel is written "upon the heart of every believer, to be interpreted only by the sense of charity and inward persuasion."[1] This picture is appealing but also deeply misleading. It distorts the real intricacies of interpretation and belief in any religion of the book.

In fact, you can't found a religion on a book. If you try, you'll be confronted with two questions: "Why this book?" and "What does this book mean?" And these questions necessarily cannot be answered by the book itself. For if you look there for an answer to the first question, you will have already presupposed that the book in question is *the* book to look to. Likewise, claims about the meaning of the book found in the book are useless unless you already know what such claims are supposed to mean.

How would you go about deciding which text, or which version of a text, is to be scripture? Unless your decision is to be arbitrary, you must appeal to some principles or reasons that favor some text over others. One can either get such principles from a source external to the text or from the text itself. But to get them from the text would be to presuppose an answer to the question at issue; namely, is *this* text credible? The situation is the same even if the text is the product of divine inspiration. It might seem self-evident that one should take as scripture those texts that have been divinely authored. And yet this recommendation, the Principle of Divine Authorship, is not a self-evident truth that is beyond all possible doubt. It is one hypothesis about how to select a body of accepted scripture, or a canon. As such, if it is not to be blindly accepted, it must be supported by reasons, and these reasons must be independent of the scripture itself. The Principle of Divine Authorship can justify the selection of a text, but the text cannot justify the selection of the principle.

Of course, in the real world, sacred books are not the work of one person, a secretary of the invisible. They have complex histories. They are the products of many people acting over much longer periods of time, sometimes centuries. Most people think that the Christian belief in the Resurrection—that Jesus of Nazareth was crucified, died, and brought back to life three days later—was originally based on accounts of the Resurrection given in the four Gospels of the New Testament, the books of Matthew, Mark, Luke, and John. But historically it was just the other way around. The Gospels were written between the years 65 and 100 CE, a generation after the apostle Paul and others began preaching the story of the risen Christ to early Christian communities. The Gospels were not written by Jesus' disciples or any other eyewitnesses to his life. In fact, almost nothing is known about the authors except that they were partisans of a new religion built around belief in the Resurrection. The Gospels we are familiar with were produced by a careful process of selection, editing, and rewriting undertaken over an extended period by early Christians in order to record the approved theology of the emerging Church and aid its missionary expansion.

Similarly, the story of the Quran is in some ways more interesting than the stories in it. According to Islamic tradition, Muhammad was said to have received a revelation from the angel Gabriel while in a cave in the desert. However, he apparently did not write it down and was probably unable to read or write at all. After his death in 632, various followers began an attempt to collect in written form the sayings attributed to Muhammad. As Islam spread, these various collections came to be housed in centers of learning and scholarship at Mecca, Medina, Basra, Kufa, and Damascus, where different scholars employed different principles of canonization to determine which passages and sayings were to be standard, accepted parts of the Quran. The caliph Uthman made the Medinan text canonical, but competing manuscripts remained in use for centuries. Over the history of Islamic scholarship, over forty different Qurans were available, depending on the methods one adopted to determine what counts as a part of the canon. By the 1920s, an Egyptian edition of the so-called Hafs transmission became a standard, although the competing Warsh transmission persisted in west Africa and northwest Africa. One Islamic scholar has found over a dozen versions used across the globe.[2] Even in Islamic studies today there is no *textus receptus*, a single universally accepted form of the Quran, as there is in studies of the Hebrew Bible.

A further difficulty is that books do not read books. Only people read books. And any book interesting enough to inspire a religion will be capable of being read in different ways by different people, with significantly different meanings. Here again the Quran is illustrative. Perhaps more than any other, this scripture has an aura of transparency and purity for believers, owing in large part to the supposed specialness of the language in which it is written. Whereas an English-language translation of the Old and New Testaments is considered a Bible, any translation of the Quran from Arabic is considered an interpretation, a distinct work with altered religious significance. As one historian of Islam has put it, "Arabic is not just the original language of the Qur'an, it is the language of the Qur'an."[3] The language itself is held sacred.

Sacred aura or not, the original manuscripts could hardly have been less transparent. They were written in Arabic that was not "pointed"; it lacked the dots and dashes that mark the vowels and that distinguish consonants such as *z* from *r* or *b* from *t*. As a result, a great many readings were possible depending on how the text was pointed and vowelized. Thus, early traditional commentators sometimes came up with as many as forty explanations for a single word. Perhaps the greatest of these commentators, Jalal al-Din al-Suyuti, who died in 1505, concluded that only God knows what some of the words mean. In the first three Muslim centuries, scholars came to recognize thousands of variants on the Quran corresponding to different schools of interpretation.

Like the question "Which text?" the question "What does this text mean?" cannot reasonably be resolved by reference to the text alone. For suppose you found in it a sentence of advice such as: "Use methods x, y, and z to interpret this text." You would be unable to follow this advice because you wouldn't yet know *how to interpret that sentence.* Muslim scholars looked outside the text to make the case for the particular methods of interpretation they employed. And so it is with any would-be holy words. In order to get a religiously useful document out of them one needs not only a canon of accepted texts but also a canon of accepted methods of interpretation. The rationale for these canons must come from outside of the texts themselves.

So, Western religions are of the book, but more important, they are of tradition, the tradition of forming and defending canons. The business of forming and defending canons is the essentially nonprivate business of communities of scholars and believers discussing and arguing with one another. The Talmudic tradition in Judaism makes this explicit, as the Talmud contains an accumulation of commentaries in conversation with one another over time. A better name for the religions of the book might be the religions of the conversation. And it takes at least two to converse. When believers read a scripture, they are entering into this talk whether they know it or not. The words they read and the thoughts they think about the divine are shaped by the choices of countless individuals.

Words themselves are public. The commonsense view is that the meaning of our thoughts and words is determined solely by what happens inside our heads, but this is far from the specialist's view. To see why, imagine an original portrait of Rasputin hung on the wall of my study. One night, the picture is secretly removed and replaced with a replica that is indistinguishable to me despite the fact that the replacement is a forgery. Subsequently, I might notice that the picture frame is not level and think to myself, "Rasputin looks a little crooked." Clearly, my thought would be a thought *about the forged picture*, not about the original, genuine picture, because it is the crookedness of the former that caused my thought. And yet, you could not tell just by looking at the contents of my brain that I am thinking about the forged picture, since for me it is indistinguishable from the genuine. The meaning of my thoughts and words is determined by the contents of my brain, plus the objects and events in the external world that cause what happens in the brain. Furthermore, the rules of the languages with which we express our thoughts are inherently public. These are not my words. They are ours.

Can we escape the publicity of religion by retreating to faith, to Luther's solitary "tower experience"? He couldn't. The ideas of this theological individualist were novel, but no novelty is absolute. Luther was part of a wider conversation. As a young man, he heard great preachers treat the subjects of sin and repentance at the church in Eisenach, where he had gone under the direction of his pious mother. Theological unrest was not unknown to him. His teachers were sympathetic to an intellectual movement known as nominalism, which challenged the dominant view among faculty of theology. Nominalists denied that the universal terms used in language—like *ravens* or *black*—refer to some abstract categories with an existence independent of our minds. Black ravens are real, but "ravenness" or "blackness" are nominal. Luther's attacks on the corruption and decadence of the Church were prefigured by Erasmus, all of whose books found their way onto the Index of Prohibited Books.

Reformation was an intensely social phenomenon, an epidemic of sermons and books. It was a linguistic happening, a publishing event. By the end of the sixteenth century, translations of the Bible had become available in most of the European national languages. As William Tyndale argued in England, God had spoken to the prophets in their native language, and the apostles had preached in the vernacular; so contemporary believers have no less right to receive the Word in their mother tongues. While this publicizing of scripture put it within the grasp of ordinary individuals, contact with the Gospel typically came through other people, in sermons preached before congregations. According to one leading historian, a favorite Bible passage for Protestants was "Faith cometh by hearing, and hearing by the word of God" (Rom. 10:17). "Many insisted that hearing the Word preached was the only means of salvation. Not even reading the Bible would work. Some doubted whether deaf people could be saved."[4]

What, then, is faith? One possible meaning of faith is a kind of trust, as when you "give someone the benefit of the doubt" or "place your faith in" someone. About friends, spouses, or business partners you say, "I have faith in him; he wouldn't betray me." In the same way, each time you get into your car, you place your trust in it. Your trust is warranted and reasonable in light of past performance. But if you were trying to sell your car and a potential buyer asked about its reliability, you probably would not get away with saying you have *faith* in it. You'd produce evidence of its past performance and current state of repair to inspire the buyer's confidence in its future. Faith as trust is not an alternative to reason but an instance of it.

Sometimes we speak of faith as believing something in the face of uncertainty, as in, "I'm not sure whether this is the right path to take; I'll make a leap of faith." This is faith as fallible belief, or belief that could possibly turn out to be incorrect. (Of course, for many people, faith is associated with certainty or at least the feeling of certainty.) However, this kind of uncertainty is consistent with warranted belief, or knowledge. Just because you are not 100 percent sure does not mean you don't know. With the possible exception of mathematical or so-called analytical truths (like "All bachelors are unmarried"), knowledge just is fallible.

But where faith can be described as belief in the face of doubt, we can always ask how much doubt one has about any particular belief, in comparison with other beliefs. We can ask about relative degrees of uncertainty. For example, one might feel very uncertain about the precise nature of the afterlife, while being much more relatively certain about the existence of a personal deity. Given the possibility of degrees of uncertainty, there are two ways we could elaborate the meaning of faith. On the first understanding, it becomes shorthand for holding on to a belief when the probability of its being true falls somewhere between 50 percent and 100 percent, in your estimation. In this case, faith collapses into reason. Apportioning your degree of confidence in a belief in accordance with your estimation of its probability of being true is precisely what we mean by rationality. We believe that alcohol in moderation has health benefits. But we could be wrong. Is that faith? No, it's just doing the best we can with the evidence at hand. We go to belief with the evidence we have, not the evidence we wish we had.

The alternative is to say that faith consists in picking beliefs utterly without regard to our rational confidence in them, following "intuition" or a "gut feeling." Faith is the invisible means of support for a belief when reasons fall out from under it. This is faith as intuition. Unfortunately, consulting entrails has never been a reliable guide to truth, even when those entrails are your own. As Nietzsche put it, a casual stroll through a lunatic asylum is enough to convince us that faith alone proves nothing. For the members of the Heaven's Gate cult, it may have just felt right to strap on their sneakers and drink poison in anticipation of hitching a ride on a passing comet. Guts are important. Your guts are what digest things. But it is your brains that tell you which things to swallow and which not to swallow.

Sometimes people long for the time when God spoke to humanity regularly, as he is portrayed as doing in the Old Testament. In truth, we find ourselves besieged with voices today—voices from Madison Avenue, Hollywood, Tehran, the Vatican. The problem is not the absence of revelations but a cacophony of revelations. Which ones should be heeded, if any, and why? Once you ask that question, you have gone beyond raw intuition and have reentered the realm of reason. Faith as intuition is a kind of faith that no thinking person should aspire to.

On every plausible understanding of faith, then, it is not a real alternative to reason or evidence as a source of belief. Faith as trust bleeds into evidence because it is based in past reliability. Faith as fallible belief folds into reason because it is based on assessments of what is more or less likely to be true. Here is another way to see the incomplete nature of faith. Take any belief "based on faith." We can always ask, and reflective people do ask if given a chance—*why* believe that? In asking and investigating this question, we are asking for reasons for belief and looking at the connection between the belief and other things we know. In asking why believe this faith claim, one turns from faith to reason. So reason is inescapable in a way that faith is not. When faith stands trial, its appeals must go to the court of reason.

At this point someone might object that the whole project of asking for reasons for faith is wrongheaded. When we see or hear something, and our faculties of sense perception are functioning properly, we don't need any additional reason or evidence to convince us of what we see or hear. The functioning of our senses *is* the evidence. The beliefs they produce are warranted because they reliably report on features of the real world around us. What if the same were true of our sense of religious truth? What if every human being were created with a "sensus divinitatus," a faculty that produced religious beliefs, like the belief in God? Insofar as this faculty were functioning properly, then the beliefs it produced would be warranted or justified.[5] We experience God directly, just as we experience the world with our ordinary senses. To demand additional evidence to justify belief is to misapprehend the very nature of religious knowledge.

This theory of religious knowledge, sometimes called "reformed epistemology," gets its confidence from an analogy between this postulated religious sense and the ordinary senses, like sight, hearing, and touch.[6] If it could be shown that religious experiences are similar to ordinary sensory experiences in relevant respects, one could conclude that they are also probably similar to sensory experiences in being veridical; that is, accurate perceptions of their apparent object. Ordinary sensory experiences like seeing or touching this book are *perceptual*—that is, caused by an object existing independently of the experience, and they are *veridical*—conveying accurate information about the object. Not every experience is like this. When I hit my head and "see stars," I am not really perceiving anything that exists independently of my experience. There is no doubt that people have religious experiences. The question is whether they are typically perceptual and veridical in character.

In fact, the analogy with ordinary sense perception is irreparably flawed. As a number of philosophers have shown, so-called religious experiences are totally different.[7] We can predict a person's future sense experiences on the assumption that the experience is veridical— I can predict that you will hear a noise when I slam a door shut. Yet we cannot make similar predictions in the case of religious experiences. We also find a high degree of agreement between the sense experiences reported by different people exposed to the same conditions. Yet we find very little agreement in the reports of religious experiences. Furthermore, we typically have an idea of what it means for a sense experience to be caused in the right way. If you are on a hallucinogenic drug trip, then we disqualify your visual experiences from being veridical because we know they were not caused by an independent object in the right way. Yet there is no caused-in-the-right-way test that is generally accepted for religious experiences. Indeed, the mystics can't make up their minds on this. Some think that being on drugs helps you tune in to the divine, whereas others think that it makes your experiences nonveridical. Religious experiences, then, are quite unlike sense perception, so our trust in the latter cannot be extended to the former.

At the same time, neuroscience research is revealing that by stimulating certain areas of the brain, it is possible to generate mystical episodes in the laboratory: feeling an overwhelming sense of oneness with the environment, sensing the presence of mysterious intelligent forces, and so on. This is not to say that all people who have mystical religious experiences are delusional, only that there is a plausible alternative to the explanation that such experiences are perceptions of God. For all we know, they could be like hearing a song in your head, just another curious nonperceptual experience for which we can thank our endlessly strange and amazing brains.

Some say that those who sincerely seek God with an open heart will find him, and that closed hearts explain why experiences of God are not as widely and reliably distributed among people as experiences of rocks, trees, and Volkswagens. But wouldn't those with closed hearts be precisely those most in need of an experience of God? Why would he leave them, of all people, in the dark? Anyway, shuttered-heart syndrome fails as an explanation of divine shyness. To test the explanation, we need to know what constitutes a hardened heart in order to see whether it in fact makes people less likely to report experiences of God. But we don't know what constitutes a hardened heart, except that it tends to block the experience of God. Suppose my car won't start and you say, "Maybe it's a bad spark plug." If I ask, "What makes you think it's the spark plug?" and you say, "Well, the car won't start," you haven't yet told me anything to make me favor your explanation over alternative explanations, like an empty fuel tank. It might be convenient for theism if there were some particular spiritual or psychological state that prevents people from seeing signs of the divine, but we have been given no independent grounds for thinking that there is such a state.

The last, desperate attempt to explain why God is absent from experience supposes that God has his reasons for remaining mysterious that our minuscule nerve cells just cannot grasp. His hiddenness serves purposes that we cannot know. That could be. Then again, it could be that God revealing himself to everyone would serve purposes that we cannot know.[8] There is no more reason to believe in unknown purposes for hiding than to believe in unknown purposes for revealing, and therefore no reason to expect divine shyness instead of exhibitionism. In the words of one mystical poet, there are things we know, things we know we don't know, and things we don't know we don't know. How does the believer know which reasons he doesn't know about? He doesn't.

In an open society, religion is private and free like this: it is none of the government's business. However, it does not follow that religious belief is private and free in the sense of being subjective or immune from scrutiny by others. Freedom from coercion does not entail freedom from reason. Text-based faiths are inherently open to the public, given the nature of language and the conversational process of forming canons of writings and interpretive rules.

5.

Has God Found Science?

Her skin, saffron toasted in the sun,
Eyes darting like a gazelle.
That god who made her,
How could he have let her go? Was he blind?
This wonder is not the result of blindness:
She is a woman, and a sinuous vine.
The Buddha's doctrine thus is proved:
Nothing in this world was created.

—Dharmakirti, Sanskrit poet and philosopher
Late seventh century

The earth was without form, and void; and darkness was upon the face of the deep. And the RNA polymerase ribozyme moved upon the face of the waters. And Jack said, let there be light. It was another day at the office for Jack Szostak, at the laboratory where he and his colleagues are synthesizing life. Over the last several years, the Szostak Lab at Harvard Medical School—a kind of Genesis Lab—has been building primitive cellular components from scratch. These protocellular structures are capable (just barely) of replication and evolution by natural selection; which is to say, they're alive. Since 1953, when University of Chicago biochemist Harold Urey and his doctoral student Stanley Miller cooked up amino acids by electrifying a mix of gases, scientists have been claiming that they are on the brink of creating life in the lab. Now, for the first time, a critical mass of researchers working with new techniques has put this possibility within the reach of the current generation.

What is happening at Harvard, and at over a hundred research centers around world, is not creation ex nihilo. Scientists have the familiar molecular building blocks of organic chemistry to work with. And now, some have uncovered a possible inorganic ingredient of genesis. It's *clay*, appropriately enough—montomorillonite, to be precise (if not the clay "moistened by a heavy mist" from which the first man is molded in Genesis 2). Montomorillonite had been known to catalyze the polymerization of RNA, and in the October 2003 issue of *Science*, Szostak and his coauthors, Martin Hanczyc and Shelly Fujikawa, reported that it also accelerates the conversion of fatty acids into spherical membranes that tend to divide spontaneously upon reaching a certain size. RNA absorbed to clay can become trapped in such membranes, creating the preconditions for its role as genetic material. Their research suggests that "[t]he formation, growth, and division of the earliest cells may have occurred in response to similar interactions with mineral particles and inputs of material and energy."[1]

Synthesizing life in the lab raises profound questions. Is it inexcusable hubris to tinker with the tools of the Creator? The Old Testament prophet Isaiah asks, "Will the pot contend with the potter, or the earthenware with the hand that shapes it?"[2] It turns out that we may have no choice, insofar as we want to understand how life began. For in this instance, it seems that we must learn by doing: scientists know of no way to discover how life might have started than by seeing how they might start it themselves. And so, the theological injunction to know God's handiwork, and the caution against "playing God" cannot, in the end (or rather "in the beginning") be jointly satisfied.

In this age of bioscience, it is no longer credible that religion is private and free from objective inquiry. Religion and science are in conversation, and this would be impossible unless both could be held to publicly available standards of truth.

As science peers into the origins of life, it is pressing into areas that traditionally have been the province of religion. This has prompted religious thinkers to reflect on the interconnections between their beliefs and the modern biological outlook. The extraordinary progress in genetics and molecular biology over the last century has only strengthened the contemporary evolutionary theories of the origins and diversity of life. Perhaps for that reason new pockets of resistance have sprung up to wage a rearguard action against advancing science. The latest is called intelligent design theory, or ID.

The idea of ID is that biological structures such as the blood-clotting mechanism in vertebrates and the flagellum of bacteria are "irreducibly complex": they are composed of so many interdependent parts that they could not have arisen by gradual, piecemeal steps as required by evolution by natural selection. The intelligent design challenge to evolution is a latter-day version of a challenge that Darwin confronted in his own day, the problem of "incipient structures." What good to an organism is part of an eye, or part of a wing? There are two solutions to the problem of incipient structures. The first is that functionality is not always all-or-nothing. As Richard Dawkins observes, a 1 percent increase in the sensitivity of a proto-eye gives an organism 1 percent more vision than it had before, and while incipient wings aren't as good as full wings, they provide a good deal more lift than no wings at all.[3] The second solution is that functions can change over time, so that a trait evolved to perform one function can come to be adapted to quite a different function.

That is just what happened in the history of the blood-clotting system. The key proteins involved are copied and modified versions of proteins that evolved for use in the digestive system for other purposes.[4] What's more, contrary to the claims of intelligent design theory, it is not the case that the system cannot function without all its parts.

Whales and dolphins lack one part of the system called Factor XII, yet their blood clots just fine. Or consider the bacterial flagellum. ID predicts that without all of forty to fifty biochemical components, none will be functional. But this is demonstrably false. If you take away all but about ten components you get something called a type-III secretory apparatus, the very micromachine used by *yersinia pestis*, the organism that caused the Black Death.[5] Would that it were nonfunctional!

The first cosmonaut in space reported that he found no God up there. But some theologians and scientists report new evidence for God's existence coming from theories of cosmic origins in astrophysics and cosmology. Some see God on the other side of the big bang, claiming it as empirical confirmation of the creationist doctrine that the universe began to exist from nothing. That's not how many mainstream physicists would characterize it. Brian Greene, professor of physics and mathematics at Columbia University, writes in *The Fabric of the Cosmos*:

> A common misconception is that the big bang provides a theory of cosmic origins. It doesn't. The big bang is a theory . . . that delineates cosmic evolution from a split second after whatever happened to bring the universe into existence, but it says nothing at all about time zero itself. And since, according to the big bang theory, the bang is what is supposed to have happened at the beginning, the big bang leaves out the bang. It tells us nothing about what banged, why it banged, how it banged.[6]

As physicists trace the expansion of the universe backward in time, they reach a point at which current theory breaks down. Many cosmologists think that a full account awaits a new insight that synthesizes Einstein's relativity theory with quantum mechanics, which describes the behavior of very small systems. There are many contenders for such a unified theory, but no clear victors as of yet. In 2002, the National Research Council reported on eleven unanswered questions in physics and astronomy. One of them is, how did the universe begin? It is fair to conclude that our scientific knowledge of the origins of the universe is nowhere near complete. Therefore, it would be premature to use it as a premise in an ambitious theological argument.

In any case, the postulation of a *transcendent* cause of the cosmos would be of no help. This is because it presupposes a radically new and mysterious kind of causation. The causes that we know about precede their effects in time. By contrast, God's creative action does not precede its effect in time (since he is supposed to transcend time). How could a timeless cause give rise to a temporal effect? God is a person who transcends the natural order. But what could that mean? Persons as we know them do things in time. Furthermore, causation as we know it involves the rearrangement of preexisting material, as when you create a sand castle by rearranging the sand on a beach. God's action produces its effect out of *nothing at all*. A familiar objection against an atheist universe is ex nihilo nihil fit, "out of nothing, nothing comes." Yet God's act of creation is no less guilty of getting something for nothing.

Metaphysical cosmonauts point to this intriguing finding: research into the basic features of the physical universe—its initial conditions, or properties of the basic particles of matter and energy—has revealed that if these features had not possessed precisely the quantitative values that they in fact do, then the emergence of human life, and all life as we know it, would have been impossible. Astrophysicist Stephen Hawking points out that the universe is expanding at just the rate necessary to avoid collapse: "We know that there has to have been a very close balance between the competing effect of explosive expansion and gravitational contraction which, at the very earliest epoch about which we can even pretend to speak (called the Planck time, 10^{-43} sec. after the big bang), would have corresponded to the incredible degree of accuracy represented by a deviation in their ratio from unity by only one part in 10 to the sixtieth."[7] Such features that are preconditions for life are called *anthropic coincidences*. Educated opinions as to the number of genuine anthropic coincidences vary, but most agree that at least a dozen such features are found in the universe as we now know it. If any one of them had been altered even minutely (the number 1 in 10^{60}—1 followed by 60 zeros—is unimaginably small), life would have been precluded. Some now argue that the best explanation for this fact is that somehow the anthropic coincidences are there *in order that life could emerge*. The universe, it is said, is exquisitely "fine-tuned" for life. We would expect such fine-tuning if theism were true, because the creator would design a universe friendly to life.

Critics respond that the fine-tuning of the universe would imply theism only if we knew that the life-permitting values of the fundamental constants are brute facts that won't be explained by any deeper physical laws.[8] However, there is no consensus in physics about this. According to Sir Martin Rees, former director of Cambridge University's Institute of Astronomy, "The status and scope of anthropic arguments, in the long run, will depend on the character of the (still quite unknown) physical laws at the very deepest level. [Steven] Weinberg hopes that a 'final theory' exists, and that we may someday discover it. . . . What we call the fundamental constants . . . may be secondary consequences of the final theory, rather than direct manifestations of its deepest and most fundamental level. . . . We just don't know."[9] It is simply too soon to say what the naturalistic, nontheistic explanation of cosmic fine-tuning might be. Meanwhile, it would be folly to base a sweeping metaphysical conclusion on a highly speculative, unfinished frontier of advancing science.

In any case, one has to ask, fine-tuned for *what*? When you fine-tune the picture on your television screen, the fine-tuning itself guarantees the desired result: whatever your preferred levels of resolution, brightness, and so on. By contrast, we are quite sure that there is nothing in natural law that *guarantees* the evolution of human beings, or eukaryotes, for that matter. The theory of evolution by natural selection tells us how things evolve—random mutation and differential survival—but it cannot tell us which kinds of things *will* evolve. Some kinds of bacteria may be inevitable (as you may have noticed, they completely overrun this particular planet) but not people. For this reason, it is misleading to say that the universe is fine-tuned for intelligent life. Unlike TV screen fine-tuning, cosmic fine-tuning would only *permit* the outcome, not ensure it: not what one would expect from a tuner interested in life. (Since they are relevant to the conditions for carbon-based life as such and not human life per se, the coincidences might more accurately be called "biotropic coincidences," or maybe "carbontropic coincidences.")

The point is not that any particular take on big banging or fine-tuning has prevailed. The point is that, no matter what the ultimate conclusion, religion and science are in conversation. That would not be possible if religion were shuttered from objective investigation altogether.

Not everyone accepts that science and religion can speak to one another. Instead, some say, religion and science are two independent and autonomous lines of inquiry. Let's go back to origins. The authors of the book of Genesis were not natural scientists. They were not interested in presenting empirical evidence for or against any answers to the question, Why does this universe exist, rather than some other? For them, such questions would have been beside the point. The point was to locate humanity in a *moral and theological model* of the cosmos—somewhere between the angels and the beasts. Typically, origins narratives serve to designate the special status of people among the rest of nature and set one group apart from others. They establish a relationship between a people and the transcendent. In origins myths, the moral *is* the story. The questions that now animate cosmologists, physicists, and biologists simply were not on the agenda when the traditional Western religions were born. In this way, some might argue that like origins narratives, religious narratives in general should not be taken as competitors or companions to scientific narratives. Scientific and religious narratives are talking about different things and hence are talking past one another.

One problem with this view is that whatever their beginnings, traditional religions now find themselves in an age of empiricism. The success of the modern scientific outlook exerts a gravitational pull on everything around it in the cultural environment. In this environment, in which quantitative, causal, historical explanations are privileged (and rightly so), the significance of religious narratives is altered. Either they are assumed to be attempts at empiricism or they have some kind of nonempirical aim that stands in need of explication, by comparison to science. In reaction, religionists can argue that their narratives are on a par with scientific narratives. Or they can explain how and why they should be regarded in some nonempirical way. What they cannot do is go back to an era in which the significance of the religious narratives can remain implicit and unexplicated, an object of veneration rather than investigation.[10]

Especially since Darwin, many theologians and ordinary believers alike began to defend the biblical traditions as alternative theories of biology, geology, and cosmology. Hence "scientific creationism." More subtly, some argued that God revealed the origins of life to the authors of Genesis in an extremely rough outline, since they would have been unable to grasp the mechanics of heredity, the scale of bil-lions of years of evolutionary time, and so on. The discovery of evo-lution by natural selection represents God's scheduled update to his revelation. It expresses the spirit of Genesis in the latest empirical vocabularies.

The late, great paleontologist Stephen Jay Gould took the other route to the independence of science and religion, defending a princi-pled division of labor between the empirical and nonempirical, which he dubbed "non-overlapping magisteria," or NOMA.[11] On this view, religion and science can peacefully coexist in neighboring yet isolated domains. The magisterium of religion, Gould said, is "to define meaning in our lives and a moral basis for our actions,"[12] while the magisterium of science is "to understand the factual character of nature." Religion gives us the Rock of Ages, while science gives us the ages of rocks.

A number of cracks are apparent in Gould's neighborly rock fence. NOMA prevents the overlapping of the magisteria by using an implau-sibly narrow understanding of faith. Under this definition, religion contains no claims or knowledge about the world. By implication, it cannot even include the statements "There is no god but Allah" or "Jesus healed the sick." It is difficult to see how this understanding of religion could be acceptable to a sincere and reflective believer. No religious worldview could get off the ground without making some factual statements about the world.

Improving on Gould's proposal, we might admit that both science and religion deal in truth-claims but insist that their claims are about very different kinds of things. Scientific claims concern natural phenomena whereas religious claims concern *supernatural* phenomena—like God, souls, and immortality—that fall outside of their proper purview. In the scholarly literature, this understanding of the sciences is sometimes called "methodological naturalism." Methodological naturalism means scientists are committed to explaining the world solely in terms of natural entities and causes. As such, science neither confirms nor denies the supernatural. It has nothing to say about it. With the scope of science restricted to the natural, conversation between science and religion is blocked.

There are two things to note about methodological naturalism. First, it is too restrictive. While it makes sense for scientists to prefer naturalistic explanations, there are no good grounds for ruling out supernatural explanations necessarily and in principle. Second, even if methodological naturalism were correct, it would not preclude the possibility of science-religion conversation. The sciences are naturalistic, but not in principle or by definition. Rather they exhibit a more modest naturalism that is provisional and a posteriori, or based in experience, according to which there is a powerful presumption in favor of natural explanations over supernatural explanations.

What would it mean to say that the sciences are naturalistic? To clarify what is being asked here, define *supernatural* roughly as things that are not a part of the physical universe but can cause changes in the physical universe. In this sense, immaterial souls and transcendent deities are supernatural. Are the sciences precluded by their very nature, in principle, or from postulating such entities or processes? Are they barred in principle from using methods of inquiry—like divine revelation—that presuppose the supernatural? The key here is whether precluding the supernatural is a criterion or part of the definition of what counts as scientific.

The sciences cannot preclude the supernatural in principle for the general reason that there is no way to legislate in advance what may or may not be used in our scientific exploration of the world. The history of science is filled with examples of novel entities, processes, and methods of inquiry that were once unknown or disregarded but that came to have important places in science.

For example, from its beginnings in the sixteenth and seventeenth centuries, modern science had confined itself to entities that are directly observable by the naked eye or with the aid of instruments such as the telescope. Yet in the 1800s, this standard was eventually revised so that by the end of the century, leading researchers found it perfectly acceptable to invoke unobservable entities, such as electromagnetic fields. Why? Because their hypotheses explained a great many facts, pointed to interesting new insights, and found support in persuasive *indirect* evidence; namely, the observable effects of the unobservables.

Until the twentieth century, the concept of causation in science involved a local interaction between entities continuous with one another in space, as when one billiard ball bounces off another. With the discovery of the weird quantum world of subatomic particles, however, physicists have been compelled to give up this bedrock notion and admit that one event can cause another event even if it is not continuous with it. Again, this novel process was accepted because of the extraordinary empirical corroboration, explanatory power, and fruitfulness of the theory in which it is embedded.[13]

The attempt to preclude these novel approaches via methodological rule would have been futile, because some of them could not have been foreseen. It also would have inhibited scientific progress. A signature strength of scientific inquiry is its open-endedness. It is not defined in advance by a list of the kinds of things it may or may not use in trying to understand the world.

However, while inquiry may be open-ended, time and resources are not endless. So, a rational inquirer will choose those avenues of investigation that look most promising. Just because it's unreasonable to preclude the supernatural in principle doesn't mean it's always reasonable to pursue it. In fact, it would have to pass a very high bar before being worthy of serious consideration by science. While a modest naturalism does not absolutely rule out the transcendent, it presents a powerful presumption in favor of natural causes. This is not an atheist dogma. It is a conclusion made on the basis of cumulative evidence.

This evidence begins in everyday, commonsense reasoning about the world. When you hear a bump in the night, your first thought is probably not ghosts but cats. Why? Because it turned out that there was a natural explanation for the last bump you heard, and the bump before that, and so on. The rational response to this past experience is to assign to a supernatural explanation a far lower likelihood of truth prior to investigation, relative to a natural explanation. Adding to this commonsense experience are over three centuries of progress in modern science in which naturalistic theories have supplanted previously accepted supernatural theories, as germs cast out demons, natural selection displaced the designer, and DNA made obsolete the élan vital. God has been outsourced. Even in cases where a naturalistic explanation was not obvious, when people looked in the right way in the right place, they found it. By contrast, supernatural explanations have a very bad track record in science.[14]

Furthermore, an important criterion for evaluating a hypothesis is the extent to which it fits with the rest of what we know about the world. If we are considering two alternative explanations for some phenomenon, all else being equal, we should prefer the one that is more consistent with the rest of our well-established theories and observations. Since the existing body of well-established theories and observations are naturalistic, it stands to reason that a natural explanation will usually produce a better fit with our background knowledge.

How strong is the presumption of naturalism? Strong enough to prevent anyone from crying, "God did it" whenever there is a gap in our understanding of natural causes. As philosopher Paul Draper puts it, "Very strong reasons to believe there is no *hidden* naturalistic explanation would be required as well. In other words, the search for natural causes should continue until the best explanation of the failure to find one is that there is none." This modest naturalism is strong enough to block the "god-of-the-gaps" move, in which any gap in the present scientific understanding can be filled by declaring, "God did it!" According to modest naturalism, there is an overwhelming presumption in favor of natural explanations in the sciences (in light of their past success in other cases). Appeal to the supernatural is acceptable only as a last resort and when we have some reason to think a natural explanation will not be forthcoming. This is provisional naturalism rather than in-principle naturalism.

These features of modest naturalism can be illustrated with an example. Although there is a growing body of scientific knowledge about autism, the basic nature and root causes of the illness remain largely mysterious. There are significant gaps in the current naturalistic understanding of autism. Yet you don't hear anyone calling for a supernatural explanation, the "intelligent design" of autism. Why not? First, there is the general confidence based on past experience that natural causes will be forthcoming. Second, there is a body of background knowledge concerning the roots of other disorders in genes and environment or some complex mixture of the two. A naturalistic account of autism would fit with this background better than a supernaturalistic account. Finally, the present gap in our understanding of autism is not at all surprising given the relatively immature state of our understanding of the brain, which turns out to be the most complex entity ever encountered. Therefore, the best explanation for the present inability to find the natural causes of autism is not that there are no natural causes but that we just don't know enough about the brain yet. Since scientific inquiry is a process that consumes time and resources, which are finite, the rational thing to do is to refrain from pursuing lines of inquiry that start out with a very low likelihood of success. In the present state of knowledge, that would mean ignoring nonnatural explanations of autism.

So according to modest naturalism, there is an overwhelming presumption in favor of natural explanations in the sciences, in light of their past success in other cases and their coherence with the rest of what we know about the world. Appeal to the supernatural would be acceptable only if we can think of no other way to account for our failure to discover natural causes.[15]

Suppose that all of this is mistaken and the more constrictive methodological naturalism is correct. Science cannot in principle invoke the supernatural. Still, it would not follow that science and religion are totally independent. For even though current science might not *invoke* the existence of anything supernatural, this would not show that it has no *implications* regarding the supernatural. Even if science and religion stick to two different modes of inquiry, one can still ask what can be concluded about one on the basis of the other. Can theology learn anything from the sciences? Can the sciences learn anything from theology? Once the question is put in this way, it becomes clear that the answer is yes.

Return to the evolution-creation debate. Perhaps the most common way of reconciling evolution with a creator god is through some sort of doctrine of theistic evolution. Theistic evolution is a kind of theological creationism, appropriate to the modern age, which demotes the creator from an artisan to a factory supervisor. He designed the evolutionary process, which set about churning out living things in the way Darwin and his successors describe. This sort of scenario faces a challenge. If I design a widget-making machine that produces widgets to my precise specifications, then it makes sense to say that I have designed not only the widget-making machine but also the widgets. Not so if the machine I design incorporates massively randomized elements, so that its end product is totally unpredictable even by me. Similarly, if the contingent evolutionary process is the cause of living things, then it cannot be said that God is the *designer* of anything. Yet surely this is essential to any creationism worthy of the name. In order for someone to count as the designer of something, his intentions must somehow explain that thing's important traits.

The last refuge for theistic evolution would be to say that God inaugurates the evolutionary process, observes the results, and stands prepared to intervene should they ever diverge from the results he intends, but they never do, so he never intervenes (imagine an artist who exposes her canvas to the elements, then watches and permits it to discolor in precisely the ways she *would have* painted it).[16] Here God's intentions belong in any full explanation of why evolution proceeded in the way it did, even though God never intervenes in the process. Of course, there isn't a scrap of evidence for this bare-bones creationism, but it shows there is no logical contradiction in imagining that life is the product of Darwinian forces *and* God's design.

Bare-bones creationism also illustrates how evolutionary science and theology could have something to say to one another no matter how thin the theology. If it were correct, then among other things it follows that everything in natural history was intended by God (or at least, everything that was not for some reason unavoidable). Theological insights tumble out: the creator has—in the phrase attributed to the geneticist J. B. S. Haldane—an inordinate fondness for beetles (or better yet, bacteria, which appeared on Earth two billion years before any other living thing and continue to dominate the planet in sheer numbers and distribution); the creator is prepared to sacrifice any number of innocent creatures as research subjects in his experimentation with life. On the other hand, if bare-bones creationism were true, then neo-Darwinians would be mistaken to describe human origins as blind, purposeless, or unsupervised. In that case, we would be evolved but also designed. Even if biology says nothing about the supernatural, it can still have implications for theology.[17]

The idea that the religious conscience is private is closely linked to a particular picture of the self, mind, and meaning—as interior, hidden, ethereal—that has deep roots in the Western intellectual tradition as well as in popular psychology. But developments in neuroscience, linguistics, and philosophy are revealing a portrait of an inner life that is much more public than it might appear. According to the prevailing theories, mind and meaning are wholly a part of the natural, material world.

In the model of the person owing to Plato, neo-Platonist Christian theology, and Descartes, the self is an immaterial and unobservable substance or soul that is the subject of conscious experiences. Individuals have a special kind of knowledge of their own minds that is in principle unavailable to others, often called "privileged access." Cogito, ergo sum, and no one but you can have your Cogito. However, by now the Cartesian model of the person has been almost universally rejected and replaced by a materialist model, according to which minds are (somehow, in ways we are only beginning to grasp) the activities of purely physical objects—brains. This "physicalist" model of the mind is not necessarily a so-called "reductionist" model. It need not deny the reality of beliefs, intentions, or consciousness, or the usefulness of psychology to explain behavior. It only insists that each instance of these mental events is the same thing as some physical event. Where reductionism says the mind is *nothing but* the brain, nonreductive physicalism says that the mind is *everything and* the brain.

The Cartesian model of the person was dustbinned for two main reasons. First, it is not at all clear how an immaterial soul could cause changes in the physical body. Consider: Souls are thought of as purely nonphysical—they can't be weighed, split in half, heated or cooled; they lack mass, electric charge, and so on. But then how could they possibly have a cause-and-effect interaction with bodies, which have exclusively physical properties? Second, there are many specific correlations between mental phenomena and brain activity. For example, language use and spatial reasoning appear to be localized in particular areas of the brain. Brain injuries cause very distinctive changes in perception, cognition, and even personality. Some mental diseases like schizophrenia have a genetic component. But why would any of this be if the mind were independent of the brain? After all this evidence, anyone who still believes in the Cartesian model ought to have someone else's head examined.

Likewise, the idea of privileged access cannot survive the new neuroscientific understanding of the mind. By monitoring the electrical activity around your hippocampus, others can know better than you whether you can successfully recall the name of a person you just met. It is true that no one can have your mental experiences for you. Then again, no one can take your stroll in the park for you either. That kind of privileged access does not put the mind in some special metaphysical category divorced from the shared, public world.

Where does all of this leave science and religion as ways of knowing? They are nonidentical but intersecting inquiries. In an age of empiricism, they share an ambition to explain the structure of the physical universe and the history and purpose of life. The claims of each can have implications for the other. Religious claims, then, are objective in the sense that they are capable of being true or false, and their truth or falsity is not determined by how we feel about them. In this way, the religious conscience is open.

Yet aren't there some avenues of inquiry that should stay closed? Isn't there a mystery surrounding life's beginnings that is worth preserving, sacred even? In fact, scientific explanations have a way of decomposing one mystery into many puzzles. That's just what happened when vitalism gave way to mechanism in biology. Vitalism was the idea that living things are distinguished from nonliving things because they possess a single mysterious life force, élan vital, or "protoplasm," whereas mechanism held that living things are just quantitatively different arrangements of nonliving matter. Dismissing the life force meant taking on more than a century's worth of hard questions about how the machinery of cells actually functions. Scientific demystification leaves us with *more* to wonder about, not less.

The Genesis Lab may well yield a number of scenarios of how protocells can arise naturally without determining which scenario actually played out in natural history. An intellectually satisfying response to the question of how life began need not be *an answer*. Even the book of Genesis presents multiple versions of the story: the "Let there be's" of chapter 1 come from a source that biblical scholars call "P," which speaks of a transcendent divinity, while chapter 2's more anthropomorphic sculptor-creator comes from the "J" material that was written much earlier.

Today's empiricists are sculptors too. Science itself is fashioned from the plastic of human minds and concerns. It is the Golem, the lumbering automaton of animated clay who defended the ghetto in Jewish folklore—obedient, if sometimes unwieldy, oblivious to its own enormous power, our guardian against the pogroms of nature: want, disease, disaster.[18] Empiricists, too, have their way to revere life. They try to do as it did. They imitate it. And isn't that the highest form of praise?

$6.$

Darwin Made Me Do It

"According to nature" you want to live? O you noble Stoics, what deceptive words these are! Imagine a being like nature, wasteful beyond measure, indifferent beyond measure, without purposes and consideration, without mercy and justice, fertile and desolate and uncertain all at the same time; imagine indifference itself as a power—how could you live according to this indifference?

—Friedrich Nietzsche

The beginning of the end of civilization can now be traced to 1859. Since its publication in that year, Charles Darwin's *On the Origin of Species* has been widely decried as an assault on the idea of morality and society itself. By reducing human beings to zoological specimens, the Darwinian, naturalistic worldview removed humanity from the moral order. The final insult came in Darwin's second-to-last book, *The Descent of Man, and Selection in Relation to Sex*, published in 1871, in which we learn that "man is descended from a hairy, tailed quadruped, probably arboreal in its habits, and an inhabitant of the Old World."[1] *Origin of Species* had forecast that in the future, psychology would be placed on a new foundation, and "light will be thrown" on the origins of humanity. *Descent of Man* explored the continuities between moral behavior in people and social behavior in other mammals.

Darwin's contemporaries got the message. "Society must fall to pieces if Darwinism be true" declared the *Family Herald*, read by some two hundred thousand. A former colleague exposed "the entire naked truth as to the logical consequences of Darwinism," that if morality is a "development of brutal instincts" then all sense of right or wrong would perish.[2] An American Protestant intellectual wrote, "It is a mistake to suppose that I am forbidden, by nature's laws, to take the life of a member of the race to which I happen to belong, if I choose to do so, any more than is the porpoise or the playful panther. Still harder is it to show that, by nature's laws, a man may not appropriate his neighbor's goods or indulge and gratify his appetite whenever and wherever he chooses to find the means."[3]

From the primordial ooze of Darwinism would slither atheism. When accounting for the order of living nature, we would now have no need of the hypothesis of a creator god. And godlessness would breed amorality, as the created would no longer be beholden to a creator.

Darwin himself was an agnostic, according to his own description. The Christian faith of his upbringing was utterly gone by at least 1851, when he and his wife were devastated by the loss of their beloved daughter Anne, ten years old. He could not reconcile the brutality and wastefulness of evolution with a benevolent creator: "for what advantage can there be in the suffering of millions of the lower animals throughout almost endless time."[4] Yet in abandoning his faith he did not abandon morality. Darwin himself was exceptionally conscientious (some have said exceedingly) and caring toward others in his personal and professional life. For him, evolution would not undermine morality but explain it:

> The moral sense follows, firstly, from the enduring and ever-present nature of the social instincts; secondly, from man's appreciation of the approbation and disapprobation of his fellows; and thirdly, from the high activity of his mental faculties, with past impressions extremely vivid; and in these latter respects he differs from the lower

animals. Owing to this condition of mind, man cannot avoid looking both backwards and forwards, and comparing past impressions. Hence after some temporary desire or passion has mastered his social instincts, he reflects and compares the now weakened impression of such past impulses with the ever-present social instincts; and he then feels that sense of dissatisfaction which all unsatisfied instincts leave behind them, he therefore resolves to act differently for the future,—and this is conscience.[5]

Darwin's insights have led to the revolutionary field of evolutionary ethics. Many secular, scientific-minded people, inspired by these insights, have come to believe that evolutionary science can tell us all we need to know about ethics: humans are highly social mammals in whom moral behavior evolved to facilitate social cooperation. Some even proclaim the birth of an evolutionary "science of good and evil" that can help us make ethically wise choices.

There is such a thing as science (or rather, the methods and accumulated knowledge of the sciences), and there are such things as good and evil. There is even something we could call knowledge of good and evil, or moral knowledge. It is just that this knowledge is not scientific. There are theories of ethics—in the sense of accounts that are systematic, rigorously reasoned, and responsive to real-world consequences— and these theories draw on the knowledge of the sciences. That does not make them scientific theories. Similarly, there are accounts of effective corporate management, sound pedagogy, and how to be a good friend or spouse that are based on careful reflection and practical wisdom. But it would be little more than a marketing gimmick to say that there is a "science of friendship" or a "science of marriage."

Evidence about human nature from evolutionary science helps explain our social and moral behavior, but it alone cannot justify or undermine ethical claims and principles. In that task, there is no substitute for consulting our conscience and critical intelligence in communication with the sciences. Until physics uncovers, alongside quarks, gluons, electrons, and protons, a new fundamental moral particle—the moron?—the quantity of which we can measure in everyday actions, we cannot hope for, and do not need, a purely scientific measurement of good and evil.

Some fans of Darwin have followed his critics in thinking that evolution must dissolve ethics. These evolutionary skeptics use the science to contend that the claims of morality are in one way or another not all that they are trumped up to be. There are two broad themes in evolutionary skepticism about ethics. One theme is that our conscience is just a device designed to help us survive and reproduce, not a faculty that puts us in touch with objective moral facts. As one prominent Darwinian has it:

> Morality is a biological adaptation no less than are hands and feet and teeth. Considered as a rationally justifiable set of claims about an objective something, ethics is illusory. I appreciate that when somebody says, "Love thy neighbor as thyself," they think they are referring above and beyond themselves. Nevertheless, such reference is truly without foundation. Morality is just an aid to survival and reproduction . . . and any deeper meaning is illusory.[6]

According to this view, our sense of moral right and wrong is merely an evolutionary adaptation designed to help us navigate our peculiar environmental niche, which includes other people with whom we must cooperate in order to survive and reproduce. Our feeling that certain things are virtuous or odious is like the sense that certain odors are pleasing or repulsive. It is there to propel us toward what is beneficial to our organism and repel us from what is damaging. We aren't drawn by the scent of dung; but dung beetles are. It makes no sense to ask who is *correct* about the value of dung.

Of course it is true that the kind of things we value has to do with the kind of things that we are, and evolutionary science helps to account for that. It does not follow that those values are unreal or subjective. Think of the faculty of vision. Seeing is accomplished by brain equipment that evolved because of its contributions to survival and reproduction. But that doesn't imply that the objects of vision—the rivers, faces, street signs—are any less real. Indeed, the reality of the objects around us helps explain why we have the faculty to detect them. Evolved faculties can connect us with objective facts.

Another form of evolutionary skepticism about ethics has it that evolution made us egoists. According to this view, all of human behavior—from a mother's love to an act of neighborly reciprocity—is about one thing and one thing only: getting more copies of our genes into the next generation. We scratch the back that scratches ours because that is what it takes to get ahead in a species for which cooperation is as vital to survival as food and shelter. Every esprit des corps is a facade masking self-assertion at the more fundamental level of the "selfish gene."

Of course, when evolutionary biologist Richard Dawkins coined the marvelous phrase "selfish gene," he didn't imagine that genes are egoistic. Being microscopic chunks of chromosome, they don't have minds at all, let alone motivations that could be selfish or otherwise. The phrase was chosen to communicate the indispensable insight that, when we think about what evolves under natural selection, it is useful to look at the situation from the gene's point of view, rather than the perspective of the organism or the "good of the species." Dawkins did not confuse this explanatory technique with a description of how genes or people think.

There are two kinds of selfishness: evolutionary and psychological. Egoism is a view about psychological motives that cause one's behavior. The egoist believes that our ultimate motives are always self-regarding and never other-regarding. But it is an open question whether a process that is selfish in an evolutionary sense will produce an end-product that is selfish in the psychological sense. As philosopher of biology Elliott Sober puts it, "If our behaviors are evolutionarily selfish, should we expect them to be implemented by a mind that is psychologically selfish?"

Consider, for example, the behavior of parental care. Parents enhance their own fitness by helping their offspring. Fitness, don't forget, reflects both the organism's chances of surviving and its prospects for reproductive success. In our species, as well as in many others, organisms that care for their offspring are fitter than organisms that do not. If individual selection has favored this behavior, and if the proximate mechanism for producing the behavior is to be a mind equipped with beliefs and desires, the question remains of what sorts of preferences that mind will contain. One possibility is that parents are made to care enormously and irreducibly about the welfare of their children. This paramount other-directed preference would mean that parents are altruistically motivated.[7]

There is no reason why evolutionary selfishness necessarily would be paired with psychological selfishness. It might be in the interests of your genes to make you act in other people's interests. Indeed, there are good grounds for thinking that evolution would have favored a mix of self-regarding and other-regarding ultimate motives in human beings.[8] This conclusion can't be disputed by insisting that altruistically motivated actions *really*, *deep down* are selfish (because they benefit one's genes). Once again, the concepts of altruism and egoism apply to the psychological motives for acting, not the evolutionary effects of those motives. Genuine altruism is sometimes the best way for selfish genes to get ahead. As professional actors know, it is all about sincerity: once you can fake that, you've got it made.[9]

Even if it were true that evolution had made us highly egoistic, that wouldn't make it right. From the fact that we often act only out of self-interest it doesn't follow that we morally ought to act only out of self-interest. In fact, it is highly implausible that we morally ought to act only out of self-interest. To appreciate this, consider the influential argument for egoism: if people were too altruistic, we'd all be worse off. Altruism is inefficient because each individual knows best what is best for him or her. This reasoning is sometimes advanced as a justification for free market capitalism. However, if you scratch it, you find that the underlying moral justification for self-interested behavior is not egoism but the promotion of the happiness of all.

Other arguments for egoism attempt to show that abiding by moral norms (such as keeping promises and respecting the property of others) has the effect in the end of furthering one's own ends—morality is a part of "enlightened self-interest." It is very difficult to maintain that morality never diverges from self-interest (where is the personal advantage in anonymously donating money to help disaster victims whom you will never meet?). Still, even when behaving morally does serve self-interest, one can ask whether self-interest provides the best reason, or the strongest motive for so behaving. Without thinking twice, a fifty-one-year-old man jumps onto the tracks of a Harlem subway station to save a young stranger, a fellow passenger who has fallen. As news of his act spreads, he becomes a minor celebrity and receives the city's Bronze Medallion, a year's supply of subway passes, and $10,000 cash from a local businessman.[10] Clearly his regard for the interests of the stranger had the effect of furthering his own. Nevertheless, furthering his own interests was not his *reason for acting*. He leapt to the rescue because of his concern for another person. Love of self is real and important; so is love of others.

So much for the skeptical implications of evolution for ethics. Subjectivism and egoism about ethics are not inevitable consequences of evolution. What about the constructive implications of evolution? Is it possible to support an objective ethics by drawing on the evolutionary sciences? There are several distinct kinds of evolutionary ethics with varying degrees of viability ranging from no-brainer to nonstarter.

Broadly speaking, the different approaches can be broken down into empirical or factual evolutionary ethics, which attempts to describe why we are the way we are or how we got that way, and prescriptive or normative evolutionary ethics, which attempts to prescribe what would be rational, morally right, or otherwise warranted for us to do.

The factual claim is that evolutionary sciences can explain why we have the faculties that make moral thinking and feeling possible at all. There is already ample support in the scientific literature for this general claim. A major area of study is how social cooperation could evolve in a population of interacting individuals (and probably did evolve among prehuman hominids).[11] These interactions are often modeled with a multiplayer game called an iterated prisoner's dilemma, in which the players receive payoffs and suffer costs depending on their choices to cooperate or not, and the way their choices combine with the choices of the other players. It turns out that the most successful strategy in such games—dubbed Tit for Tat—is to cooperate in the first round and thereafter to do whatever the other player did on the previous round (the tendency to occasionally forgive an opponent's noncooperation also helps). Translate the payoffs and costs into effects on survival and reproduction, and you get a tantalizing model of how our sense of reciprocity and fairness could have arisen through natural selection.

Something like this sense of proto-justice seems to be exhibited by chimpanzees. They are more likely to share food with others who have groomed them in the past. Chimpanzees also exhibit empathy, peacemaking, and collective punishment of individuals who transgress the norms of the group.[12] Evolutionary psychologists have discovered that people are relatively lousy at detecting violations of generic logical rules, but extremely good at spotting violations of social rules that have the same logical structure.[13] Emerging brain research on "mirror neurons" promises to uncover neurobiological roots of empathic concern.[14]

Some neuroscientists now suggest that our very sense of self and the self's responsibility for actions may have evolved to facilitate social coordination among our ancient ancestors. At first glance this research is somewhat counterintuitive. But once one fully understands its implications it becomes wildly counterintuitive. In the activities of an ordinary day—walking, lifting, deciding, interjecting, apologizing—nothing could be more obvious than the reality of being a person or self who is the originator of free choices (my hand raised because something raised it, and that something is me). The experience is underscored by the unavoidability of the first-person singular in language. "I" is everywhere. It is easy to forget that selves are not inevitable, from an engineering standpoint. If you were designing an animal from scratch, you would not necessarily need to give it a sense of self.

Daniel Dennett explains that an animal's brain is a collection of devices that cause its body to exhibit adaptive behavior in response to the right inputs from its environment: "In general, causes work just fine in the dark, without needing to be observed by anybody, and that is true of causes in animals' brains as anywhere else. . . . A bundle of situation-action links of indefinite sophistication can reside in the nervous system of a simple creature and serve its many needs without any further supervision."[15]

If, however, in the course of its evolution, an animal's behavioral repertoire becomes sufficiently complex, it will become "capable of considering different courses of action in advance of committing to any one of them, and weighing them on the basis of some projection of the probable outcome of each."[16] Now the creature needs "a level of self-monitoring that keeps track of which situation-action schemes are in the queue for execution, or in current competition for execution—and which candidates are under consideration in the faculty of practical reasoning." So far we are not in distinctively human territory. But suppose a creature comes to depend for its survival and reproduction on complicated coordination with fellow members of the species, coordination that is effected through communication between individuals. Now it needs to keep track of *who* is monitoring what and why, in order to express its desires and intentions to its fellows, thereby rendering it a reliable agent in social coordination. "It is only once a creature begins to develop the activity of communication, and in particular the communication of its actions and plans, that it has to have some capacity for monitoring not just the results of its actions, but of its prior evaluations and formation of intentions as well."[17]

In human beings, the meta-monitor of the brain-body's complex internal economy comes in the form of a more-or-less permanent, unified self that evaluates options and consciously wills actions. The conscious will, according to the theory developed by Daniel Wegner, is a feeling that we experience, a "feeling of doing." Like the feeling of knowing, the feeling of familiarity, or even the feeling of confusion, the feeling of conscious will serves to "inform us about the status of our own mental systems."[18] The feeling "marks our actions for us. It helps us to know the difference between a light we have turned on at the switch and a light that has flickered alive without our influence." The will "makes the action our own far more intensely than could a thought alone. Unlike simply saying, 'This act is mine,' the occurrence of conscious will brands the act deeply, associating the act with self through feeling, and so renders the act one's own in a personal and memorable way."[19]

A will is a human being's way of keeping track of those events in its environment that were caused by it. This ability is crucial to interactions with other members of a social group over time, in determining who is responsible for what occurrences and who therefore deserves the corresponding rewards or penalties. In order to follow social customs, make reliable threats, and keep promises, I need to remember who I am (and who I was). Imagine that when you try to collect on a debt owed you by a friend, he turns naive Buddhist: "There is no 'I' here. The ego has been overcome. There are experiences, but no experiencer. Who it was that borrowed your money yesterday cannot be said. But he is not here today and will not be here tomorrow. Sorry." Suffice it to say you would not lend that person money again.

The details are sketchy, but the general picture is of the evolution of the self driven by social interaction facilitated by language. "Nonhuman animals can engage in voluntary action of sorts. The bird that flies wherever it wants is voluntarily wheeling this way and that, voluntarily moving its wings, and it does this without benefit of language." With the introduction of language, we have "added a layer on top of the bird's (and the ape's and the dolphin's capacity to decide what to do next. . . . We can ask each other to do things, and we can ask ourselves to do things. . . . We can answer inquires about what we are doing and why. We can engage in the practice of asking, and giving, reasons."[20] By giving a reason for a behavior we claim responsibility for it—we assert it was not something that just happened to us; it was something we did. Without the capacity for exchanges of reasons and claims of responsibility, we could not be moral creatures at all.

This line of thought promises nothing less than a revolution in our self-concept. Traditionally, the self and its reasons were understood as originating from within the private states of the individual and projecting out onto the shared, public world. That traditional understanding is being turned inside out. The inner life begins in the outer world. The self would not exist were it not for others.

Taken together, all this research can leave no doubt that the faculties enabling our moral thinking and feeling were significantly shaped by our evolutionary history. Some specific moral norms may have an evolutionary history as well. For instance, it may well be that the norm—found in cultures around the world—discouraging incest is a product of selection. Does all of this add up to a "science of good and evil"? Hardly, since evolutionary psychology can only say how or why it is that we make the moral judgments we do. It says nothing about which, if any, of them are justifiable or true. Factual evolutionary ethics is accumulating some weighty science on its side, but it is light on the good and evil.

A more daring form of evolutionary ethics is based on the idea that knowledge from the evolutionary sciences can provide warrant or justification for specific moral norms or values, and hence claims about what we ought to do. Call this the prescriptive or normative form of evolutionary ethics. The project faces one colossal obstacle: the fact that something evolved does not make it morally right or permissible (and the fact that something is nonevolved does not make it morally wrong or indifferent). If that were so, then at the very least there would be something morally objectionable about choosing not to have children (do you really want to count that against the Buddha or Florence Nightingale?).

It should be no surprise that evolutionary adaptation does not track goodness, because the process of natural selection is inefficient, wasteful, and indifferent to everything we care about. When people create something, we try to devise the best design in advance and then build the thing according to that design. Natural selection, the main engine driving evolution, works by randomly trying a huge number of possible designs and discarding all the errors. This would be like a person who attempts to build a bridge by randomly trying every possible configuration and letting it collapse until through dumb luck one stays standing. That's not design. That's lunacy.

Additionally, because evolution must operate by making gradual modifications to preexisting structures, it leaves organisms with many traits that are functionally useless or even dysfunctional. The openings in our throats for breathing and swallowing are so close together that we often choke. The birth canal is too small, increasing the chances of injury, even death, during delivery. The list goes on. What's more, we know that almost every species that has ever existed on Earth is now extinct. Every museum of natural history is a scrapheap of failed experiments. An engineer whose designs were this intelligent would not have a job for long.

Evolution is a like a game with one rule: have more kids (and grandkids) than your neighbors, by any means necessary. One would hardly expect the outcomes of this game to be praiseworthy to any but the most depraved of spectators. As David Hume observed, with some melodrama, in his 1779 *Dialogues concerning Natural Religion*, what we get is "perpetual war [that] is kindled amongst all living creatures":

> Necessity, hunger, want, stimulate the strong and courageous: Fear, anxiety, terror, agitate the weak and infirm. . . . The stronger prey upon the weaker, and keep them in perpetual terror and anxiety. The weaker too, in their turn, often prey upon the stronger, and vex and molest them without relaxation. . . . And thus on each hand, before and behind, above and below, every animal is surrounded with enemies, which incessantly seek his misery and destruction.[21]

Sometimes people talk as though such deprivation and suffering is necessary to preserve a "balance of nature." There is nothing redemptive in balance. Any balance of nature is just a state of equilibrium; that is, a state of a system such that, when the system enters that state, it tends to stay in it. That says nothing about the value of the state. The most stable balance of nature is everything being dead. In the evolving world of living things, the balance of nature is a pound of flesh on each side. In our case, there is ample evidence that evolution made us, among other things, easy to indoctrinate; relatively polygamous and philandering; prone to dangerously xenophobic in-group, out-group thinking and racial and ethnic stereotyping. Males especially are hypersensitive to markers of social status and dominance, so much so that the majority of the homicides on Earth consist in men killing other men over perceived losses of social standing.

In 1844 Darwin wrote to his friend Joseph Hooker to disclose his belief that all living things have descended, with modification, from a common ancestor, a germinal idea of what would become *Origin of Species*. He told Hooker it felt like "confessing to a murder." Darwin found out (as did Alfred Russel Wallace) how the living world came to be, how it continues to be, through the struggle for existence, speciation, and extinction. For him, this secret was a terrible one, because it would turn so many people against him and destroy or unsettle so much of his own culture. But Darwin's secret was terrible, too, because of what it revealed about nature itself: that we live in the midst of a great conflagration, which was begun, and which can be stopped, by no one. We now call it evolution by natural selection.

The Sage of Down House, who worked more closely than anyone with the supposedly toxic substances of evolutionary theory, was not morally contaminated. He did not look for ethical guidance from evolution, which he knew to be blind and wasteful ("horridly cruel" even, he said). His understanding of the unforgiving realities of nature did not dampen his care and concern for others, and may have heightened it. Not long after his confession to Hooker, Darwin wrote an emotional indictment of slavery and its "heart-sickening atrocities":

> I thank God, I shall never visit a slave country. To this day, if I hear
> a distant scream, it recalls with painful vividness my feelings, when
> passing a house near Pernambuco [Brazil], I heard the most pitiable

moans, and could not but suspect that some poor slave was being tortured. . . . I have seen a little boy, six or seven years old, struck thrice with a horse-whip (before I could intervene) on his naked head, for having handed me a glass of water not quite clean.[22]

Darwin's friend and most able public advocate, Thomas H. Huxley, was explicit that a foundation for ethics could never be found in evolution. He saw the activity of ethics—people reasoning together about how they ought to live—as totally opposed to natural selection:

The practice of that which is ethically best—what we call goodness or virtue—involves a course of conduct which, in all respects, is opposed to that which leads to success in the cosmic struggle for existence. In place of ruthless self-assertion it demands self-restraint; in place of thrusting aside, or treading down, all competitors, it requires that the individual shall not merely respect, but shall help his fellows; its influence is directed, not so much to the survival of the fittest, as to the fitting of as many as possible to survive.[23]

Today's evolutionary ethicists have read Huxley and they have a counterargument prepared, a kind of sleight-of-mind trick. They agree with Huxley that an evolutionary origin alone is not enough to vindicate a practice that (for independent, non-Darwinian reasons, often unstated) they already reject, say, male control over female sexuality. But then they go on to use evolution to vindicate a practice, such as the Golden Rule, that they antecedently approve (again, on the basis of non-Darwinian assumptions). This won't do. If evolutionary origins can't vindicate an abhorrent practice, neither can they validate a laudable one.[24]

Anyway, the Golden Rule in its common form is neither evolutionarily nor morally sound. The Golden Rule does not win an iterated prisoner's dilemma. It counsels cooperation always (assuming that is what we would want done unto us). But the Tit for Tat strategy counsels us to cooperate only if the other players do. If they defect, then they get the same done unto them. The Golden Rule is also indefensible as an ethical principle, since it is satisfied by wicked actions so long as the actor is consistent: the genocidal Nazi executioner who, upon discovering that he is Jewish, consents to his own execution. He does not do unto others anything he would not want done to himself. There must be more to morality than the Golden Rule.

Where does this leave evolutionary ethics? At its best, ethical theorizing is done in constant dialogue with the natural and social sciences. It does not attempt to read our duties off of the genome, but it draws on knowledge from the sciences to guide our thinking about morality. It is ethics in a naturalistic key.

You were born a physicist. Your mind, like the mind of all other statistically normal human beings, came built with a set of assumptions about the nature of the objects around you and how they interact in space: implicit knowledge of causation, motion, acceleration. Experimental psychological evidence shows that these assumptions emerge early in childhood and persist despite one's level of education.[25] Your natural-born physics, as it turns out, is a bit off. It does all right as a commonsense or intuitive theory of ordinary-sized objects. But in its basic principles it is closer to the dynamics of Aristotle, obsolete since the seventeenth century, than contemporary physical science. For instance, when people see an object flying across a room, they explain that it is kept in motion by a kind of internal force that gradually diminishes over time. This is strikingly similar to the pre-Newtonian notion of impetus and directly at odds with the Newtonian notion of inertia, which entails that objects in motion will stay in motion unless acted on by some other force.

How did we discover inertia? Not by escaping our intuitions altogether. Rather, we harnessed other of our natural faculties—those that permit memory, careful observation, quantitative reasoning, and symbolic communication—we applied them systematically to our experiences, and we discussed together the meaning of those experiences. In a word, we experimented. (Actually, Galileo did most of the work.) Shared reason and experience permitted us to transcend our intuitive physics, so that while our minds remained Aristotelian, our understanding could become Newtonian (and now, Einsteinian). With this same experimental method, psychologists could later explain why pre-Newtonian physics seems so irresistible despite its shortcomings and how it might nonetheless have served the needs of our evolutionary ancestors (since it was good enough to get by with).

There is now growing evidence that just as you were born a physicist, you were born an ethicist. Like your intuitive physics, your intuitive ethics consists in implicit knowledge and dispositions by which you make sense of the world, in this case the world of yourself and other persons. And like intuitive physics, your intuitive ethics is not the final say. It may have been shaped by ancient evolutionary pressures, but today through shared reason and experience we can examine its limitations to see how it fits into a more complete picture.

To take one example, Harvard psychologist Marc Hauser has conducted a large-scale cross-cultural study of people's judgments about hypothetical moral dilemmas involving the permissibility of killing another person. The study involved several thousand subjects from more than one hundred countries and a wide variety of populations: "adults in different countries, with different demographic and cultural backgrounds; children prior to the age at which school might impact their moral attitudes; patients with selective damage to different parts of the brain believed to be relevant to moral analysis; and studies of animals that may have access to some of the central psychological distinctions involved in generating a moral verdict."[26] Hauser reports that the study produced three striking results:

> First, the effects of demographic and cultural variables on the pattern of moral judgments are insignificant. Second, there is a dissociation between judgment and justification, such that people rarely produce coherent justifications for their moral verdicts of right and wrong. And third, there are three principles that appear to unconsciously guide people's judgments, when consequences are held constant: People judge intended harms as worse than foreseeable harms, harms resulting from action as worse than harms resulting from omission, and harms involving physical contact as worse than those involving no contact.[27]

On the basis of these findings, Hauser has hypothesized that a shared "moral grammar" shapes the moral reasoning of all normal human beings, a set of universal assumptions embedded in our psychology. He draws a parallel to the universal grammatical structures that have been found in all natural languages. The best explanation for these complex adaptive structures is that they that were shaped by natural selection among our distant ancestors.

Suppose that something like Hauser's hypothesis is correct, and nature has endowed us with a moral sense with a particular structure. What can we conclude, ethically speaking? Is it justifiable to claim, in accord with the common intuition, that harms resulting from action are worse than harms resulting from omission? Certainly the intuition doesn't hold up in the case of the man who deliberately walks past a small child drowning in a pool whom he could save with no effort and at no risk to himself. In that case, omitting to save seems no better than causing the death. Ethicist Peter Singer famously claims that citizens of affluent societies have a moral duty to use their disposable income to aid the sick and starving in poor societies, arguing that there is little moral difference between allowing these strangers to perish—when they could be aided at no great personal sacrifice—and causing their deaths. Singer invokes Hauser's research to explain why the distinction between causing and allowing *feels* so natural and right to us, despite being morally indefensible upon reflection. If our moral duties in this case are counterintuitive, he contends, it is because our moral intuitions evolved to serve the reproductive interests of our ancient ancestors, who are thought to have lived in small, relatively independent groups of fewer than two hundred individuals.[28] There is no reason to think that they will point us in the right direction today.

In this case, the evolutionary story doesn't justify the moral norm. It explains why the norm seems justified despite the fact that, upon reflection, we can see that it is not. In deciphering the ethical lessons to draw from this research, we must go beyond the scientific facts and ask what can be supported by reason. In part, this means looking at the matter from a common, impartial point of view, testing for consistency across cases, and seeking coherence with our background understanding. It means appealing to conscience.

Research on a universal moral grammar demonstrates how ethics can and should be empirically grounded without being evolutionary or strictly scientific. If we wish to construct a defensible objective ethics from secular resources, we will have no choice but to enlist our own reason and compassion in the experimentation. There will be no substitute for thinking critically about our own good and the good of others.

Just before midnight, on Monday, April 17, 1882, Charles Darwin was awakened by wracking pain. He was on his deathbed, and on that night he had what was to be his last conversation with his wife, Emma. Despite the apocryphal accounts of his deathbed return to Christianity for last-minute salvation, Charles's mind was in fact not on his own interests. He was thinking of other people. "My love, my precious love," he strained to get out. "Tell all my children to remember how good they have always been to me. I am not the least afraid to die." Two days later, in his last lucid moment on Earth, Charles asked after Emma. Hearing that she was in bed resting, he exclaimed, "I am glad of it."[29]

7.
Original Virtue

I believe in original sin. I also believe in original virtue.
Look around!

—Kurt Vonnegut

In the run-up to his election as pope, then-cardinal Joseph Ratzinger warned that Western culture was sliding toward "a dictatorship of relativism which does not recognize anything as for certain and which has as its highest goal one's own ego and one's own desires."[1] In his first encyclical, *Deus Caritas Est* (God Is Love), he faults modern people for missing the transcendent meaning of love and caring for each other just because we feel like it. Is this relativism, and if so, is it wrong? Like cholesterol, relativism comes in good and bad varieties.[2] It turns out that while some varieties of so-called relativism are confused and even pernicious, others are essential to any serious, well-developed worldview. Even the pope's.

The pope is not the only one confused about relativism and ethics. The deeper question he raises is whether objective ethics is possible outside of a religious framework, whether goodness necessarily is next to godliness. Many secular liberals want to believe in objective ethics, the idea that moral questions can have right and wrong answers and that the answers are somehow determined by the way the world is, not just the way we feel about it. But they find this idea difficult to reconcile with their liberalism. They get nervous around "absolute truth." This feeling is unfounded. With a little work, one can have liberalism and moral truth too. What secular liberals cannot have is a so-called private conscience that issues in private moral truths. If conscience is private in that sense, then ethics is not objective. Those trying to hold on to both have lost their grip on moral reality. Thank goodness, there is such a thing a nonreligious objective ethics. In fact, there is no alternative to it. Conscience is secular by its nature. Not only is the secular conscience possible without religion, the religious conscience is impossible without it.

Strictly speaking, of course, if relativism makes the desires of each individual supreme, then a dictatorship of relativism would be at worst an extreme form of government bureaucratic redundancy—the ministry of forcing citizens to do what they feel like doing anyway. Pope Benedict's real worry, expressed in writings and addresses over several years, is that individual autonomy has been elevated above moral absolutes.

Ethicists distinguish between what they call defeasible and indefeasible moral claims. Defeasible claims are rules of thumb that nevertheless can be overruled for countervailing moral reasons. Surely many moral principles are defeasible and in that sense relative. We all recognize that although lying is wrong as a general principle, under certain circumstances—to protect someone's life, for example—it is justifiable to lie. Yet the fact that a moral rule can sometimes give way for good cause does not show that it is mistaken or groundless, any more than traffic laws are invalidated because ambulances get to run red lights. Indeed, the exception proves that the rule holds at a more fundamental level.

This is a point Benedict can appreciate. His first substantive instruction to the Church came in a November 2005 directive on gays and the priesthood, which states that bishops "cannot admit to the seminary or to holy orders those who practice homosexuality, present deep-seated homosexual tendencies or support the so-called 'gay culture.'"3 At the same time, the document enjoins respect for gays and disavows discrimination. It leaves open to interpretation the distinction between "deep-rooted" and "transitory" tendencies, leading some observers to suggest that it would permit the ordination of a sexually mature, celibate homosexual. Most significantly, it does nothing to get current gay priests to come out of the cassock. If homosexuality is, as the catechism holds, "objectively disordered," why not an outright ban? One weighty reason is the priest shortage. An objectively disordered order is better than none. Nonabsolute standards, anyone?

So, one question about ethics is, can a sound moral principle have exceptions? This is the worry over *defeasible versus indefeasible* ethics. The answer is, sure. It is no objection to objective ethics to acknowledge that principles have exceptions, so long as they are principled exceptions.

Maybe the problem with secular standards in particular is that they can never be certain—another meaning of "relativism." However, the alternative to certainty is not ignorance but fallibility, the idea that a belief can be reasonable even though it is not justified conclusively or beyond all possible doubt. If that's all relativism means, then it is not the enemy of truth or morality, for fallible knowledge is knowledge nonetheless. Being fallible doesn't keep us from thinking that we're right (as Benedict no doubt recalls from his pre-papal days). It just keeps us from thinking that we couldn't possibly be wrong. And that's a good thing. The ability to revise beliefs in light of new information is part of what makes having a mind worthwhile. It worked for a young German theologian who (according to biographer John Allen) in the late 1960s began to morph from Vatican II reformer to enforcer of the faith.4 The Church itself has been known to self-correct every once in a while (see Galileo, Darwin).

This second source of consternation about ethics is over *certain versus fallible* moral knowledge. Here the question is, can moral claims be known with a degree of confidence less than certainty? Again, it would not bankrupt the idea of morality to admit that moral knowledge is imperfect and revisable in light of future experience. After all, the most successful ways of knowing that we know of are found in the natural sciences. In the sciences, fallibility and revisability are virtues. Why should moral knowledge be held to a higher standard? There is room for us to wonder whether we are wrong about what is morally right. That alone does not mean we *are* wrong.

What else could relativism mean? It could mean that apart from a transcendent order, nothing is better or worse, right or wrong, period. Truth is opinion, and "objective moral truth" is opinion on stilts. Taken to the extreme, this is just nihilism, the doctrine that nothing really matters. It is hard to argue that nihilism is the reigning ideology of our time, except perhaps at certain dance clubs and on cable TV between the hours of 11 p.m. and 4 a.m. Just ask yourself how many nihilists you've met today (if they found a reason to get out of bed in the morning, they probably weren't nihilists). Or perhaps the ideology of our time is egoism, the idea that only *my* interests matter. There are in fact at least four distinct worries about morality mixed up here that need to be sorted out. Here they are.

Would anything be valuable if there were no beings doing the valuing? If the universe doesn't care about anything, does anything really matter? Call this the worry over *relational versus nonrelational values*. A value is relational when it is valuable in relation to some valuer. It seems obvious enough that nothing matters unless there is someone to whom it matters. Of course, the universe does contain creatures like us, for whom many things—like love, knowledge, and loneliness—hold value and disvalue. What remains to be seen is whether the valuing of mere mortal, finite creatures is enough to make its objects "really" matter, in the last analysis. A satisfying answer would have to show that our values are not somehow unreal because they are relational values.

Can the same moral claim be "true for" one community, society, or time period but not others? This is the worry over *universal versus relative norms*, and it is crucial. Morality would lose most of the wind from its sails if it turned out that moral judgments are not universal. Without the assumption of university, when egalitarians objected to homegrown white supremacists, or when the Committee to Protect Journalists denounced totalitarian repression in some other part of the world, they would be talking to themselves, strictly speaking. Moral norms would be relative to communities, and so there would be no point in addressing a criticism *to* the members of another community. Sure, genocide is wrong, but not if you are one of the perpetrators. Again, this kind of skepticism is a challenge to the viability of ethics.

Do an individual's attitudes alone make it the case that something is valuable? Is the moral permissibility of an option determined by the way one feels about it? This is the worry over *objective versus subjective values*. Skepticism about ethics would prevail if "infidelity is wrong" turned out to have the same status as "I don't like ice cream" and "icky!" Finally, there is the related worry: Are there any moral obligations to anyone other than one's self? This is the question of egoism, or *self-regarding versus other-regarding concerns*. Some people claim that their only obligations are to themselves, to promote their own ends, whatever those may be.

Confronted with these confounding questions—over relational versus nonrelational values, universal versus relative norms, objective versus subjective values, and self-regarding versus other-regarding concerns—many secular liberals are tempted to take refuge in the Privacy Fallacy and the Liberty Fallacy. If moral conscience is a private matter, then we don't need to answer such questions together. Each of us consents to a social and political framework that gives us the freedom to make up our own minds on moral matters, and none of us presumes to declare our ethical standpoint to be *the* ethical standpoint.

However tempting it may be, the haven of privacy is a mirage. For if it matters at all, the privacy of conscience is itself a value that is objective, universal in scope, and that implies concern for others. We cannot avoid passing moral judgment by insisting on the freedom of conscience, for the freedom of conscience is a moral judgment.

What Benedict calls "relativism" are actually the values of secular liberalism: individual autonomy, equal rights, and freedom of belief. But it is easy to conflate *what liberals affirm* with *the way they affirm it*. Liberalism tells us that our way of life is up to us (within limits), not that the truth of liberalism is up to us. It entails that we tolerate even claims that we doubt, not that we doubt even the claims of tolerance. Liberals themselves are prone to this confusion, the Liberty Fallacy, and fall into an all-values-are-equal relativism (especially common among students in introductory ethics classes, at least until the instructor informs them that since all grades are equally valid, everyone will be receiving a failing grade for the course).

Freshman ethicists also conflate the making of a truth-claim with the determination to force others to believe it. But there is nothing illiberal about asserting an objective truth, a claim that is made true by the way the world is. You do it every time you give the time of day to someone who asks. You don't thereby *coerce* your neighbor into believing it is noon, you give him a reason to believe it. Consider these six statements:

1. I'm right, but I could be mistaken.
2. I'm right.
3. I'm right, you're wrong.
4. I'm right, you're wrong, here's why you should change your mind.
5. I'm right, you're wrong, go to hell.
6. I'm right, you're wrong, change your mind or be killed.

Rank these statements on an Intolerance Scale, a scale of one to ten, where the unit of measurement of intolerance is a *stal* (in honor of Joseph Stalin). Statement (6) is the most intolerant, earning 10 stals. By making statement (6) I not only assert a claim that you disagree with but I threaten you with real harm unless you conform. This is coercion of the most vicious kind. At the opposite end of the scale, statement (1) is accompanied by no coercive force, and the claim itself is hedged with uncertainty. Clearly statement (1) has 0 stals. Statement (2), while more self-confident than (1), remains within the comfort zone of liberal relativists, as it says nothing about whether others are "entitled" to their truths that might contradict mine. Give it 0 stals as well. Where many relativists lose their nerve is at statements like (3). The assertion of the other's wrongness, they fear, is judgmental, intolerant. The relativist's impulse is to broadmindedness, but there are some things that a mind cannot fit no matter how it is stretched. When I claim that Connaught Place is in New Delhi, and you claim it is in Dublin, then my being right will amount to your being wrong. If condom use is advisable, then those who hold it to be morally abominable must be mistaken, as moral abominations are not to be recommended. One cannot make a claim without being committed to denying its denial, any more than one can wish one's team to win the World Cup without wishing that everyone else's will lose. In most cases, then, a statement (2) will imply a statement (3). It is not intolerance to think that another is wrong; it is the nature of thinking. If (3) were intolerant, then intolerance would be inescapable and the accusation of intolerance therefore empty.

Statements (1)–(3) ranked 0 stals on the Intolerance Scale. Could it be that the significant move in the direction of intolerance is the move from (3) to (4)? Here I am not only believing but proselytizing, attempting to convince others to change their minds. But there is nothing objectionable in principle about this.[5] By pointing out the position of the hands of my watch to an inquiring stranger, I am giving him a reason to change his mind about the time of day. Nothing could be further from intolerance. Giving reasons to others is the laudable *alternative* to imposing my will on them. A statement like (4) earns no stals. But suppose my attitude of cognitive superiority—of being right—were accompanied by an attitude of personal or moral superiority and of contempt, hatred, or ill will toward those who disagree, something like (5): I'm right, you're wrong, go to hell. These attitudes, depending on their severity, can put me into positive stals, anywhere from 1 to 9. Conversation gets dangerous, and deserving of the cautionary label of intolerant, when disagreeing is joined by basic disrespecting and disregarding of the persons on the other side. This kind of intolerance is a powerful and volatile chemical that must be handled with care. But even liberal peoples will often have need of it. It is no vice to despise the knowing purveyors of a genocidal or misogynistic ideology. Still, contempt falls far short of actual coercion with the threat of real harm.

All of this is a far cry from just asserting the truth of a claim or the rightness of a course of action. To be meaningfully described as intolerant, it is not enough that I assert the true or right, or even that I attempt to convince others through reason to see things my way. Intolerance involves the addition of some coercive force or a fundamental disrespect for those who disagree. So the scruples of broadmindedness should not prevent liberals from holding their truths without apology. Having glimpsed the final destination of this train of thought, some liberals may choose not to get on it at all. But in so doing they would be giving up the chance to engage in serious public argument. Every serious argument is at least a statement of type (3), and often, under favorable conditions, a statement of type (4).

Benedict is correct. Secular values can turn a society inside out. In post-Christian Europe, entire nations have been plunged into endemic health, skyrocketing education, and hopelessly low rates of violent crime. Perhaps a future papal encyclical will target the kind of relativism that leads to real harm. This is the misguided multiculturalism that keeps Western liberals from criticizing the oppression of women, religious minorities, and apostates in Islamic societies for fear of being accused of "Islamaphobia." The solution is not to shrink from the ideals of autonomy and equality but to affirm them openly for what they are: objectively defensible principles of conscience. The important contrast, then, is not between absolutism and relativism, as the pontiff would have it, but between these secular values and their traditional religious alternatives. He can accuse secularists of believing in the wrong things, but that's not the same as believing in nothing.

✼ ✼ ✼

What about love? Isn't love enough? What more do we need for meaning, for morality? *Caritas, eros, agape*—the Latin Church had words for forms of love that are lost in the English *love* and the French *amor*. But they are not lost in life. Almost all of us have known *agape*, the solidarity with brothers and sisters in the family of humanity, the awareness of the other as another self, another creature as conscious and fragile as we are. Almost all of us are moved when one person gives up his life for another, or even just a seat on the bus. To love like this is to desire the good of the other for the sake of the other, to take the true interests of the other as our own reasons.

Agape was not invented by the Christians—although it was their supreme virtue—nor by the Jews, who were the first to see in all human beings the image of God. It was not invented at all, but discovered, in many places and many times by many peoples. Not all of them made love an ethical ideal. Aristotle was not a fan; the Greeks and Romans esteemed temperance, prudence, courage, and justice. The Confucian thinkers did discover and extol love. The Confucianism that shaped Chinese civilization is not a supernatural religion but a humanistic ethical philosophy. Its central concept is *ren*, a virtue of the ideal man variously translated as benevolence, love of others, humaneness, human-heartedness, or compassion. *Ren* is an affectionate concern for the well-being of others in the community.

Surely, love—*agape, ren*—is not enough. We need reason and truth, for we can be mistaken about how and when to love, about what do to about it. Existence takes courage too, if compassion is to have a fighting chance. All of these are sustained by hope, and in turn sustain it. So, love is not sufficient for all of life's demands, but is it sufficient unto itself? Can it support the claims of other-regarding concern? When someone fails to recognize the force of the reasons of love, can we say he is objectively wrong? Some would say that even in its domain, *ren* is not sovereign, that its authority is the grant of something transcendent. Ethics, some suggest, cannot make use of love without first laying its metaphysical anchor outside of ordinary human experience.

I submit that this is not how we ordinarily experience love. Ask yourself, if there were no divine creator or life everlasting, would you love your friends or family any less? Would your care for a child be diminished by the discovery that you were the only one caring? Were the heavens empty, would your heart no longer be full? It is worth wondering what sense can be made of the religious alternative, that the objective moral worth of humanity depends on God. How would that work? Could it be that God simply *decides* that we have value? That doesn't seem right, for we don't suppose that God could simply decide that a lump of coal is as valuable as a person. Rather, it must be that God *recognizes something about us* that is morally important: maybe our capacity to suffer, or to have interests and plans. But if that is so, then God drops out of the picture. It is these morally important features that determine our value. And these we have in virtue of facts about us, not facts about God.

What Would Jesus Do? is a good question. But a more important question is, *why* would he do it? Presumably Jesus's injunction in Luke 18:22 to "sell all that you own and distribute money to the poor" was not a whim. He must have had some reasons for it (for starters, he thought the world was coming to an end soon). If there are such reasons, then they must be binding on Jesus's choices and therefore exist independently of those choices.

Why Would Jesus Do What Jesus Would Do? is what Socrates would want to know. It was, of course, Socrates who, in Plato's telling of his dialogue with Euthyphro, took the same scythe to the idea that morality could have religious foundations. Socrates encounters Euthyphro on his way to bring a lawsuit against his own father, and this sparks a discussion on the nature of piety, or holiness. As the dialogue unfolds, Euthyphro defines holiness as what is loved by the gods. To this Socrates responds with his all-time best question: Is it holy because it is loved by the gods, or do the gods love it because it is holy? Neither answer to the question, now known as the Euthyphro dilemma, looks inviting to the religious moralist: If holiness is just whatever the gods love, then the gods' evaluation appears arbitrary or subjective. If, on the other hand, holiness is loved because it is holy, then the gods' evaluation appears superfluous.

The independence of the moral conscience from faith is not some secular heresy. It is integral to Christianity and Judaism. In fact, it can be found in the Hebrew Bible and the New Testament. Romans 2:14–15 acknowledges the existence of a moral conscience among pagans, those who are outside of the covenant with Yahweh: "When Gentiles, who do not possess the law, do instinctively what the law requires, these, though not having the law, are a law to themselves. They show that what the law requires is written on their hearts, to which their own conscience also bears witness; and their conflicting thoughts will accuse or perhaps excuse them." The moral law is written on the heart of all, believer and unbeliever.

In the New Testament, conscience is also open in the sense of being fallible, susceptible to two kinds of error. In the first, a false negative, conscience fails to detect a wrong that, by God's standards, has been done. In the second, a false positive, conscience is convinced a wrong has been done, when in fact—again, by God's standards—it has not. In 1 Corinthians 4:4–5, it is said that conscience can be satisfied when God is not: "I am not aware of anything against myself, but I am not thereby acquitted. . . . Therefore do not pronounce judgment before the time, before the Lord comes, who will bring to light the things now hidden in darkness and will disclose the purposes of the heart." And 1 John 3:18–20 states that our conscience may condemn us even when God is satisfied: "Little children, let us love, not in word or speech, but in truth and action. And by this we will know that we are from the truth and will reassure our hearts before him whenever our hearts condemn us; for God is greater than our hearts, and he knows everything." Later, medieval Christian Scholastic theologians would develop an elaborate theory of conscience as a faculty and a judgment that is guided by some ultimate principles of practical rationality, the rules of reason governing action.[6]

The Old Testament speaks of the promptings of the "heart" on matters of right and wrong. For the ancient Israelites, as for the Greeks, the heart was not just the center of sentiment, but also of thinking and will—the center of the entire person. The lesson of the Euthyphro dilemma is also found (at least in between the lines) in the familiar story of Abraham and Isaac from the book of Exodus:

> And it came to pass after these things, that God did tempt Abraham, and said unto him, Abraham: and he said, Behold, here I am.
>
> And he said, Take now thy son, thine only son Isaac, whom thou lovest, and get thee into the land of Moriah; and offer him there for a burnt offering upon one of the mountains which I will tell thee of.
>
> And Abraham rose up early in the morning, and saddled his ass, and took two of his young men with him, and Isaac his son, and clave the wood for the burnt offering, and rose up, and went unto the place of which God had told him.
>
> Then on the third day Abraham lifted up his eyes, and saw the place afar off.
>
> And Abraham said unto his young men, Abide ye here with the ass; and I and the lad will go yonder and worship, and come again to you.
>
> And Abraham took the wood of the burnt offering, and laid it upon Isaac his son; and he took the fire in his hand, and a knife; and they went both of them together.
>
> And Isaac spake unto Abraham his father, and said My father: and he said, Here am I, my son. And he said, Behold the fire and the wood: but where is the lamb for a burnt offering?
>
> And Abraham said, My son, God will provide himself a lamb for a burnt offering: so they went both of them together.
>
> And they came to the place which God had told him of, and Abraham built an altar there, and laid the wood in order, and bound Isaac his son, and laid him on the altar upon the wood.

And Abraham stretched forth his hand, and took the knife to slay his son.

And the angel of the Lord called unto him out of heaven, and said, Abraham, Abraham: and he said Here am I.

And he said, Lay not thine hand upon the lad, neither do thou any thing unto him: for now I know that thou fearest God, seeing thou hast not withheld thy son, thine only son from me.

Imagine: God speaks to you. Bring me your son, he says, your only son. You know that God is sovereign. You know that he is good. And he wants you to kill your son. What do you do?

Abraham obeys, so the story goes, and God rewards his obedience by sparing Isaac. The awful command is a test, and Abraham has passed. The story is revered as a meditation on the nature of faith (not sadism and megalomania, as a straightforward reading of the text could suggest). Abraham is remembered not just as a father to Isaac but also to Judaism, Christianity, and Islam. The story is thought to communicate two essential features of these great monotheisms—that the moral order of the world flows from the will of God, and that the proper relationship of human beings to that will is submission. Had God allowed the sacrifice to continue, Abraham would have been justified in carrying it out.

Take another look at the story of Abraham and Isaac and it becomes a meditation on the nature of conscience. For although Abraham faces the Almighty, he remains free to disobey. Had he been necessitated to obey, had he been psychologically incapable of lowering the knife and leading his son back down the mountain, then the gesture of faith would have been meaningless. In the same way, the gesture would have been meaningless had Abraham been thoughtless or indifferent to its gravity, carrying out the ritual in a perfunctory funk. His act is an act of faith only insofar as it comes from Abraham's own judgment about what he has most reason to do. When Abraham reflects on the reasons that flow from his love of Yahweh, and on the reasons that flow from his love of Isaac, and still in freedom chooses to obey, then and only then could his action be pleasing to God.

The Danish philosopher Søren Kierkegaard proposed an ingenious —devilish, even—alternative analysis of Abraham's choice. He distinguished between ethical obligation and religious obligation and showed that our religious obligations could sometimes come apart from our ethical obligations. He acknowledged our revulsion at the thought of killing an innocent child, and conceded that this attitude is in fact appropriate. As a father and a human being, Abraham was obligated to disobey God's command. Ethically speaking, he was bound to love his son more than himself or else become a "murderer."[7] But somehow his singular devotion to God as an individual impelled him to go beyond the ethical sphere of universal rules itself, to "suspend" the ethical in order to embrace the divine person: "By his act he overstepped the ethical entirely and possessed a higher *telos* outside of it, in relation to which he suspended the former."[8] Kierkegaard's analysis complicates the connection between God and morality, but it doesn't escape the primacy of Abraham's judgment. The move outside (above, below?) the ethical realm is still a move *made by Abraham* and so involves no less of an exercise of his judgment.

Read in this way, the story of Abraham and Isaac turns on its head the conventional belief that conscience depends on religious faith. Here the genuine act of religious faith depends on a prior act of conscience. For unless your moral life is one of arbitrary, unprincipled choice or abject, mindless obedience (a state most adults could not keep up even if they tried), you will find yourself thinking about what you have most reason to do, all things considered. Then it is the instruction of your own conscience, not the voice on the mountaintop, that guides your hand. The only moral sense worthy of the name is secular.

While Confucianism was a tradition-bound ethics preoccupied with *li*, the customary rules of proper behavior, it also stressed *yi*, the ability and the responsibility of the individual to make particular judgments on a basic sense of rightness. The parallel with what is called conscience in the West is irresistible. The great Confucian philosopher

Mencius, active three hundred years before Christ, elucidated the uses of *yi* with the story of Shun's marriage. Shun decided to marry without first securing his parents' permission, an action that would normally constitute a serious violation of the duty of filial piety, something very prized in Confucian ethics. Nevertheless, Shun was justified in his action for two reasons. One is that of the things that are disrespectful of one's parents, leaving no posterity is the worst of all. The other is that had Shun been refused by his parents, whom he knew would have disapproved of his choice of partner, he would have ended up far more bitter toward them and hence a bad son.[9]

The ethically superior man (yes, man) does not blindly follow his presumptive duties. Rather, he interprets them in light of individual circumstances, and arrives at a judgment about what he has most reason to do on the basis of all the relevant considerations. The sense of rightness is not a raw intuition, unanswerable to criticism. Instead, it is a craft of practical reasoning that can be learned through careful attention to historical examples from the experience of others, which are themselves open to challenge and revision.

A defender of religious ethics might respond that conscience may be prior to religion, but it cannot be prior to God, because it is ultimately God's creation. According to the Christian conception, my conscience is a law written on the heart, but not a law written by me. In the words of the Second Vatican Council:

> In the depths of his conscience, man detects a law which he does not impose upon himself, but which holds him to obedience. Always summoning him to love good and avoid evil, the voice of conscience when necessary speaks to his heart: do this, shun that. For man has in his heart a law written by God; to obey it is the very dignity of man; according to it he will be judged. Conscience is the most secret core and sanctuary of a man. There he is alone with God, Whose voice echoes in his depths.[10]

Can it make sense to speak of conscience without reference to the divine author? The dilemmas of Abraham and Euthyphro show that conscience must come before faith in deliberations about what one ought to do. But they do not show that conscience unaided will come through with any answers. They point out that in the search for moral truths there is no substitute for the secular conscience, not that the search must succeed. For it could be that God is no foundation for objective moral values because there is no foundation for objective moral values to be had. It could be that religious *and* secular ethics are doomed.

There are three separate questions that have to be disentangled here. One is the question of *moral motivation*: can you be a good person and decent citizen without belief in God or supernatural religion?[11] I have already suggested that love unaided is enough to give us reasons to consider the interests of our neighbor. Evidence abounds for this independence of religious and moral motives. The most generous philanthropists, dollar-for-dollar, in the history of the world have been secular, freethinking people: Bill Gates, Warren Buffett, Andrew Carnegie, and George Soros. Gates, in the ultimate statement of agnosticism for the multitasking age, told *Time* magazine, "Just in terms of allocation of time resources, religion is not very efficient. There's a lot more I could be doing on a Sunday morning."[12] The second-most generous nation on Earth as of this writing (measured both in individual charitable contributions and in government aid to developing countries) also has one of the lowest rates of regular church attendance (and the highest level of self-reported fulfillment in life): Denmark.[13] Christopher Hitchens's challenge remains unmet: name a single morally praiseworthy act by a believer that could not have been performed by an unbeliever. (At the same time, research shows that secular Americans are significantly less likely than religious Americans to do anything for charity to help the poor).[14]

What these discussions about moral motivation never question is the assumption that the good behavior of the religious is *caused by religious motives*. What might appear obvious is actually extraordinarily difficult to demonstrate. Human motivation is as multivariate as the weather. A single action may be caused by a number of different desires interacting, much as low- and high-pressure systems combine to produce a storm front. Suppose the motivational system of a religious believer contains the religious desire to please the deity and the altruistic desire to aid persons in dire need. There is no reason to think that the altruistic desire must be reducible to some more ultimate religious desire. It could be love of neighbor for its own sake. Now, when the believer gives to the poor, how do we know which was operating as the cause of the behavior—the religious desire, the secular altruistic desire, or a combination of the two? It won't settle the matter to ask the believer himself. As psychologists can tell you, people are notoriously unreliable observers of their own motivations.[15]

Perhaps the secular conscience is taking too much credit for itself. Ethical secularists in the West, it could be argued, are spending the moral capital accumulated by millennia of Judeo-Christian civilization. The moral knowledge and practices of the secularist—such as the affirmation of the inherent dignity of the person—are actually parasitic on religious tradition. According to this moral capital argument, European societies have survived secularization because they remain culturally Christian.[16] First, setting aside the historical experiences of China, South Korea, and Japan, where civil morality obviously is not the afterglow of monotheism, it must be said that the moral capital argument gives short thrift to contributions to European civilization by the pagan Greeks and Romans, to say nothing of literal capital—values such as prudence, temperance, and honesty probably flourished in bourgeois society in part because they are nurtured by capitalist commercial activity.[17] Further, there is no evidence that the benefits of the Judeo-Christian moral heritage, whatever they may be, are going to be expended and exhausted over time. An alternative hypothesis is at least as plausible: owing to its particular historical course, the West discovered *agape* by way of monotheism, but once having done so will not lose it, even if it should lose its religion.

Maybe the moral capitalists have unacknowledged debts of their own. The secular conscience is not a derivative of the history of religious ethics; rather, it is part of that history. Whenever believers have appealed to their own reason and compassion in order to determine which biblical laws to follow and which to reinterpret or retire, which punishments to apply and which to abjure, they have exercised the secular conscience. The tenth-century Jewish philosopher Saadya Gaon, influenced by the Kalam school of Islamic theology, saw the Torah as a shortcut to moral wisdom available to common reason. The Catholic natural law tradition bypasses scripture altogether, determining our good by looking (in St. Thomas's theory) to our natural inclinations or (in the "new natural law theory" of Germain Grisez, John Finnis, and Robert George) to self-evident principles of practical reason. Whenever scripture and clerical authority have been insufficient to settle a moral question (judging just from disagreement among the Christian denominations, such questions include war, theocracy, capitalism, slavery and white supremacy, the death penalty, divorce, blasphemy, apostasy, homosexuality, contraception, abortion, and the equality of women), thoughtful believers have wondered, as Anne Hutchinson did, "How do we know which voice is the voice of God?" The answer could only come from themselves, and each other.

Secularists are not out of the woods yet. Apart from the question of moral motivation is the matter of *moral knowledge*: can you find out what is right and wrong without help from revelation, clergy, or scripture? Finally, there is the question of *moral reality*: are objective values and moral truths possible apart from a religious worldview? Absent a transcendent, does it make sense to believe in a realm of relational yet real and objective values that support moral claims that are in some important sense universal and that go beyond egoism to posit other-regarding duties? The answer is yes. This answer is the consensus conclusion of the countless philosophers, theologians, and others who have thought carefully about the nature of ethics. Their open inquiry can be called secular ethics, and subsequent chapters will explore it.

8

The Search for the Theory of Everyone

What gods can exceed these that clasp me by the hand, and with voices I love call me promptly and loudly by my nighest name as I approach?

What is more subtle than this which ties me to the woman or man that looks in my face?
Which fuses me into you now, and pours my meaning into you?

We understand then do we not?
What I promis'd without mentioning it, have you not accepted?
What the study could not teach—what the preaching could not accomplish is accomplish'd, is it not?

—Walt Whitman

W hen I ride my bicycle to work, the particular path I choose to take—along the river, through the park, or down the avenue—reflects my personal mood, tastes, and partialities at the moment. But when I collide with a pedestrian, my choice about whether to flee or remain at the scene has to be considered in light of the interests of all affected. The reasons for which others sanction or condemn my actions, if they are to be compelling, must apply not just to me but to anyone else in a similar situation. As David Hume put it, in thinking about a situation from this point of view, a person "must here therefore depart from his private and particular situation, and must choose a point of view common to him with others."[1] A point of view that is "impartial, but equally concerned with all those potentially affected"[2]—this is what we mean by morality.

The Golden Rule, which has been discovered by diverse civilizations across the globe, reflects this urge to universality and impartiality. Do Unto Others As You Would Have Them Do Unto You is not a bad thing to remember. Still, it is a long way from a full account of the moral life. For starters, it is not self-vindicating; it says nothing about why one should follow it (leaving aside for the moment the question of how to follow it), instead of the more appealing Do Unto Others Whatever You Feel Like Doing. Those who worry about such questions are drawn to construct more comprehensive and systematic accounts of morality and test them against their reason and experience. These accounts, which can be called theories of ethics, aim to find out whether there are defensible reasons or principles that can be universally applied and that give impartial consideration to all.

For some time this was the Holy Grail in the exploration of ethics by Western philosophers and theologians. Just as physicists dream of a Theory of Everything, ethicists dreamed of a Theory of Everyone. A Theory of Everyone would show that everyone has reason to do the right thing and that these reasons respond to a moral reality that everyone shares—values are in some important way objective, not mere projections of our individual desires and dislikes onto the world. In so doing, a Theory of Everyone would resolve two interrelated issues that have confronted just about everyone who has thought carefully about moral questions. The first has to do with the nature of moral reasons and motivation: Why be moral? What makes morality *normative*, something that we should go along with? When your self-interest diverges from what morality expects of you, why not serve yourself and follow the principle Do Unto Others Whatever You Feel Like

Doing? The second question has to do with the nature of moral claims. Are there, alongside the facts of geography, psychology, and history, such things as *moral facts*—facts about what one morally ought to do? Is morality real? Are there moral truths, and what makes them so?

The question of moral normativity and the question of moral objectivity are intertwined but not identical. It might be, for example, that there are moral truths available to everyone, but not everyone is moved by them. Morality could be real, but dead to some of us. Or it might be that everyone is constituted so as to be moved by moral truths, but in fact there aren't any. Despite this apparent independence, there is a venerable tradition in Western ethics that tries to wed moral reality to moral motivation. According to this tradition, if there are any moral facts, then they are essentially motivating, giving reasons to all rational beings.

Perhaps the most widely discussed attempt to make good on the Theory of Everyone comes from Immanuel Kant. Kant's moral philosophy begins with the thought that when you take an action, you must think of yourself as acting freely. Acting freely does not mean acting arbitrarily or capriciously but rather abiding by rules of one's own making. For Kant, this means setting aside all "contingent" or accidental influences on the self—the push and pull of changing appetites, the prejudices of the blood and country you happened to be born into—and listening only to the laws of one's own will, which is to say the laws of reason itself. Your actions will have moral worth, and you will be autonomous, or self-governing, to the extent that you act out of a duty to reason, which is a duty to your own fundamental nature.

And what do the laws of reason say? Kant postulates, taking a page from Newtonian science, that we know they must have the defining feature of all laws: universality. Hence his famous Categorical Imperative: "Act only in accordance with that maxim through which you could at the same time will that it become a universal law." The Categorical Imperative, which Kant presents as one formulation among four different formulations of "precisely the same law," is a test of the moral permissibility of our actions. A "maxim" is a kind of principle of action, such as the Promise-Breaker's Maxim: "Break your promises whenever it suits you to get want you want." To apply Kant's test, ask yourself what you are willing by making a promise you intend not to keep. You are willing to make a promise. At the same time, since the laws of reason are universal, you are willing that everyone (all rational beings) adopt the Promise-Breaker's Maxim. But in willing that everyone adopt the Promise-Breaker's Maxim, you are willing a world in which promising is impossible because no one would take a promise as binding. So by acting on the maxim, you are willing simultaneously that promising is both possible and impossible. You are caught in a contradiction of the will, a practical inconsistency. This is why, according to Kant, breaking a promise is morally prohibited.

Despite its elegance, the Categorical Imperative fails as a reliable test of right action. Some maxims that do not pass the universalizing test are not obviously immoral; other maxims that are morally problematic pass it. "Always arrive ten minutes late" would not survive universalizing (if everybody did that, no one would be late). Yet it is impolite at worst, not wicked. On the other hand, a maxim can be made to pass Kantian muster by building in enough specificity that its universal adoption would amount to nothing. Consider the maxim "When it suits you, lie in your testimony before the grand jury on August 17, 1998, in the Map Room of the White House." Still, most ethicists believe that Kant was on to something essential when he placed universality at the heart of morality. Many believe that where he overreached was in holding that moral values must provide reasons to everyone simply in virtue of their rational nature, no matter what their other appetites and natures: the quest for the Theory of Everyone.

The quest has also led some skeptics to conclude that objective morality is a sham. It goes like this: no values can get a motivational grip on everyone who apprehends them, and (assuming the theory) objective moral values would have to do just that; therefore, there are no such things. One such skeptic about ethics is J. L. Mackie, who argued that "if there were objective values, then they would be entities or qualities or relations of a very strange sort, utterly different from anything else in the universe":

> Something's being good both tells the person who knows this to pursue it and makes him pursue it. An objective good would be sought by anyone who was acquainted with it, not because of any contingent fact that this person, or every person, is so constituted that he desires this end, but because the end has to-be-pursuedness somehow built into it.[3]

Mackie's objection is that objective moral values are just too weird to exist ("queer" was the term he used, in 1977). In the world as we find it, with the aid of the natural sciences, we have found nothing with this extraordinary feature of *to-be-pursuedness*. If you find out the time or the temperature, you haven't thereby found out what to do about it. That depends on your purposes, what you desire and intend to do. All the facts we have ever encountered are motivationally inert. They do not speak. They do not tell us where to go. Our past experience and background knowledge alone make it incredibly unlikely that there could be such a thing as an essentially motivating fact, a moral fact.

Along with this metaphysical objection about the nature of values, Mackie presents an epistemological objection, an objection about our ability to come to know about values. What we know about the rest of the world comes to us ultimately through sense organs that are designed to perceive certain properties of nature, such as color, taste, and timbre. With what organ could we perceive the to-be-pursuedness of moral facts? As Mackie puts it, "If we were aware of them, it would have to be by some special faculty of moral perception or intuition, utterly different from our ordinary ways of knowing everything else."[4] Again, we are clueless in principle as to how such a faculty could operate and so we are justified in rejecting the whole idea. All our high-sounding words about objective values are unwitting fiction and wishing thinking.[5] The problem with Mackie's argument is the problem with the Theory of Everyone: it is asking too much.

It is too much to ask that a moral fact necessarily motivate anyone who recognizes it. If that were correct, then we couldn't conceive of people who are basically rational, who recognize what would be morally right for them to do, but who just don't care. But such people are conceivable. We call them sociopaths. They are no less intelligent or perceptive than you or me. In fact, they typically have a better sense for social norms than the average person. They just aren't affected by the prospect of hurting others or by the ideal of helping them. The good leaves them cold. Not only are sociopaths conceivable, they are responsible for thousands of murders and violent crimes each year.

If someone commits a horrendously bad act for its own sake (what we call an evil), such as mutilating and killing a child, you and I would not alter our judgment if we discovered that the perpetrator is some kind of sociopath who lacks the commitments that lead us to see the situation from the moral point of view. We would still hold the act to be an evil, even while we recognize that this particular person—tragically—had no reason to avoid it on that account. In this lies the difference between the subjective and the objective. Why not give up the judgment? Why not conclude that the killing was "bad for us" but indifferent "for him"? Simply, because ethical judgments aren't like that. This is nothing remarkable about ethics. It is common to most norms that structure social interaction. If someone violates the standards of etiquette, we don't have to inspect his motivations before judging that he was rude. And if we were to find that he just doesn't care about the standards of etiquette, we would not withdraw the judgment that he made a mistake, by the standards of etiquette. We would conclude that he made a mistake that he doesn't care about. Whether he should care about it is another matter.

Of the monstrous person for whom the child's suffering does not and could not ever matter, we cannot say: he had reason to avoid the evil. We can say: he did evil. We do say it, and there are many arguments for saying it. One argument is that we wish as many people as possible to recognize the importance of a child's suffering, and calling the sociopath's action evil is part of that effort. Another argument is that the motivations of a person are very complex and difficult to know fully, even in our own case. So, it is difficult to know whether a person cannot possibly be moved to adopt the moral point of view. We begin with the hopeful assumption that there is something in his motives that commits him to the moral point of view and we relinquish that assumption only when forced to do so by the facts.

Not every human being has a reason to adopt the moral point of view. The Theory of Everyone is false. But in giving up on the theory, we are not giving up on the idea of objective morality. Quite the contrary, we come to understand how objective morality could be understandable and how it could enter into explanations of our actions. Moral facts are not some bizarre, mysterious entities with to-be-pursuedness built into them. They are everyday, honest-to-goodness, natural facts; facts, perhaps, like the fact of another's pain or the self's well-being. Moral facts take hold of the agent only because of some other commitments that she has. But this is not cause to abandon the ideal of universality. We are committed to a world in which as many people as possible are responsive to moral reasons. Perhaps the theorists of everyone were looking for the right thing—a special kind of impartiality and universality in reasoning—but looking for it in the wrong place.

The subway trains of New York City are notoriously unpredictable. No schedules are published, and routes are subject to sudden change, sometimes while en route. City dwellers soon learn that the most reliable source of information about the behavior of a train is to be gathered in real time from those who are riding it. So it is common for a rider just boarding a train to step inside the doors and ask passengers onboard about precisely where the train is going and how it is getting there. Picture yourself stepping onboard and asking a passenger, "Is this train stopping at 96th Street?" The passenger responds, "Yes," and you take your seat, having heard what you wanted to hear.

As simple as it may seem, there are some complex assumptions and expectations at work, without which the exchange would have been unsuccessful. A basic assumption is that you and the other share the ability to form beliefs and make judgments about a subject of which you have some common understanding. You and your interlocutor are engaged in believing about the same object; in this case, the same train. Suppose a second passenger were to speak up after the first, claiming that the train is not in fact stopping at 96th Street. You would not take this for mere noise or for a belief about another subject. You would take it for a disagreement about a common subject and a discrepancy to be resolved. One of the two must be correct, and the other incorrect.

Along with the assumption that differing beliefs constitute a disagreement about a shared reality is the assumption that some mutually available evidence will probably suffice to resolve the disagreement. There is a fact of the matter about whether the train is stopping at 96th Street, and one should expect to find indicators of this fact that could settle the discrepancy between the passengers' two reports, at least in principle ("The conductor just announced that this train is now making express stops only, so the next stop is 125th Street").

By engaging one another in talk that aims at truth (rather than, for example, pleasantries, bartering, humor, flattery, or abuse), conversation partners invest each other with a certain degree of authority on the subject. Authority is not superiority or infallibility, but the partners take each other, by default, to be authoritative enough to be worth talking to. This confidence can be withdrawn if the person in question turns out to be off the rails. If a passenger were to respond to your schedule question by shouting that you must get out of his bedroom or by singing "L'Internationale," you would in fairly short order decide to ask someone else. This might take another exchange or two. The conversational expectation of authority is strong enough that you might first explore the possibility that your interlocutor was shouting at someone else over his cell phone or concentrating on practicing for a musical performance, oblivious to your inquiry. Barring that, the conversation would be over.

These assumptions are part of what it means to engage another in serious truth-seeking talk, to adopt what some have called the "conversational stance": the conversation partners share the ability to form beliefs and make judgments about a subject of which they have some common understanding; each is granted some authority on the subject; and it is expected at least provisionally that disagreements can in principle be resolved by appeal to mutually available evidence.[6]

Another way to put these assumptions is to say that conversation partners are expected to be basically reason guided. They must be capable of recognizing reasons in favor of certain beliefs, evaluating the strength of these reasons, and responding by bringing their thinking into accord with them. To say that there is a reason to believe a claim is to say that something weighs in favor of the truth of that claim; that one would be right or correct to believe it; that there are some principles or norms according to which one *ought* to believe it. The norms might be things like: believe a claim if and only if that claim is true; believe a claim if and only if that claim is supported by the total evidence available to you; believe a claim if and only if its truth is implied by other beliefs and is not inconsistent with any of your other beliefs. Without these assumptions, there could be no expectation on the part of your interlocutor that you will revise your belief in light of the evidence (for example, taking the conductor's announcement as a good reason to give up the belief that the train will stop at 96th Street).

Now imagine that you were to ask your fellow passengers, "How can I get to 96th Street?" One person answers that you should step off the train at 59th Street and take a different train uptown. Another says that you should ride the present train to 125th, and from there take a train downtown. Here the conversation is not about what to believe but what to do; it is an instance of practical reasoning. If you desire to get to 96th Street, and the most efficient way to get there is by way of 59th Street, then there is a strong reason for you to go to 59th Street. You ought to go there, all else being equal. If instead the most efficient way to get there is by way of 125th Street, then there is a strong reason for you to go to 125th Street. You ought to go there, all else being equal. Of course, all may not be equal. There might be other, competing reasons that bear on your action: maybe you left your umbrella at the 59th Street station.

When you act, it is not as a passive marionette pulled about by the strings of desire but as a person who is capable of deliberating over your desires, evaluating whether they provide good reasons for action, and acting accordingly (at least sometimes). To say that there is a reason to take an action is to say that something weighs in favor of taking that action; that one would be right or correct to take it; there are some principles or norms according to which one *ought* to take it. Some candidates for such norms are: form your desires in light of the total evidence available to you; if an action is necessary to achieving an end you desire, intend to perform that action; if you intend an action, pursue that action unless presented with some reason not to.

As with conversation about belief, conversation about what to do is based on an expectation that the conversation partners are basically reason guided. Each assumes that there are some norms governing desire and action and that the other is capable of recognizing and responding to such norms. When a passenger tells you to go by way of 125th Street, he does not expect you to follow his advice out of awe for his authority or out of fear of repercussions. He assumes that you are a reason-guided person and that there are some norms that make it the case that you have a reason to do—you ought to do—as he says. In this case, you have a reason to take those actions necessary to achieve your desired ends. Such norms are not up to the attitude or whim of either of you. They are a given, shared backdrop of conversation. In that sense they are as objective as the language you use and platform on which you stand.

Deliberation about moral questions is deliberation about what to do. Moral reasoning is a species of practical reasoning. (May I lie to protect a friend's feelings? Can we allow genetic engineering to violate human dignity? How much aid should rich countries give to poor countries?) There are as many different practical "oughts" as there are kinds of practical reasons. There are reasons of aesthetics, like "the lamp ought to go over there." There are reasons of etiquette, like "you ought to apologize." There are reasons of prudence or self-interest, like "you ought to get to work on time." There are also reasons generated by the interests of others, such as "you ought to help that pedestrian who was just hit by a bicycle." When we speak of the moral ought, we are speaking of the ought that takes into consideration all of these reasons. The moral ought is the "all-things-considered" ought: I can see that the action would not be tawdry, or rude, or imprudent, but would it be the right thing to do?

So, just as with a serious conversation about which subway stop to take, serious conversation about moral questions presupposes some objective standards of good reasoning that are open to public examination. The activity of giving and receiving reasons for action presupposes, as Simon Blackburn puts it, that "what I advance as a reason, a reason from my point of view, can be appreciated from your point of view. If this were not so, conversation about practical matters would seem to be reduced to one side saying 'Me, me, me,' and the other side saying the same. There would then be no possibility of each side sharing an understanding of the situation, or coming to a common point of view on the factors in virtue of which something is to be done."[7]

To say that the implicit norms guiding practical reasoning are common and objective is not to say that they are unquestionable. All are open to question, and when a conversation about what to do is driven to an intractable disagreement, it may be because the conversation partners embrace different, incompatible understandings of the relevant norms. "If you advance a reason for the choice that I do not share, we can go on to deploy general standards for whether such a factor should itself count as a reason. There is no guarantee that we will come to the same conclusion of course, but there is a guarantee that we might do so."[8] That modest guarantee is enough to make it worthwhile to go for dialogue as a first move.

We cannot assume that deep down everyone will agree on some basic values or principles. But we must assume that everyone—if only implicitly—will agree on how to talk about them. There may be no common ground, at least not enough for everyone to stand on. But there is a shared language and framework for conversation: a common commitment to the existence of objective standards for what counts as a good reason, and a common openness to examining those standards.

A number of theorists[9] have remarked that underlying the practice of reason trading is a desire for our actions and beliefs to appear reasonable or at least comprehensible in the eyes of others: "The whole activity of presenting my reason for acting to you implies a kind of hope that you will see my reason as having been permissible. I want you to acknowledge that it was all right to act like that, in that circumstance, for that reason. So long as I need that recognition, I need to seek justification from the common point of view."[10] If this desire to appear reasonable is real and widespread, it gives us yet more cause to expect that people will take the moral point of view when evaluating their choices.

A reason is a step in a social dance that commits one to making other steps, whether leading or following. If I claim that someone ought to do something, I am committed to following through, if called upon to do so, by providing further justification—I am committed to making good on my claim. That means I am committed to some objective norms governing what counts as a good reason. I may not have thought through those norms carefully. But by entering into serious conversation about what to do, I take such norms for granted and I take it for granted that you do too. By its very nature, then, serious moral debate is open, not private, and freedom of conscience means conscience is free to be evaluated, not delivered from evaluation.

The Theory of Everyone collapses under the weight of its grand ambitions. There can be no guarantee that every rational person will have most reason to do the morally right thing. However, it is enough to show that almost all people do, and that there are good arguments for sticking to our moral judgment that the sociopath has done wrong, even if he couldn't care less. In other ways, though, the theorists of everyone have been vindicated. In our reasoning about ethical choices, as in all practical reasoning, we adopt a point of view that is universal in the sense of being open and accessible to all. The theorists of everyone were also correct to seek something like objective moral facts. Thankfully, we can give up the notion that moral facts are essentially action guiding without giving up on their objectivity.[11] They will be objective if they turn out to be facts about the world that are indispensable to the best explanation of why we do what we do, and why we sometimes regret what we have done.

9.
Ethics from Below

There are few prophets in the world; few sublimely beautiful women;
few heroes. I can't afford to give all my love and reverence to such
rarities: I want a great deal of those feelings for my everyday fellow-
men, especially for the few in the foreground of the great multitude,
whose faces I know, whose hands I touch, for whom I have to make
way with kindly courtesy.

—George Eliot

If there were a sacred scripture for secular liberals (there isn't), it
surely would be *On Liberty*. The author, the British philosopher,
businessman, politician, and social reformer John Stuart Mill, is unar-
guably one of the most important influences on the Western liberal tradition. His 1859 essay lays out the ungospel truth: that people ought to
be free to think and do what they want so long as they don't harm
others, that the sphere of my liberty extends into social space until the
point where it touches those of my neighbors. At the heart of *On Liberty* is the bold thesis that scholars refer to as the Harm Principle or,
more agreeably, the No Harm Principle or Liberty Principle:

> The sole end for which mankind are warranted, individually or collectively, in interfering with the liberty of action of any of their number, is self-protection. That the only purpose for which power can be rightfully exercised over any member of a civilised community, against his will, is to prevent harm to others. His own good, either physical or moral, is not a sufficient warrant. He cannot rightfully be compelled to do or forbear because it will be better for him to do so, because it will make him happier, because, in the opinion of others, to do so would be wise, or even right. . . . The only part of the conduct from which it is desired to deter him must be calculated to produce evil to someone else. The only part of the conduct of any one, for which he is amenable to society, is that which concerns others. In the part which merely concerns himself, his independence is, of right, absolute. Over himself, over his own body and mind, the individual is sovereign.[1]

Some secular liberals may think that this is the last word on the subject. In a way, they are right. Mill's basic insight about the primacy of liberty has withstood all challenges. In another way, the Liberty Principle is only the beginning of the story. It is the story of secular conscience, of objective morality that is based in reason and experience and open to debate. It is worth asking what Mill, whom one expert has called the "wisest of liberals," would make of contemporary liberalism. Unlike many of his intellectual heirs, Mill did not prefer liberalism because he thought ethics and values are private or subjective. In other writings, he devoted much attention to developing his theory of human happiness as an objective moral value.[2]

The whole point of a secular, liberal society, some will say, is that moral questions are private: they are not on the communal table. No one gets to tell anyone else what to think on moral matters. Our public institutions are devised to bracket moral questions—to place them to one side, without taking sides—and in this way leave them up to each individual.

At first blush, Mill's Liberty Principle may seem like a philosopher's gloss on the popular admonition against meddling in others' private beliefs, which go by the slogans: live and let live, to each his own, and who am I to judge? But that would be getting Mill exactly backward. As he later puts it in *On Liberty*, the principle is not "one of selfish indifference, which pretends that human beings have no business with each other's conduct in life, and that they should not concern themselves about the well-doing or well-being of one another, unless their own interest is involved. . . . Human beings owe each other help to distinguish the better from the worse, and encouragement to choose the former rather than the latter."[3] In fact, Mill is explicit about this when he first introduces the Liberty Principle. Just as soon as he has said that a man "cannot rightfully be compelled to do or forbear because it will be better for him to do so, because it will make him happier, because, in the opinion of others, to do so would be wise, or even right," he clarifies: "These are good reasons for *remonstrating* with him, or *reasoning* with him, or *persuading* him, or *entreating* him."[4] The only thing that is forbidden by the Liberty Principle is "compelling him, or visiting him with any evil in case he does otherwise." This makes the critical difference between the Liberty Principle and the Liberty Fallacy.

But why should we remonstrate, reason with, persuade, let alone entreat, our neighbor? What's it to us? Mill answers: Liberty is not an end in itself. It is not to be protected for its own sake but because it leads to greater happiness for ourselves and others. For Mill, the ultimate moral measure is the happiness of humans, or indeed of any being that can experience well-being and freedom from suffering. For creatures like us, one of the essential elements of well-being is "the free development of individuality." Because of the diversity of the human personality, one life does not fit all: "To give any fair play to the nature of each, it is essential that different persons should be allowed to lead different lives." Some social engineers, whom Mill calls "Calvinists," would have all lives squeezed into a single prefabricated design:

> All the good of which humanity is capable, is comprised in obedience. You have no choice; thus you must do, and no otherwise; 'whatever is not a duty is a sin.' Human nature being radically corrupt, there is no redemption for any one until human nature is killed within him. To one holding this theory of life, crushing out any of the human faculties, capacities, and susceptibilities, is no evil: man needs no capacity, but that of surrendering himself to the will of God: and if he uses any of his faculties for any other purpose but to do that supposed will more effectually, he is better without them.[5]

The Calvinist theory is false and harmful, writes Mill, because "human nature is not a machine to be built after a model, and set to do exactly the work prescribed for it, but a tree, which requires to grow and develop itself on all sides, according to the tendency of the inward forces which make it a living thing":

> Different persons . . . require different conditions for their spiritual development, and can no more exist healthily in the same moral, than all the variety of plants can in the same physical atmosphere and climate. The same things which are helps to one person towards the cultivation of his higher nature, are hindrances to another. The same mode of life is a healthy excitement to one, keeping all his faculties of action and enjoyment in their best order, while to another it is a distracting burthen, which suspends or crushes all internal life. Such are the differences among human beings in their sources of pleasure, their susceptibilities of pain, and the operation on them of different physical and moral agencies, that unless there is a corresponding diversity in their modes of life, they neither obtain their fair share of happiness, nor grow up to the mental, moral, and aesthetic stature of which their nature is capable.[6]

The moral climate of liberty is meant to nourish all those unique capabilities of particular people, so that they may blossom into unique excellences, admirable in their own right:

It is not by wearing down into uniformity all that is individual in themselves, but by cultivating it and calling it forth, within the limits imposed by the rights and interests of others, that human beings become a noble and beautiful object of contemplation; and as the works partake the character of those who do them, by the same process human life also becomes rich, diversified, and animating, furnishing more abundant aliment to high thoughts and elevating feelings, and strengthening the tie which binds every individual to the race, by making the race infinitely better worth belonging to. In proportion to the development of his individuality, each person becomes more valuable to himself, and is therefore capable of being more valuable to others. There is a greater fulness of life about his own existence.

So at the root of the Liberty Principle we find not agnosticism about values but an affirmation of values. This must not be forgotten. Those of us who are lucky enough to live in the kind of open society Mill championed often find ourselves thinking something like this: we all do our own things, choosing different ways of life. And yet, many of us find these incompatible ways of life fulfilling. So, there must be nothing that makes a way of life good, except that one chooses it. Call it subjectivism about the good. Something is good (for me) just because and only in the sense that I happen to like it. Can anything more be said about the good? What can be said about those of us who prefer pinball to poetry, or who choose the life of a contract killer over the life of a loving parent? Are any of these pursuits objectively better or more advisable than others? Who's to say? Who else, but us.

You may have devoted your life to sculpture, and I, who have devoted mine to designing computer software, may not appreciate sculpture at all. I may be unable to distinguish excellent work from trash, or spot artistic talent when I see it. That doesn't mean there is no value there to be appreciated; it may be that I have not developed the capacities necessary to appreciate it. That is not to say I ought to have developed them. For the life I have constructed through the develop-ment of my faculties is well suited to my particular nature; and it is rich in valuable experiences and achievements that may be as inaccessible to you as yours are to me. Maybe the subjectivist is correct, and there is such diversity of satisfying yet incompatible forms of life because there are no objective values.

Or maybe there are too many. Maybe life offers an embarrassment of riches, a superabundance of values, and hence the possibility of more varieties of lives fulfilled in the pursuit of different values than any one person could hope to pursue. Subjectivists can say that the diversity of satisfying lives is precisely what one would expect in a world where values are up to us: with no objective good to guide our choices, the paths of human lives meander through the space of possible lives, led by differing tastes. But it is at least as reasonable to say that diversity is what one would expect in a world where values are objective and superabundant and the capacity to experience and engage with these values varies from person to person.

Skeptics' lips may be curling at all this talk of objective standards of what makes a life worth living as opposed to enjoyable. Forget about the Good, they snort, just give me a good time. It's all about individual pleasure. Life is short; get it while you can. Not so fast, says Ronald Dworkin. He points out that often this attitude just amounts to the belief that "a long life full of pleasure is the best kind of life you can live. In that case you actually do think it is important to live well, though you have a peculiarly hedonistic conception of what living well means."[7] The alternative is to not care at all about whether your life as a whole is well lived, to seek only pleasure now and in the future. But it is extremely difficult to find people who have this attitude, at least in their reflective moments: "People who say that they want only pleasure out of life do not in fact want only as much pleasure as they can have right now or in the future. They also want their lives to have *been* full of pleasure. They regret pleasures missed or foregone; they complain that they should have had more sex or traveled more or had more of other kinds of fun in the past."

Most of us would find it extremely difficult to do without the idea that there are objective standards of what makes a life go well, that we can be mistaken about what makes a life go well, and that it is hugely important that we not make such mistakes: "If we abandoned that assumption, we would find it difficult to make any of the important decisions we now make. . . . We cannot make such decisions, for instance, just by trying to predict what we will enjoy, because whether we enjoy doing or having something depends too much on whether we think enjoying it is part of living well."[8] Even hedonists believe in an objective measure for success in life, objective in the sense that it is not up to them. When they trumpet that pleasure is the only good, they don't just mean "hedonism pleases me." They mean hedonism is true, whether we like it or not.

Having heard all this, a skeptic could snarl on: pound the table all you like about objective standards for a life well lived, but just name one.

Okay, begin with desire. Desire isn't perfect. Specifically, there is a problem with using it to determine what makes a person's life go well. People desire all kinds of things, some of which are not at all good for them, as evidenced by the fact that they later regret desiring them: "It seemed like a good idea at the time (until I found out that the stout beer I desired was actually motor oil)." So, raw desire is too crude to supply the kind of power that we expect the good to have. We expect the good to have *normative* power: it should be something that pulls us in its direction, but it should also provide the basis by which we can evaluate our current desires and find that they sometimes fall short. If our good were identical to our current desires, then we could never coherently say, as we do all the time, that something seemed like a good idea at the time but wasn't. (The unexamined life might be more worth living than nothing, but it certainly is not worth repeating if you can help it.) It must be possible that our desires sometimes point us to what we ought not to do, even from our own perspectives. As Mill put it, the desired must not be the same as the desirable.

However, if the connection between current desires and the good is stretched to the point that the two are totally unconnected, then the good becomes too weak. It will no longer explain why we care about our good, why we do what we do and sometimes regret not doing otherwise. Yoga might be a good for some people, but if nothing in my desires could ever possibly lead me to it, how could it be part of *my* good? If, despite this, you insist that yoga will enhance my well-being, I will conclude that your talk is just your presumptuous way of saying, "I wish you would do yoga." It doesn't get at anything real or objective about me. Here then is one of ethics' longest-running wrestling matches. How can the good be normative—how can it support statements to the effect that you *ought* to be moved by it; and how, at the same time, can the good be objective—how can it be more than just happy talk?

Imagine a tourist named Lonnie who has fallen ill while traveling in a foreign country.[9] Lonnie is feeling miserable, and in thinking about what would settle his stomach, he finds himself craving a comforting glass of milk. Lonnie desires milk. However, one can ask whether it is desirable for him; that is, whether it would be good for him, whether it would make his life go better. In fact, Lonnie is suffering from dehydration, something common to on-the-go tourists but difficult for them to self-diagnose. Milk, difficult to digest as it is, would only make Lonnie's condition worse, whereas a long drink of water would quickly improve it. Now, if Lonnie were in possession of all the relevant information about his situation, he would see this. The fully informed Lonnie—call him Lonnie-Plus—would realize that what Lonnie needs is water, not milk. If Lonnie-Plus were not only fully informed but also rational, he would use this information to further his underlying goal of feeling better. So, if Lonnie-Plus were advising Lonnie, he would want Lonnie to drink water rather than milk. What is good for Lonnie—what satisfies a real interest of Lonnie—is what Lonnie-Plus would want Lonnie to want.

Lonnie is a creation of the philosopher Peter Railton, but we've all been in Lonnie's shoes. We've all been in situations where we found out only later what was best for us at the time. Railton uses the case to illustrate a general blueprint for a person's interest, or good:

> Give to an individual *A* unqualified cognitive and imaginative powers, and full . . . information about his physical and psychological constitution, capacities, circumstances, history, and so on. *A* will have become *A*+, who has complete and vivid knowledge of himself and his environment, and whose . . . rationality is in no way defective. We now ask *A*+ to tell us not what he currently wants, but what he would want his nonidealized self *A* to want—or, more generally, to seek—were he to find himself in the actual condition and circumstances of *A*.

According to this "full-information" account of well-being (or the A-Plus account), a person's objective interest is "what he would want himself to seek if he knew what he were doing." Because the account requires full information, vividly entertained, and rationally applied, it puts the right amount of distance between current desires and a person's good. Since no actual person is ever fully informed and rational, the good is an ideal, a norm that can be approached if never perfectly followed.

The notion of A-Plus is a useful tool for talking about whether something contributes to a person's good. But strictly speaking, Lonnie-Plus doesn't exist. He is a construct. So, if the good for Lonnie is what Lonnie-Plus would want for Lonnie, isn't that just another way of saying that there is no such thing as the good for Lonnie? No. What does exist are certain psychological and physical facts about Lonnie and his environment, facts about "his existing tastes and his ability to acquire certain new tastes, the consequences of continued dehydration, the effects and availability of various sorts of liquids."[10] It is these facts that make statements about Lonnie's objective well-being true or false. They are facts about ordinary, natural properties of the world we all inhabit. As such, they can play a role in objective explanations of why he would regret a glass of milk in his current condition and why over time he might gravitate, through trial and error, perhaps not even knowing why, toward liquids containing more water. Now it makes sense to say that Lonnie's good is not just an idea but something real and objective.[11]

Now it makes sense to think of values as real and objective even while they are not supernatural or transcendent, part of some eternal symphony. A value is always a value *to someone*—it contributes to the well-being of some person or sentient creature. Take away all the beings to whom anything can matter, and nothing matters. But so long as we live here, in this world, values live with us, and they don't disappear when no one is looking at them. They are relational—they exist in relation to us—but they exist objectively. In the same way, colors and sounds exist in relation to our eyes and ears, but they don't change depending on what we think about them. Our good helps to explain our desires, decisions, aspirations, confusions, and regrets. And that makes it as real as anything.

In one sense, if-you-knew-what-you-were-doing is a simplistic formula: full-information, vividly entertained, and rationally applied to one's current situation. The formula may be simple, but it is not easy, because no one is A-Plus. A-Plus is an ideal that can only be approximated by us, imperfectly rational creatures that we are. No wonder we often come to regret what seemed like a good idea at the time, and why our friends and family often know better than we do what really is good for us.

A theory of objective well-being like the one sketched above gets us closer to the moral point of view, but not quite there. The A-Plus point of view transcends your present point of view, but it is still a view *of your good*. The next move in the direction of the moral point of view is to transcend your own good, to rise to a scale from which you can survey your good and the good of others with equal, impartial concern. Our guides are Scottish Enlightenment philosopher Adam Smith and his "impartial spectator."

Adam Smith is not known as a people person. He is known as the greatest theorist of modern capitalism and defender of the individualism, competition, and inequality that are bound up with it. The line of Smith's writing that is perhaps most repeated comes from *An Inquiry into the Nature and Causes of the Wealth of Nations*, his celebrated masterpiece of political economics: "It is not from the benevolence of the butcher, the brewer, or the baker, that we expect our dinner, but from their regard to their own self-interest. We address ourselves, not to their humanity but to their self-love, and never talk to them of our own necessities but of their advantages."[12] Here, it seems, is a model of society and of the person perfectly egoistic, amoral even, in which human relationships begin and end in the satisfaction of self. A model upheld by some, but not by Adam Smith, professor of moral philosophy.[13]

Wealth of Nations cannot be understood, and would have been impossible for Smith to write, were it not for his first book, this one a masterpiece of ethics called *The Theory of Moral Sentiments*. Since its publication in 1759, *Theory of Moral Sentiments* has been regarded as a crowning achievement of the tradition of ethics known as moral sense theory, a tradition led by Smith's mentor, Francis Hutchenson, as well as the great Scottish skeptic David Hume. In this work Smith lays the moral foundation for the open-market society he would go on to describe a decade and a half later in *Wealth of Nations*. The foundation is conscience. For Smith, conscience resides "in the breast" of each individual. But it is not private. It is that which transcends the self and joins with others in "fellow-feeling." The words "other people" appear over and over in *Theory of Moral Sentiments*. Conscience is that within us that accesses a point of view accessible to all and held by no one in particular, the moral point of view. Man is the immediate judge of man, says Smith, but everyone can appeal "to a much higher tribunal, to the tribunal of their own consciences, to that of the supposed impartial and well-informed spectator, to that of the man within the breast, the great judge and arbiter of their conduct."

Smith sees that humanity is prone to selfishness, greed, and cruelty but also given to generosity, kindness, and self-sacrifice. How is it that we are capable of both? "When our passive feelings are almost always so sordid and so selfish, how comes it that our active principles should often be so generous and so noble? When we are always so much more deeply affected by whatever concerns ourselves, than by whatever concerns other men; what is it which prompts the generous, upon all occasions, and the mean upon many, to sacrifice their own interest to the greater interests of others?"

Some might think that the answer lies in the complex nature of human emotion. The heart has many chambers, enough to hold benevolence and fellow-feeling as well as selfishness, and so other-love can compete with and sometimes triumph over self-love for mastery of our motives. Smith sees something of a different order.

> It is not the soft power of humanity, it is not that feeble spark of benevolence which Nature has lighted up in the human heart, that is thus capable of counteracting the strongest impulses of self-love. It is a stronger power, a more forcible motive, which exerts itself upon such occasions. It is reason, principle, conscience, the inhabitant of the breast, that man within, the great judge and arbiter of our conduct. It is he who, whenever we are about to act so as to affect the happiness of others, calls to us, with a voice capable of astonishing the most presumptuous of our passions, that we are but one of the multitude, in no respect better than any other in it.

What is conscience, and how does it work its "stronger power" over our selfish natures? Smith explains using the metaphor of sight. Just as objects closer to our eyes appear larger than they are in reality, interests nearer to our own appear more important than they are, from the moral point of view.

> As to the eye of the body, objects appear great or small, not so much according to their real dimensions, as according to the nearness or distance of their situation; so do they likewise to what may be called the natural eye of the mind. . . . In my present situation an immense landscape of lawns, and woods, and distant mountains, seems to be out of all proportion less than the chamber in which I am sitting. I can form a just comparison between those great objects and the little objects around me, in no other way, than by transporting myself, at least in fancy, to a different station, from whence I can survey both at nearly equal distances, and thereby form some judgment of their real proportions.[14]

To grasp the real size and relationship among objects, we must complete our partial vision with reason and imagination. We must do the same to understand the real importance of our own interests in relation to the interests of others.

> In the same manner, to the selfish and original passions of human nature, the loss or gain of a very small interest of our own, appears to be of vastly more importance, excites a much more passionate joy or sorrow, a much more ardent desire or aversion, than the greatest concern of another with whom we have no particular connexion. His interests, as long as they are surveyed from this station, can never be put into the balance with our own, can never restrain us from doing whatever may tend to promote our own, how ruinous soever to him. Before we can make any proper comparison of those opposite interests, we must change our position. We must view them, neither from our own place nor yet from him, neither with our own eyes nor yet with his, but from the place and with the eyes of a third person, who has no particular connexion with either, and who judges with impartiality between us.[15]

This point of view—neither our own nor our neighbor's—is what we call the moral point of view. It belongs to the "impartial spectator," and the voice of the impartial spectator is the voice of conscience: "It is from him only that we learn the real littleness of ourselves, and of whatever relates to ourselves, and the natural misrepresentations of self-love can be corrected only by the eye of this impartial spectator."[16]

The spectator is not impartial in the sense of being uncaring or dispassionate. When our conscience cries out, says Smith, it is with the emotions of approval or disapproval, praise or blame, and it is on these emotions that moral judgments are grounded. The spectator is impartial in the sense that it gives no more weight to the interests of any one person simply in virtue of whom he or she happens to be. It considers the differences between people only insofar as they make a moral difference. The fact that a person shares my family name or my skin color (or that the person happens to be me) makes no difference to how he should be treated from a moral point of view.

Further, the conscience transcends the partiality that comes from having incomplete information about the situation at hand. The eye, looking out over the distant mountain vista, lacks visual information that could correct for the size distortion of faraway objects. To arrive at an impartial judgment as to the rightness of an action, the spectator needs all the relevant information. As a partial spectator, I may think you have done me a good turn by buying me a drink. The fully informed, impartial spectator would know that you slipped poison in my drink and therefore that you have done me a great wrong.

The impartial spectator sees what we often lose sight of: that if our interests matter, then so do the interests of our neighbors. What we ought to do is what we ought to do all things considered, and that means having considered their interests as well as our own. Think about why it is so difficult for an honest, thinking person to be an egoist, someone who holds that his interests alone determine what he ought to do. Try to put yourself in the mind-set of the egoist: You believe that your interests matter, in the sense that they provide strong reasons for action (for example, your interest in not starving provides a strong reason why you should get your next meal). If your interests matter, what about the interests of your neighbors and fellow beings? Is there something special about you that your interests should be taken into consideration while theirs should not? True, you are you and they are they. But why should that make a difference? Like you, they think their interests matter, too. So if anyone's interests matter, everyone's interests matter.

Here is the moral point of view, which takes into account everyone's interests, the reasons of self-love as well as the reasons of other-love. The question is, *how* should they be taken into account? In our own case, we evaluate the options in light of our interests and select those options that we anticipate will bring about the most good ("expected utility," in the jargon of economics and decision theory). Does the same procedure make sense with the good of all? This question is pursued through the approach to ethics known as consequentialism.[17]

✤✤✤

Consequentialism is the radically simple notion that the morality of our actions is determined solely by their *consequences*, by how much good they bring about. Consequentialism is a theory about how we ought to respond to values. If anything matters, if anything is really better or worse than anything else, the question that arises is what we should do about it. There are at least two responses to a value. One response is to protect it or honor it, to keep it from being somehow violated or undermined. The other response, the consequentialist response, is to promote the value, to act so as to bring about more of the value where possible. It is the commonsensical suggestion that good things are to be promoted, bad things minimized, and the appropriateness of our actions depends on the extent to which they succeed in bringing this about.[18]

We are all consequentialists, at least when it comes to some values. Most of us agree that the proper response to many of the goods in life is to promote them, not merely to protect them. Think of knowledge, or friendship. Because these things are valuable, we are not content merely to refrain from doing something to undermine them (after all, that is consistent with having no education or friends at all). Rather, we cultivate them actively. Consequentialism says that this same response should apply, at least as a default assumption, to goods of all sorts, including the good of well-being, the objective interests of others.

A great advantage of consequentialism is that it comports well with our natural response to value. By contrast, nonconsequentialist theories must explain why certain important values like well-being should not be treated in the same way we treat friendship or education. Nonconsequentialist ethics, among them most traditional religious systems, must show that a wrong action is made wrong by something intrinsic to the action, regardless of its effects on things of value. This is no easy task. Suppose that you are confronted with the opportunity to kill a man who is surely about to murder his family. Your choice is between allowing several murders that you could have prevented, and becoming a murderer yourself. According to most nonconsequentialist ethics, you may not kill no matter how much good that killing might do. But what could be the rationale for this prohibition? If there is some property of murdering that makes it morally wrong, how could you remain indifferent as to whether more or less of this property comes to be? What reason could there be—based on the wrongness of killing—that you should refrain from murdering even when by so refraining you help to bring about world in which more murdering takes place?

Another advantage of consequentialism is its flexibility. It tells us what makes right actions right, but it leaves open how we are to go about making up our minds on moral questions in everyday life. Often by deliberately aiming at promoting a good, we would do worse at attaining it than if we were to aim somewhere else. For instance, parents will usually do better at promoting the good of their children by unconditionally loving them than by calculating every decision by some consequentialist metric. Often the best advice for resolving a moral dilemma will not be to think like a consequentialist, but to try to be a good parent, child, sibling, friend, colleague, or citizen; to practice the virtues of love, justice, fidelity, or courage. Does this mean consequentialism fails? Not at all, since the ultimate moral justification of these virtues, habits of mind, and rules of thumb lies in their promotion of goods worth caring about. In grappling with the complexities and struggles of life, human beings develop rich theories, ideals, and narratives of virtues, of rights, of duties. Consequentialism is the moral measure we apply to them in moments of reflection about how best to arrange our lives. The great power, scope, and simplicity of consequentialism account for its longevity and lasting appeal, even after centuries of dispute.

John Stuart Mill held that individual happiness is the only thing good in itself. Yet it is easy to imagine situations in which people experience the greatest degree of happiness but still appear to be missing things that contribute to a life well lived. Imagine an experience machine (like in *The Matrix* films) that creates totally comprehensive and convincing experiences. In this perfect virtual reality simulator, you can be made to experience any life you like, as a Nobel Prize–winning scientist, a star athlete, or the parent of brilliant children. Of course, this life is an illusion. Would you choose a life in the experience machine over an actual life, with its risks and discontents? The thought experiment shows that happiness (as an experience) is not the only thing worth caring about. We also care about achievement, connecting with other people, making an impact on the future, and much else. Although happiness is part of objective well-being, it is not everything. (For one thing, it can't buy you money.)

Mill would have taken the point. No doubt he wanted not only to experience happiness but *to have lived* a meaningful life. And he did. Mill's work suggests how secular liberalism can be deeply rooted in a moral affirmation of objective standards of what makes a life worth living. Secular liberals follow Mill in wanting people to be left free to choose a course in life, so long as no one else gets hurt. They should follow him in believing that some courses in life are objectively better or more worthwhile than others; that personal freedom of choice is the best policy not because all choices are equal, but because individual experiments in living are the best method for humanity to discover which choices are superior. Crucially, part of the method is that we discuss the design and results of these experiments with each other. Personal choice is free from coercion by god, government, and society, and freed for public criticism, for our mutual remonstrating, reasoning, persuading, and entreating.

Whether we can articulate it or not, most of us care about more than just having a good time. We care that our lives will have been objectively worthwhile or valuable. The A-Plus account gives us a way to understand what makes a life go well or what contributes to objective well-being: a person's good is what she would want for herself if she really knew what she were doing. Well-being is sufficiently connected to your current beliefs and desires to be normative for you but sufficiently independent of your current beliefs and desires to be objective. Your good is not whatever you think it is. The theory also accounts for how the good can be part of the real world, because the desires of A-Plus ultimately just are a set of ordinary, natural (albeit stupendously complex) facts about our psychology, our history, and our environment. So while the A-Plus account gives us the normativity and objectivity we crave, it comes in a thoroughly secular and naturalistic flavor.

If objective well-being is a value, consequentialism offers the natural response to that value: promoting it impartially. In evaluating our actions in light of the objective interests of all affected, we adopt the moral point of view. By thinking through the best practical strategies for promoting well-being, we develop a complex system of rules, virtues, and decision procedures, some of which promote well-being only indirectly. In this way, conscience plus time equals ethics. Operating in individual experience and over human history, conscience leads to the discovery of reliable practices of ethical conduct.[19]

10.

The Umma and the Community of Conscience

I am a secular human being.
—Wafa Sultan

In September 1998, Hojat al-Islam wa al-Moslemeen Sayyed Mohammad Khatami comes to New York City to stand before the United Nations and call for a dialogue of civilizations. On behalf of the Islamic Republic of Iran, President Khatami expresses the "earnest hope that through such a dialogue, the realization of universal justice and liberty may be initiated":

> Among the worthiest achievements of this century is the acceptance of the necessity and significance of dialogue and rejection of force, promotion of understanding in cultural, economic and political fields, and strengthening of the foundations of liberty, justice and human rights. Establishment and enhancement of civility, whether at national or international level, is contingent upon dialogue among societies and civilizations representing various views, inclinations and approaches. If humanity at the threshold of the new century and millennium devotes all efforts to institutionalize dialogue, replacing hostility and confrontation with discourse and understanding, it

183

would leave an invaluable legacy for the benefit of the future generations.[1]

The General Assembly unanimously votes to declare a Year of the United Nations Dialogue among Civilizations. That year is to be 2001.

On September 11, 2001, as tons of paper fall on the streets of Lower Manhattan, heaping into six-foot drifts and catching fire, diplomatic envoys and experts from the embassies of eighteen countries have gathered in Beijing for a symposium on dialogue among civilizations that is later reported as a "complete success." The participants commend Khatami for his initiative and discuss "the effect of dialogue among civilizations on the development of international relations."[2]

On the eve of the fifth anniversary of September 11, the Shiite cleric, regal in his chocolate-colored robes, delivers a lecture at Harvard University titled "The Ethics of Tolerance in the Age of Violence," saying, "We should not be thinking about how we can kill each other better. We should be thinking about how we can live and coexist together." What he neglects to say is that during the two terms of his presidency, over a thousand citizens were executed by the Islamic Republic of Iran, and that the regime held more prisoners of conscience than any other state in the world, closing down 150 Iranian newspapers while remaining the world's largest state sponsor of Islamic terrorist organizations such as Hezbollah.

Even Khatami's name, as presented to the American audience, is a disguise. He drops the traditional title *Hojat al-Islam wa al-Moslemeen* ("Proof of Islam and of Muslims") and *Sayyed* ("Master"), which designates him as a descendant of the Prophet Muhammad.[3] He chooses his words carefully so that the listeners in Cambridge hear one thing and those in Tehran hear another. While Khatami's English interpreter speaks of "Osama bin Laden," Persian speakers hear "that gentleman" (*Aan Agha*). Talk of "sodomy" becomes "gay sex" in English. When an Iranian student interrupts the tolerance fest to ask about the imprisonment, torture, rape, and murder by the regime of the Iranian-

Canadian journalist Zahra Kazemi, Khatami smiles and tells the student he wasn't quite sure how the poor woman had died, adding that "maybe if the relatives of Kazemi had not made it into such a big political issue it could have been resolved a lot quicker and more to their liking."[4]

For this former president, who refuses to be interviewed by members of the Iranian-American media during his US visits, "dialogue" requires no precondition of openness, honesty, and transparency. He is a ventriloquist's dummy whose touring stage show is permitted by the mullahs running the country because it serves their interest in making the regime more respectable to the West. Certain Western liberals seem to need this character too, to make guest appearances in their morality play in which everyone, in the end, wants the same thing, and love and understanding are enough.

The secular, open society has met its antithesis. It comes in many forms: Salafist jihad, clerical totalitarianism, the rule of sharia law. What unites them is the willing sacrifice of freedom and human rights before a sacred order and their dependence on Islam for their existence. And yet there are millions of secular liberal Muslims, and potential alternative interpretations of the faith abound. One would think that secular liberals would be at the center of this struggle. Instead, reluctant to "impose" their values on others, fearful of the taint of American imperialism, most are submerged in silence. The result? Public discussion of Islam tends to veer between chauvinistic denunciations by conservative Christians ("Muhammad was a child molester") and useless overgeneralizations by politicians ("Islam is a religion of peace"). Words are liberals' first weapons of choice. Unfortunately, they now find themselves facing something they've sworn not to talk about—religion. If it is to rise to the historical moment and engage with both faces of Islam, secular liberalism needs a new self-understanding.

When in tenth-century Cordoba, Spain, Muslims join with Jews and Christians to translate Archimedes, Aristotle, and Euclid from Arabic into Latin, it is the search for objective knowledge that carries them across the boundaries of cultural tradition. It is reason and solidarity with humanity that orient them. The aim of this dialogue of civilizations is to ascertain what is excellent, true, or just in each. The aim of the Dialogue of Civilizations is instead to attain a state of empathic understanding. In this state, there are no mistakes or immoralities, only misconceptions or misunderstandings; and consequently, no discoveries or excellences, only "differences" to be "celebrated." In the words of the former UN secretary-general Kofi Annan, it is "a chance for people of different cultures and traditions to get to know each other better, whether they live on opposite sides of the world or on the same street."[5]

But while the recitation of the dialogue script carries on in elegant seminar chambers in New York, Cambridge, and Beijing, an ugly subplot is enacted on the streets of Europe. In September 2004, a short film called *Submission* is broadcast on television in Holland. It is the collaboration of iconoclastic Dutch filmmaker Theo van Gogh and Ayaan Hirsi Ali, a Somali-born minister of parliament known for her vocal public criticisms of the treatment of women in Islamic cultures. The film features testimonials by Muslim women who have suffered abuse and repression sanctioned by religion. In one scene, Quranic verses are shown imprinted on the exposed and brutalized flesh of a woman's back. On a Tuesday morning in November of that year, van Gogh is riding his bike along Linaeusstraat toward the center of Amsterdam when Mohammad Bouyeri steps from the side of the street. After gunning down van Gogh, slicing his throat, and leaving his corpse on the sidewalk, the twenty-seven-year-old Dutch and Moroccan citizen is wounded in the leg and apprehended by the Amsterdam police, who find a message in his pocket, a would-be martyr note: "For the hypocrites I have one final word . . . Wish DEATH or hold your tongue." Receiving a life sentence in court, Bouyeri clutches a copy of the Quran and declares, "The law compels me to chop off the head of anyone who insults Allah and the prophet."[6]

Mohammad Bouyeri has a final message for secular liberals, but so does his victim. Witnesses report that in his last moments, van Gogh attempted to engage his assassin, imploring: "Surely we can talk about this." The life and death of Theo van Gogh teaches that the invitation to dialogue must always remain open, but never for the mere "celebration of difference"; that the culture of conversation cannot survive the toleration of intolerance, intimidation, and violence. From the outpouring of shock, grief, and outrage after his murder, there are signs that the European public is beginning to understand this. Not so with the majority of spokespersons of the European establishment and the "international community." Well-practiced postcolonial guilt, dogmatic adherence to a blinkered multiculturalism, and sheer craven fear will lead them into a cycle of self-blame and appeasement. In the days following van Gogh's murder, Holland's Queen Beatrix neither attends the funeral, nor meets with Ayaan Hirsi Ali, nor utters a word about it in public.[7] Instead, she makes an appearance at a Moroccan youth center to exchange pleasantries. In Rotterdam, a street mural featuring the date of van Gogh's death and the words "Thou shalt not kill" is removed by the police after the leader of a nearby mosque calls it racist.[8] The prime minister endorses a campaign of wearing orange wristbands to symbolize "respect" and "tolerance."[9] Writing for the *Financial Times*, a Dutch journalist characterizes criticisms and satire of Islam as "Islam-bashing." In the home of Erasmus and Spinoza, what was a klaxon call to rescue freedom of conscience as a cardinal Dutch value has become an occasion to chant the mantra of multiculturalism: all cultures are equal.[10]

Across Europe, the opinions of most opinion makers are in unison. In December 2004, Britain's National Audit Office revises its tax rules because they are said to penalize Muslims with multiple wives.[11] Several members of the ultra-right-wing British National Party are arrested for saying that Islam is "vicious." The following year, the home secretary proposes a law that would make it a crime to offend the religious sensibilities of citizens. Almost alone among cultural figures, Salman Rushdie and British comedian Rowan Atkinson campaign against the bill. Atkinson (whose television program once satirically imagined that Iranian worshippers at Friday prayer were bowing down in search of the ayatollah's missing contact lens) writes to the

Times of London: "For telling a good and incisive religious joke, you should be praised. For telling a bad one, you should be ridiculed and reviled. The idea that you could be prosecuted for the telling of either is quite fantastic."[12] In a meeting with legislators, Rushdie and Atkinson ask whether their work would have been permitted under the law. They are assured that while their work technically fell under the law's purview, the officials administering it would in their discretion protect it. The bill is defeated by one vote.

In Norway, where the leader of the national Muslim Council has expressed empathy for Bouyeri and called for the critics of radical Islam to be stopped,[13] the parliament passes a similar law providing fines and imprisonment for those who make "discriminatory" or "hateful" remarks about another's race, ethnicity, religion, or sexual orientation. In Italy, author Oriana Fallaci is brought to court by the president of the Muslim Union of Italy over a passage in her book *The Force of Reason*, which is ruled to be "without doubt offensive to Islam and to those who practice that religious faith."[14] Following the July 7, 2005, suicide attacks on the London transit system, the BBC officially replaces the word *terrorists* with *bombers* in its descriptions of the suspects.

Some Europeans show a willingness to stand up for European values. In France, Nicolas Sarkozy, then minister of the interior, becomes ever-more uncompromising in his championing of *laïcité* (civil secularism). In a televised interview he confronts Tariq Ramadan, a Swiss academic and activist whose sophisticated apologetics for Islamism have made him a celebrity among many European and American liberals, asking Ramadan to prove his moderation by condemning stoning as a penalty for adultery (the most Ramadan will agree to is a "moratorium" on the practice). Denmark's queen, Margrethe, goes on record as saying that there are "certain things of which one should not be too tolerant."[15] In the wake of the cartoon jihad, *Jyllands-Posten* runs an editorial proclaiming, "There is only one answer to violence, threats, revenge killings, taking the law into one's own hands, blackmail, private justice, blood feuds, camel economics and imams who have not understood what society and what century they live in: NO!"[16]

In the face of a challenge to the future of European values, the official ideology of multiculturalism has become a pact for mass cultural suicide. No amount of dialogues celebrating difference can explain why the spirit of the Enlightenment ought to be preserved. Europe's cultural adversaries at least grasp this. Tariq Ramadan sees a rigid Islamic identity as a noble alternative to the "spiritual emptiness" of Western modernity. And here he joins hands with the smiling master Khatami. The true Other, the real obstacle to understanding, with which there can be no interchange, is secularism:

> At times, we encounter a difficult situation where we interact with a language which sounds the same as the one we use, however, the universe to which these two languages belong are very different. One of the most arduous passages in the road of dialogue among cultures arises when a party to the dialogue attempts to communicate with another by employing a basically secularist language—I'm here referring to a broad and general concept of secularism which means the rejection of any intuitive spiritual experience and any belief in the unseen, in an essentially sacred and spiritual discourse. . . . It now appears that the Cartesian-Faustian narrative of Western civilization should give way and begin to listen to other narratives proposed by other human cultures.[17]

Dialogue takes place only under the sacred canopy of faith, before which the scientific, materialist worldview must "give way." Cross-civilizational conversation is at best interfaith conversation.

Stripped of its stagecraft and pseudoacademic jargon, Khatami's proposal is not for dialogue at all. It is in fact a call for unanimity, unity in submission to God. In this, he is a voice thrown by President Ahmadinejad, who wrote to the American president:

> The God of all people in Europe, Asia, Africa, America, the Pacific and the rest of the world is one. He is the Almighty who wants to guide

and give dignity to all His servants. . . . . All prophets speak of peace and tranquility for man—based on monotheism, justice and respect for human dignity. Do you not think that if all of us come to believe in and abide by these principles, that is, monotheism, worship of God, justice, respect for the dignity of man, belief in the Last Day, we can overcome the present problems of the world, that are the result of disobedience to the Almighty and the teachings of prophets?[18]

There is a way of dialogue practiced by the scholars of medieval Cordoba, by Theo van Gogh, and by Ayaan Hirsi Ali. It is to persuade by reason, to puncture with satire, to reimagine through art. Genuine dialogue is defined by openness and honesty, guided by reason, and pointed toward knowledge. Genuine dialogue cannot be based in submission to God. It recognizes no authority save the authority of our common reason, no obedience but to the individual human conscience.

Peace-loving people at the United Nations and everywhere had hoped that interfaith dialogue would serve as a corrective and alternative to Samuel Huntington's (and Bernard Lewis's) famous thesis of the clash of civilizations. But here they were guilty of the kind of oversimplification of which Huntington is so often accused. If there is a fault to be found with Huntington's formulation, it is not with the "clash" but with the "civilizations," for civilizations cannot be parsed neatly along religious lines. The world that jihad seeks to undo is not Christendom as such; it is secular modernity—the world built of critical reason, science, and humanist values. From Iraq to Bangladesh, the contest of the culture of totalitarian faith with the culture of secularism is also a struggle *within* Islamic societies, and its warriors claim the highest number of innocent casualties among fellow Muslims. Of the victims of terrorist attacks between 2002 and 2005, 10,615 were in the Middle East, 994 in Southeast Asia, and 3,639 in East, Central, and South Asia. Fatalities in Western Europe for the same period were 272 and in North America, 3.[19]

In March 2007, nearly two dozen leading intellectuals and activists of Muslim heritage gather for the first Secular Islam Summit in the United States. Some are former Muslims, such as Wafa Sultan, a Syrian-

American psychiatrist and Middle East commentator whose fiery inter-change with a cleric on Al Jazeera in February 2006 has been down-loaded over a million times. Others are practicing believers calling for reform of their faith, like Irshad Manji, the Canadian author of *The Trouble with Islam Today*. What they share is an affirmation of secular values of reason and freedom of conscience as the necessary precondi-tion for real dialogue and progress in majority-Muslim societies. The summit issues a declaration, whose signatories include Ayaan Hirsi Ali and Mithal al-Alusi, a member of the Iraqi parliament.[20] It reads:

> We are secular Muslims, and secular persons of Muslim societies. We are believers, doubters, and unbelievers, brought together by a great struggle, not between the West and Islam, but between the free and the unfree.
>
> We affirm the inviolable freedom of the individual conscience. We believe in the equality of all human persons.
>
> We insist upon the separation of religion from state and the obser-vance of universal human rights.
>
> We find traditions of liberty, rationality, and tolerance in the rich his-tories of pre-Islamic and Islamic societies. These values do not belong to the West or the East; they are the common moral heritage of humankind.
>
> We see no colonialism, racism, or so-called "Islamaphobia" in sub-mitting Islamic practices to criticism or condemnation when they violate human reason or rights.
>
> We call on the governments of the world to
>
> - reject Sha'ria law, fatwa courts, clerical rule, and state-sanctioned religion in all their forms; oppose all penalties for blasphemy and apostasy, in accordance with Article 18 of the Universal Declaration of Human Rights;

- eliminate practices, such as female circumcision, honor killing, forced veiling, and forced marriage, that further the oppression of women;
- protect sexual and gender minorities from persecution and violence;
- reform sectarian education that teaches intolerance and bigotry towards non-Muslims;
- and foster an open public sphere in which all matters may be discussed without coercion or intimidation.

We demand the release of Islam from its captivity to the totalitarian ambitions of power-hungry men and the rigid strictures of orthodoxy.

We enjoin academics and thinkers everywhere to embark on a fearless examination of the origins and sources of Islam, and to promulgate the ideals of free scientific and spiritual inquiry through cross-cultural translation, publishing, and the mass media.

We say to Muslim believers: there is a noble future for Islam as a personal faith, not a political doctrine;

to Christians, Jews, Buddhists, Hindus, Baha'is, and all members of non-Muslim faith communities: we stand with you as free and equal citizens;

and to nonbelievers: we defend your unqualified liberty to question and dissent.

Before any of us is a member of the Umma, the Body of Christ, or the Chosen People, we are all members of the community of conscience, the people who must choose for themselves.

The event is covered by Al Jazeera, Al Arabiya, and Kuwait News, and meets with an outpouring of support from people across the globe. But Western moderate-liberal media are derelict. The Council on American-Islamic Relations (CAIR), whose self-described mission is "to enhance understanding of Islam" and "encourage dialogue," denounces the meeting as "illegitimate" and "anti-Muslim." The *Washington Post*'s only coverage comes nearly two weeks after the event, in the form of an article toeing CAIR's line and written by an invited speaker at a CAIR conference. Even Al Jazeera's reportage is more evenhanded.

Also missing from the Secular Islam Summit are Western women's organizations. One would expect that the oppression of women in Islamic societies would be a defining issue for Western feminists. Instead, as philosopher Martha Nussbaum observed in 1999, "Feminist theory pays relatively little attention to the struggles of women outside the United States." Western intellectuals' "hip quietism," she said, "collaborates with evil."[21] The Web site of the National Organization for Women lists the following as its "Top Priority Issues": abortion rights/reproductive issues, violence against women (domestic violence in the United States), constitutional equality (the Equal Rights Amendment to the US Constitution), promoting diversity/ending racism, lesbian rights, and economic justice. Yet if it is a feminist issue that some women make less than men for the same work, then it must be a feminist issue that other women are forbidden from leaving their homes unaccompanied by a man. If it is a feminist issue that some women are stigmatized for their sexual orientation, then it must be a feminist issue that others are murdered with impunity by their male relatives for the crime of "dishonor" or stoned to death by the government for extramarital sex. ("Paradise," Muhammad is said to have remarked, "lies at the feet of mothers.") Yet in a morally relativistic universe, all are given equal gravity. It is a bizarre case of moral dysmorphia that blows the failings of one's own society out of all proportion while diminishing the failings of others. And this for the sake of respecting difference.

Admirably, political leftists instinctively seek solidarity with the dispossessed and oppressed. So, when they see that the perpetrators of Islamic terror are brown-skinned people from backward societies, they assume they must in some way be allies against the common foe of Western imperialist aggression led by America. They are blinded to the fact that the enemy of Islamism—the self-professed enemy—is secular liberalism itself.

A noteworthy exception is the Feminist Majority Foundation, which launched a campaign in 1997 to call international attention to the inhumane treatment of women under the Taliban in Afghanistan. Working with human rights groups, the Feminist Majority Foundation (FMF) succeeded in persuading the United States and the United Nations to deny formal recognition to the regime. This was too much for some of their sisters. An article in the *International Feminist Journal of Politics* accused FMF of colonialism: "The FMF's campaign narrative is one of colonialist protection rather than of solidarity. . . . [It] capitalizes on the images of prominent white Western women . . . who construct themselves as 'free' and 'liberated' and thus in the best position to 'save' Afghan women."[22] For these pious feminists, the preservation of their own imagined moral purity appears more important than protecting real women's lives.

In 2006, Ayaan Hirsi Ali emigrates to the United States and publishes two popular books critiquing Islam from a woman's perspective. The reception in the liberal press ranges from condescension to hostility, while "neoconservatives" embrace her. A British feminist writing in the *Guardian* begins by agreeing that women's oppression under Islam is intolerable, and then thinks better of it: "But it is also important to remember that many women are seeking equality within, not outside Islam, and it is not as though women's oppression does not exist outside Islam."[23] It is true that countless women are seeking equality from within Islam. What has that to do with the merits of Ayaan's case? Does the author wish to insinuate that an internal critique is somehow more authentic, legitimate, or worthy of attention? Of course it is true that Islam is not the only oppressor of women, but it is certainly peerless. Most to the point, two wrongs don't make a right. Renaissance humanist Montaigne had a line from Terence inscribed on the wooden beams of his tower library: *Homo sum, humani nihil a me alienum puto* (I am human, nothing human is foreign to me). The slogan of too many Western feminists is *Tu quoque*

(You, too). Incessantly pointing a finger at their own societies, they cannot reach out to others.

Islamism is the new totalitarianism and it demands a new liberalism that places global resistance to theocratic Islam at the center of its agenda. Like the choice between communism and anticommunism for a former generation of liberals, Islamism has become the defining issue today. Historian Arthur Schlesinger Jr., a founder of Americans for Democratic Action in 1947, felt that the cold war gave liberalism a "historical re-education" in the dangers of communism. A small but growing number of liberals hope that 9/11 will reeducate the liberalism of their generation, reorienting it from a preoccupation with partisan domestic policy feuds and a reflexive aversion to the exercise of American power abroad.[24] Still, the mainstream left wing remains more fixated on embarrassing local conservative parties than on protecting women and religious minorities in the Islamic world. As Salman Rushdie put it in a speech on Manhattan's Upper West Side in October 2006, "The fellow traveling of a great section of the left with Islamic radicalism" is a "historical mistake as great as those who were the fellow travelers of Stalinist Communism in an earlier age."[25]

In the face of totalitarian Islam, secular liberalism must be reimagined. The new secularism is based on the free and open conscience as a universal, objective value. Its central mission is promoting freedom of conscience, expression, and the press, and it does not shirk from critically engaging religion. As Iranian-born journalist Amir Taheri observes:

> The only valuable dialogue between Islam, in its multiple forms, and the West, also in its diversity, can take place at a people-to-people level. Muslims should be allowed to read books and newspapers, see films, watch television and listen to the music produced in the West. In exchange the peoples of the West should be able to have direct access to Islam's cultural, artistic and philosophical production. And, yet, we know that this cannot happen as long as censorship remains a key element in the policies of most majority-Muslim states.[26]

The chair of the Secular Islam Summit was Ibn Warraq, the author of *Why I Am Not a Muslim* and editor of a series of scholarly anthologies of Quranic criticism. His pseudonym (meaning "son of a paper-seller") is taken from al-Warraq, mentor to the great ninth-century skeptic al-Rawandi. In 2006 Warraq addressed a meeting organized by the Dutch parliament in The Hague:

> If one desires to bring about an Enlightenment in the Islamic world or among Muslims living in the West, at some stage, someone somewhere will have to apply to the Koran the same techniques of textual analysis as were applied to the Bible by Spinoza and others, especially in Germany during the 19th Century. . . . Koranic Criticism, on the other hand, has lagged far behind. But surely Muslims *and* non-Muslims have the right to critically examine the sources, the history and dogma of Islam. . . . Without criticism of Islam, Islam will remain unassailed in its dogmatic, fanatical, medieval fortress; ossified, totalitarian and intolerant. It will continue to stifle thought, human rights, individuality; originality and truth.[27]

A majority of Iranians voted in favor of Ayatollah Khomeini's referendum calling for an Islamic republic in 1979. Twenty-seven years later, half the population is between the ages of fourteen and twenty-five. To them, the revolution and its aftermath are history. They know only that the theocracy was an experiment that failed. A 2002 telephone public opinion poll found that only 19 percent of Iranians support a politically active clergy.[28] According to all estimates, if they were presented with a new referendum on the option of an Islamic republic, Iranians would overwhelmingly reject it.

As in 1979, the boldest revolutionaries in Iran today are at the universities. In 1997, the students were heartened by the election of President Khatami on a platform of reform and took to the streets in massive numbers in July 1999, March 2000, October 2001, November 2002, and July 2003. But by 2004, Khatami's program had collapsed, and the students were publicly denouncing him as a fraud. This betrayal only deepened their anger at the regime.

They are overwhelmingly secular in outlook. At the age of eighteen, Soroush Danesh completed a course in Islamic education, but by the time she was a third-year college student in Tehran she was "slowly but surely" becoming an atheist. For her, God is in the Found & Lost Department. For many young Iranian secularists who stop short of atheism, religion just doesn't matter that much. In *Free Inquiry* magazine, Soroush wrote that her peers "wish to be no different than any free Westerner. Among other things, they want to date and have romantic relationships and attend parties, all of which are opposed by Islamic government and law."[29]

Today's activists are also secular in their organization. Throughout the 1990s, reformist students organized under the auspices of a national umbrella group, the Office of Consolidation Unity, or OCU, which descends from a government-backed body of religious students involved in the Cultural Revolution of the 1980s that Islamicized Iranian universities. Now reformist Islamist politics are being forsaken in favor of grassroots civil disobedience.

Akbar Ganji, an Iranian journalist, spent six years in Iran's notorious Evin Prison for his vocal opposition to the Islamic Republic and its outrages against human rights. In June 2006, he was awarded the 2006 Golden Pen of Freedom, the annual press freedom prize from the World Association of Newspapers. The Iranian authorities permitted Ganji to travel to Russia to accept the award. There, in his acceptance speech, Ganji argued for a global ethos of liberalism:

An authentic life is one wherein every individual has the right to pursue his or her own goals, and is not deemed merely a tool to be used by others to achieve their goals. If we can create equality for everyone, then this authentic life can become a reality, and people can, in cooperation and competition with one another, pursue their goals successfully, and have a chance to offer their values for scrutiny and discussion in the public domain.

Today we need to help create and strengthen a truly viable, clever, and vital public domain, and we ourselves must move in that arena, and use it to control and curtail power and criticize those politicians who have turned human beings into tools and means. Only through such a public sphere can we stand up to ideological and intellectual totalitarianism that wishes to impose its vision of a perfect world forcefully on everyone. As Kant has written, the principle of human freedom is the foundation of a democratic state and for him, freedom is when no one can coerce me to pursue my happiness according to their vision. Everyone must be free in their pursuit of their own happiness.[30]

Ganji gives voice to a secularism of conscience, which takes to the public sphere to champion a moral case for human freedom. Western secular liberals looking for allies need look no further.

11.

The Future Is Openness

It is something to be able to paint a particular picture, or to carve a statue, and so to make a few objects beautiful; but it is far more glorious to carve and paint the very atmosphere and medium through which we look, which morally we can do.

—Ralph Waldo Emerson

I n 1991 a second-year computer student at the University of Helsinki named Linus Torvald couldn't find a computer operating system to suit his needs, so he set out to create one of his own. He wrote an experimental draft of the source code, the human-readable version of the code that runs computer programs. But rather than tinkering in solitude, he took an unusual step. Torvald licensed his software under a special public license called GPL. The GPL license permitted free public access to a piece of intellectual property to any users who agree to two conditions. First, they will not try to claim a proprietary right to it. Second, any improvements they make will be shared with others in the same fashion as the original. Torvald posted the source code for his operating system on the Internet for free download and sent a message to an online newsgroup inviting other programmers to get involved in perfecting the program. The name of the system was Linux 0.01.

Three years later, "Linus Torvald's hobby claimed a 25 per cent share of the global market for server operating systems, and had consumed an estimated 8,000 person years of development time,"[1] most of them contributed by a global, networked community of volunteers who tinker with the source code and share their improvements with others. Linux sparked a worldwide "open source movement" that is transforming the Internet and industry. Major software corporations like IBM and Microsoft have been compelled to react. London think tank Demos has studied the open source method of software development and identified these ten characteristics:

> *Transparency*: "While the standard approach to ensuring innovation in competitive industries has been to keep ideas secret as long as possible, and then copyrighted or patented thereafter, the open source model turns this on its head."

> *Vetting of participants only after they've got involved*: Open source projects "allow absolutely anyone to get involved; all that matters is whether or not they deliver high quality work," as vetted by project leaders or members of the general community.

> *Low cost and ease of engagement*: "Genuine openness in any activity depends on cheap and easy ways of taking part."

> *A legal structure and enforcement mechanism*: Open development "depends on a clearly defined legal framework which shapes the incentives for participation. . . . All open source projects release their data for free, but control its use through licences that ensure that the improved work remains available for public use."

> *Leadership*: "Contrary to assumptions of anarchic, emergent behavior, we find that most open source projects normally have charismatic leaders who help motivate a more dispersed group of developers."

Common standards: Open methods rely on design and technical standards that are not only shared but "free to use, and open for scrutiny" by the community.

Peer review and feedback loops: "even complex code, millions of lines in length and of huge complexity, can be debugged reasonably quickly when there are enough people looking at different bits of it."

A shared conception of goals: Participants in an open design process do not agree on everything, and may have different motivations for participation. However, they share a notion of what would make the end product good, and agree that "the vetting they can get from peer review is a valuable resource if they want their creation to be as good as possible."

Incrementalist—small players can still make useful contributions: In many fields of development, extensive training or advanced qualifications are prerequisites for making a major contribution. An open design gets "a bit better every time someone makes a tiny change—and tiny changes are therefore sought and accepted, alongside major contributions."

Powerful non-monetary incentives: "programmers are more commonly driven by motives of social or personal fulfillment including the desire to be respected for their work."[2]

The idea of open methods for organizing human knowledge is nothing new. The sciences are the original open network, a meritocratic information-sharing collective regulated by peer review. One explanation for the dynamic success of open methods in software design and science is the power of distributed computing. Rather than attacking a problem with a single centralized intelligence, open methods mobilize many intelligences to attack different parts of the problem or the same problem in different ways. In the future of knowledge, openness may be the rule. Both the open source movement and the open access sciences provide instructive models of conscience.

The traditional image of conscience is a mirror of revelation. Not a voice from an angel in a cave or a burning bush, but a revelation from within, a "still, small voice." But from where? In the picture of conscience developed in this book, the model is not a revelation but a network. The network of open source ethics is a pubic, collaborative, and critical enterprise that builds up a storehouse of shareable answers to challenges faced by a community. The sound of conscience is the clamor of conversation, not the eerie whisper of revelation.

Emily Rosa knows something about the openness of science. When she was nine years old and living in Colorado, Emily saw a videotape of nurses demonstrating therapeutic touch, an alternative medical practice in which the practitioner manipulates an insensible "energy field" surrounding the patient's body. Proponents claim that therapeutic touch is effective treatment for numerous conditions. With the help of her parents, Emily devised an experiment for her high school science fair. Twenty-one therapeutic touch practitioners participated, and their success rate was only 44 percent. A nine-year-old with no scientific training empirically disconfirmed a pseudomedical practice that is believed by a multitude. As Galileo said, anyone can look through my telescope.[3]

Science is essentially nonsectarian. It defers to the authority of no ecclesiastical hierarchy or law-giver god, it swears loyalty to no scripture or revelation, and it opens its doors to participants regardless of creed. There is no Jewish physics or Hindu physics, despite what some so-called Vedic scientists in India might tell you. It is also a collective process. Authority flows not from a ruler or a sacred revealed text but from a freely assenting community of individuals—peer review and feedback loops. John Dewey, the great public philosopher of democracy, drew the connection between democracy and scientific inquiry, calling democracy a way of life involving inquisitiveness, openness to experience, and deliberation across differences, which are equally virtues of the scientific life. In *The Problems of Men*, he wrote: "The authority of science issues from and is based upon collective authority, cooperatively organized. Even when, temporarily, the ideas put forth by individuals have sharply diverged from received beliefs, the method used in science has been a public and open method which succeeded and could succeed only as it tended to produce agreement, unity of belief among all who labored in the same field."[4] Dewey called our attention to the experimental spirit of the democratic enterprise and the democratic spirit of the scientific enterprise, both open-ended processes of self-critical, collective inquiry and consensus formation. In both, deliberation is elevated over authoritarian rule, reason and persuasion over coercion and the contest of interests. One of the reasons Dewey favored democracy was epistemological: he believed that the public inquiry of democracy, like the public inquiry of science, would lead to an increase in important knowledge, knowledge of the social, moral, legal, and political practices that best suit human beings. Open networks grow public knowledge.

> Every scientific inquirer, even when he deviates most widely from current ideas, depends upon methods and conclusions that are a common possession and not of private ownership, even though all the methods and conclusions may at some time have been initially the product of private invention. The contribution the scientific inquirer makes is collectively tested and developed. In the measure that it is cooperatively confirmed, it becomes a part of the common fund of the intellectual commonwealth.[5]

If we think of scientific knowledge in economic terms as a good, then science is a process that produces that good as its output. What are the inputs to this process? In addition to human labor, physical resources like electricity, laboratories, and machines, there is information of various kinds: raw data, existing scientific literature, background knowledge, practical expertise, and so on. General economic assumptions lead us to expect that the output of a process will rise as the cost of its inputs falls. In the case of science this means that more access to information inputs should lead to more knowledge output. Open access to information increases scientific innovation.

It is no accident that an ethos of information sharing has been central to modern science since its beginning. Early organizations like London's Royal Institute and publications like the French philosophes' *Enclyopédie* were explicitly designed to provide cheap and reliable access to information. The Industrial Revolution was a revolution in information sharing. Artisans, mechanics, engineers, mariners, and other tradesmen with practical knowledge of emerging technologies and techniques communicated with physicists, chemists, and other experimentalists whose growing theoretical knowledge could help refine, augment, and extend these technologies and techniques in new directions.[6] Indeed, practices that would today be considered intellectual piracy were crucial to America's technological ascendance. Early American patent and copyright systems rewarded those who introduced technologies taken from European markets.[7]

At the same time, scientific knowledge is, like all knowledge, a public good, or at least a quasi-public good, in this sense: once it has been produced, the marginal cost of providing it to each additional user tends to be low to zero, and excluding anyone from using it without excluding all is impossible or impracticable. Thus, a public good invites "free-riders," making it difficult for the producers to extract value from it. Just ask the Pythagoras estate about the royalty check they don't cash each time someone calculates the area of a triangle. So, the quasi-public character of the output of the scientific process is a disincentive to those who would invest resources in it. Thus, open access to information impedes scientific innovation.

If one wants to maximize the knowledge output of science, one needs to strike the right balance between the control granted to producers and the freedom granted to users. Intellectual property rights are a legal instrument that enables this balancing. An intellectual property right to information gives the producer of that information some limited control over its use by others. In the case of science, systems of intellectual property have typically sought to offset this control by protecting only particular expressions of information, for example, an article published in a journal, while leaving the data or discoveries themselves as nonproprietary.

With the increasing digitalizing of scientific publishing, and the shift of research funding sources from public entities like governments and universities to private, profit-seeking entities like pharmaceutical companies, open access to scientific knowledge can no longer be taken for granted. Organizations such as the Public Library of Science are leading an open access movement in science aimed to keep the intellectual wealth affordable, especially for those in poor countries of the global South. There are powerful egalitarian arguments for open access. There is also a Deweyian, epistemological argument.

In 1990 the Commission on Health Research for Development estimated that less than 10 percent of the world's budget for health research and development goes toward conditions that account for 90 percent of the world's diseases, dubbing the inequality "the 10/90 gap." Since that time, global spending on health R&D has more than tripled. It remains true that most R&D is financed by rich countries and aimed at bringing products (like so-called lifestyle drugs) to healthcare markets of rich countries. The United States alone accounts for almost half of global expenditures, followed by Japan, United Kingdom, Germany, and France. Even if we could bridge the digital divide separating Internet users from nonusers in the South, there would remain a content divide: most of the content on health science available in new media would cater to the North, discussing medical problems, medications, and technologies that are largely not relevant to practitioners and patients in the world's underdeveloped regions.

In a February 2002 issue of *Nature*, two American physicians proposed that all medical journals commit at least 15 percent of their pages to issues impacting developing regions and pointed out three benefits of this shift in content: (1) "First, and most important, the journals would provide articles of interest and relevance to doctors, scientists, and patients in these regions"; (2) "Increased focus on the health-care needs of poorer countries might encourage western physicians and scientists to think about problems they might not ordinarily encounter, and to generate fresh insights or novel approaches"; (3) "The new articles might help to inform the development of ethics guidelines for clinical research done by North American and European scientists in underdeveloped regions. . . . Greater familiarity with the needs and the resources of patients in poorer nations might help ethics committees as they wrestle with these difficult but vitally important decisions."[8] Extending this point, one could argue that scientists can increase the likelihood that they will attain important truths by increasing the number and diversity of their discussion partners.

Like the sciences, conscience shares many of the key features of open source methods. Discussion of matters of conscience is transparent: its reasoning is open and accessible to all. No barriers of cost or expertise or community membership keep out some discussion partners. Contributions are judged on their merits as assessed by peer review and feedback. Discussion partners share a common goal—to seek answers to questions of meaning, identity, and value—and common standards, like the assumption that conversation is guided by objective norms for what counts as a good reason. These assumptions are themselves open to scrutiny. And while there are no final authorities, there are clearly leaders of conscience, people distinguished by outstanding contributions to religious and ethical questions. When the network of conscience produces results—such as the idea of civil disobedience or the idea of private property—they are of course not licensed. But they are protected under the legal and cultural framework of an open society, where they become part of an intellectual and moral commonwealth, to be seen, heard, and read by anyone.

You are already a contributor to open source ethics. If you are like most human beings, you probably think about what you have most reason to believe and do about central human questions of meaning, identity, and value. You think about what constitutes your good and the good of others. You try to apply your principles in action and live according to your conscience. You reflect on the results and share your findings at least with others you know, if not in public discourse such as letters to newspapers, local government forums, and online forums. You listen to criticism and feedback at least sometimes and you revise your principles and values in light of the best solutions that emerge from conversation.

As with the sciences and open source development, so in the network of conscience, everyone has an incentive to expand the pool of conversation partners, so that the chances of hitting upon defensible beliefs, values, and practices will be maximized. Conscience weighs what we have most reason to think or do. Therefore, it constantly seeks out the interests and reasons of others. This can happen interculturally as much as interpersonally.

It is now a truism that the future belongs to China and India, if they will take it (although we know that the future isn't always what it used to be). Commercial markets and mass media are globalizing faster than we can count, and yet culture, values, and ethics have remained mostly localized. Asian, South Asian, and Western societies may have much practical and ethical wisdom to gain from one another. That conversation cannot happen without some shared language of reason and value that transcends religions and borders. While there is already considerable comparative study of Asian and Western history and literature, there is to date comparatively little cross-cultural research in philosophy, religion, ethics, and social science. Such cross-cultural conversation is imperative, since many of the most pressing issues facing the coming generation—energy and environmental problems, family planning, genetic research and engineering, nanotechnology and artificial intelligence, nuclear proliferation, the automation of militaries, political Islam and human rights—will spill across national and cultural borders.

There is no guarantee that all of the divergent societies affected by these issues will necessarily share some "common ground" that is robust enough to resolve them. Yet there is no viable alternative to reasoning together. To do that, we do not need common ground, but we need common ground rules for public debate on matters of conscience. As the world becomes more interconnected, actions taken in one place affect more and more people in other places. The common, impartial point of view—conscience's eye view—expands to include more and more reasons and interests, and the commonwealth of conscience is enlarged and enriched.

This is the insight that links the Public Library of Science to the Virginia Statute for Religious Freedom, and conscience to Linux; that ties Spinoza to Jefferson, and Mill to Dewey and Torvald: open talk makes wisdom. The insight shines brightest in Mill's discussion of freedom of expression in *On Liberty*. He constructs a dilemma for all those who would suppress an opinion in an effort to safeguard orthodoxy. He shows that no matter whether the belief is false, or true, or partially true and partially false, suppression would be a mistake. What if the opinion is true? "Those who desire to suppress it, of course deny its truth; but they are not infallible. They have no authority to decide the question for all mankind, and exclude every other person from the means of judging. To refuse a hearing to an opinion, because they are sure that it is false, is to assume that their certainty is the same thing as absolute certainty."[9] Infallibility is not a real option. For it may turn out that "though the silenced opinion be an error, it may, and very commonly does, contain a portion of truth; and since the general or prevailing opinion on any object is rarely or never the whole truth, it is only by the collision of adverse opinions that the remainder of the truth has any chance of being supplied."

But suppose the dissenting view is entirely mistaken and the received opinion is correct. Even still, says Mill, it would be a mistake to protect the received view from scrutiny, since even a correct opinion has something to gain from the free contest of ideas: "If it is not fully, frequently, and fearlessly discussed, it will be held as a dead dogma, not a living truth."

> Unless it is suffered to be, and actually is, vigorously and earnestly contested, it will, by most of those who receive it, be held in the manner of a prejudice, with little comprehension or feeling of its rational grounds. And not only this . . . the meaning of the doctrine itself will be in danger of being lost, or enfeebled, and deprived of its vital effect on the character and conduct: the dogma becoming a mere formal profession, inefficacious for good, but cumbering the ground, and preventing the growth of any real and heartfelt conviction, from reason or personal experience.[10]

The Millian liberal wants liberty because she desires truth, not because she is indifferent to truth. Freedom of belief does not free her belief from examination; it frees her belief for examination.

Openness does not mean ambiguity or skepticism. Mill is not asking that we abandon all our convictions and suspend judgment. He is careful to point out that leaving our convictions open to criticism is in fact a precondition for having confidence in them:

> Complete liberty of contradicting and disproving our opinion, is the very condition which justifies us in assuming its truth for purposes of action; and on no other terms can a being with human faculties have any rational assurance of being right. . . . The beliefs which we have most warrant for, have no safeguard to rest on, but a standing invitation to the whole world to prove them unfounded. If the challenge is not accepted, or is accepted and the attempt fails, we are far enough from certainty still; but we have done the best that the existing state of human reason admits of.[11]

Openness is also the only way to discover the principles—the common standards—by which we can evaluate our beliefs. Our methods of inquiry themselves, our "Principles of Evidence and Theories of Method" are not known a priori or delivered from on high: "The laws of our rational faculty, like those of every other natural agency, are only learnt by seeing the agent at work . . . we should never have known by what process truth is to be ascertained, if we had not previously ascertained many truths."[12]

If secular liberalism is to continue to stand for reason and freedom, the separation of religion and state, personal autonomy, equality, toleration, and self-criticism, secular liberals must stand up for these values in public debate. This means returning conscience to its proper place at the heart of secular liberalism. Matters of conscience—including religion and values—are open. Like the sciences and open source methods, they are fit subjects of public discussion, they are guided by shared, objective evaluative standards, and they are revisable in light of future experience. The point of the open, secular society is not to privatize or bracket questions of conscience, but to pursue them in conversation with others. Like a free press, conscience is freed from coercion so that it may perform a vital public function: reasoning together about questions of meaning, identity, and value.

Religious institutions ought to be private, but the religious conscience is not. The Privacy Fallacy must be abandoned. Sectarian reasons cannot be barred from public debate; they can and must be held to the same critical conversational standards as all serious contributions to public debate. Religion inevitably makes truth-claims that are susceptible to examination and evaluation by others and continuous at many points with the sciences. Many beliefs that go by "faith" are actually attempts at reason: trusting on the basis of past experience; believing in the face of uncertainty. So-called religious experience is not a reliable guide to truth. The sole alternative to reason is raw, baseless, intransigent intuition, something to which no decent person aspires. But even "subjective" intuition can be evaluated and found immoral or unwise. Faith cannot escape the judgment of reason.

The open society leaves people's lives up to them, within the limits of the Liberty Principle. But the Liberty Principle is not the Liberty Fallacy: permissiveness is not a mark of indifference but an affirmation of the objective worth of lives well lived and the individual autonomy necessary to discover them. It is not, as Mill reminds us, that "human beings have no business with each other's conduct in life, and that they should not concern themselves about the well-doing or well-being of one another." Rather, we "owe each other help to distinguish the better from the worse, and encouragement to choose the former rather than the latter."

Who is to say that some choices are better or worse? Who else, but us? In our reasoning about ethical choices, as in all practical reasoning, we can't help but adopt a point of view that is universal in the sense of open and accessible to all. When we talk seriously with others about ethical choices, we presuppose that we all embrace some objective norms of what counts as a good reason. Where do these norms come from? Evolutionary science can explain why we have selves that are capable of offering and accepting reasons and responsibility for action. And it may discover that we have an evolved intuitive ethics. Ultimately, evolution makes the ethical possible; it does not define the ethical. For that, our intuitive ethics must be checked and corrected against our best theoretical ethics.

Secular ethics begins with the reality of love, the desire for the good of the other for the sake of the other. Our good or well-being is not just what we happen to want, but what we would want if we knew what we were doing. The value of well-being is real. It is constituted by facts about human nature and the world, and without these facts we cannot explain our desires, regrets, and reasons. Your good gives you reasons. Probably, it gives me reasons as well. In deciding what to do, nearly all of us have reason to take into consideration the interests of all those affected by our actions—to take the moral point of view. Secular liberals aren't skeptics about ethics. The real skeptics about ethics are those who think that human beings are incapable of fairness, responsibility, care, and compassion without divine enforcement.

In politics, a renewed secular liberalism that embraces conscience can do justice to the religious and moral convictions of the citizens of pluralistic democracies. It avails itself of all of the historically influential arguments for the open society, including the Argument from Theology and the Argument from Futility. It places on a firmer footing the traditional liberal commitment to freedom of conscience. It enables secular liberals to make an ethical case for their domestic agendas, empowers them to engage the global challenges and opportunities presented by Islam, and prepares them to deal with the transcultural moral dilemmas of tomorrow.

Conscience is what unites thinking persons and free peoples across ethnic, national, and creedal lines, and in its unfolding through public conversation, our moral lives are measured out. Conscience cannot be found in duty to God, for it is conscience that must judge where one's duty lies, and so the faithful cannot hold a monopoly on morality. Before any of us is a member of the Body of Christ, the Umma, or the Chosen People, we are all members of the community of conscience, the people who must choose for themselves.

Acknowledgments

The main themes of *The Secular Conscience* emerged from conversations with Camilla Dacey-Groth in 2000. More recently, I discussed some of the ideas or language with Daniel Dennett, Paul Draper, Richard Einhorn, Peter Hare, Elizabeth Harman, Sam Harris, Jennifer Michael Hecht, R. Joseph Hoffmann, Susan Jacoby, Nica Lalli, Richard Miniter, Alan Mittleman, Paul Nelson, Joyce Salisbury, James Stacey Taylor, and Ibn Warraq. Some of the material was developed from my graduate research, and was strengthened by the comments of my teachers and readers, especially Michael Bradie, James Child, Loren Lomasky, and Donald Scherer. Some material was published previously in the *New York Times*, *Free Inquiry*, and *The Encyclopedia of Unbelief* and appears by permission. I thank the editors for their contributions. For their courage in cutting swaths through the overgrown prose of the book's early incarnations, I recognize Philip Dacey and Robert Worth. Bob's friendship and generous support of my writing have been my greatest encouragement. When seeking a publisher I also received encouragement and advice from D. J. Grothe, Sydelle Kramer, Sarah Jordan, Michael McGandy, Chris Mooney, Peter Simon, and Lewis Vaughn. My agent, Beth Vesel, worked closely with me to shape the project. My colleagues at Prometheus Books—Paul Kurtz, Steven L. Mitchell, Chris Kramer, Jonathan Kurtz, Jill Maxick, and Joe Gramlich—have been superb. I appreciate the assistance of Rhiannon Inners, Tasha Williams, Mark Anthony Smith, the staff of the New York Public Library and the Center for Inquiry, and the various audiences before whom I presented portions of this work and whose feedback—and, sometimes, uncomprehending stares—prompted refinements. Finally, I am grateful to my friends Jahed Ahmed, Vikas Gora, Tawfik Hamid, Tariq Ismail, Shahriar Kabir, and Banafsheh Zand-Bonazzi for expanding my horizons and to Vie for breaking my concentration.

Endnotes

INTRODUCTION

1. Rory McCarthy, "Rioting with Well-Planned Spontaneity," *Guardian*, February 6, 2006, http://www.guardian.co.uk/religion/Story/0,,1703235,00.html (accessed July 18, 2007); "Let the Hands That Drew Be Severed," *Times Online*, February 3, 2006, http://www.timesonline.co.uk/tol/news/world/article725925.ece (accessed July 26, 2007); "Iranians Rename Danish Pastries," BBC News, February 7, 2006, http://news.bbc.co.uk/2/hi/middle_east/4724656.stm (accessed July 26, 2007).

2. Roman Heflik, "Editor Reflects on Denmark's Cartoon Jihad," *Spiegel Online International*, February 2, 2006, http://www.spiegel.de/international/0,1518,398717,00.html (accessed July 26, 2007).

3. Joel Brinkley and Ian Fisher, "U.S. Says It Also Finds Cartoons of Muhammad Offensive," *New York Times*, February 4, 2006.

4. "Denmark's Cartoon Jihad," *Spiegel Online International*, February 1, 2006, http://www.spiegel.de/international/0,1518,398533,00.html (accessed July 26, 2007).

5. Brinkley and Fisher, "U.S. Says It Also Finds Cartoons of Muhammad Offensive."

6. Tom Flynn, "A Time to Push Back," *Free Inquiry* 26, no. 4 (June/July 2006): 12–13.

7. Catholic News Service, "Vatican Says Freedom of Expression Does Not Mean Offending Religions," http://www.catholicnews.com/data/briefs/cns/20060206.htm (accessed July 26, 2007).

8. From the address "Pro Eligendo Romano Pontifice Homily of His Eminence Cardinal Joseph Ratzinger, Dean of the College of Cardinals," delivered at the Vatican Basilica on April 18, 2005, http://www.vatican.va/gpII/documents/homily-pro-eligendo-pontifice_20050418_en.html (accessed on July 25, 2007).

9. "Pope Ends Germany Trip with Mass for 1 Million," *Boston Globe*.

10. Christa Case, "Germans Reconsider Religion," *Christian Science Monitor*, September 15, 2006, http://www.csmonitor.com/2006/0915/p01s01-woen.html (accessed January 2, 2008).

11. The professor is Robert Simon, and he appears in Gertrude Himmelfarb, *One Nation, Two Cultures* (New York: Knopf, 1999), p. 122 (quoted in Stephen Law, *The War for Children's Minds* [New York: Routledge, 2006], pp. 78–79. The classic chronicling of relativism's effects on higher education is, of course, Allan Bloom's *Closing of the American Mind* (New York: Simon and Schuster, 1987).

12. Quoted in Law, *The War for Children's Minds*, p. 82.

13. I am referring, of course, to Sam Harris, Daniel Dennett, Richard Dawkins, Ayaan Hirsi Ali, and Christopher Hitchens. See, for example, Nicholas D. Kristof, "A Modest Proposal for a Truce on Religion," *New York Times*, December 3, 2006. See also Alistar McGrath, *The Twilight of Atheism: The Rise and Fall of Disbelief in the Modern World* (New York: Doubleday, 2004).

14. Vatican library online at http://www.vatican.va/roman_curia/congregations/cfaith/documents/rc_con_cfaith_doc_20030731_homosexual-unions_en.html (accessed July 26, 2007).

15. "Overreaching by Rome," *Boston Globe*, September 2, 2003.

16. Danny Postel, "High Flyer: Richard Rorty Obituary," *New Humanist* 122, no. 4 (July/August 2007), http://newhumanist.org.uk/1440 (accessed October 12, 2007).

17. Nicholas D. Kristof, "God, Satan, and the Media," *New York Times*, March 4, 2003.

18. Jim Wallis, *God's Politics* (San Francisco: HarperCollins, 2005), p. xviii.

19. Michael Lerner, *The Left Hand of God* (San Francisco: Harper-Collins, 2006), pp. 18, 21.

20. Ibid., p. 361.

21. See Richard Dawkins's discussion of deserved and undeserved respect in *The God Delusion* (New York: Houghton Mifflin, 2006). "I shall not go out of my way to offend, but nor shall I don kid gloves to handle religion any more gently than I would handle anything else," p. 27.

22. See Susan Jacoby, *Freethinkers: A History of American Secularism* (New York: Metropolitan Books, 2004), p. 332.

23. Frederick Douglass, "What to the Slave Is the Fourth of July," in *Against Slavery: An Abolitionist Reader* (New York: Penguin, 2000), p. 43.

24. Jacoby, *Freethinkers*, p. 118.

1. HOW SECULARISM LOST ITS SOUL

1. Isaac Kramnick and Lawrence Moore, *The Godless Constitution: The Case against Religious Correctness* (New York: W. W. Norton, 1997), p. 84.

2. Charles Taylor, *Sources of the Self: The Making of Modern Identity* (Cambridge, MA: Harvard University Press, 1989), p. 134.

3. Augustine, *The City of God against the Pagans*, trans. R. W. Dyson (Cambridge: Cambridge University Press, 1998), p. 486.

4. Patrick Collison, *The Reformation: A History* (New York: Random House, 2004), p. 63.

5. Martin Luther, *De Servo Arbitrio*, in *Luther and Erasmus: Free Will and Salvation*, trans. and ed. Philip S. Waton (Philadelphia: Westminster, 1969), p. 109; quoted in Jennifer Michael Hecht, *Doubt: A History* (New York: HarperCollins, 2003), p. 276.

6. It was with every bit of this certainly, and equal passion, that Luther spoke of the Jews of Germany, whom he called, quoting Matthew, "a brood of vipers and children of the devil." See Martin Luther, *On the Jews and Their Lies*, trans. Martin H. Bertram, in Franklin Sherman, ed., *Martin Luther's Works Vol. 14: The Christian in Society* (Philadelphia: Fortress Press, 1971), p. 277. Three years before his death, Luther authored an eight-point plan to deal with the Jewish problem, which included forced servitude, the seizure of all religious literature along with all money and property, and the prohibition of rabbinical teaching on pain of death.

Calvin was no less certain. He defined faith as "a firm and certain knowledge of God's benevolence toward us, founded upon the truth of the freely given promise in Christ, both revealed to our minds and sealed upon our hearts through the Holy Spirit." *Institutes of the Christian Religion*, 1559 ed., trans. Ford Lewis Battles (Philadelphia: Westminster Press, 1960), p. 551.

7. From Luther's *To the Christian Nobility*, quoted in Deryck W. Lovegrove, ed., *The Rise of the Laity in Evangelical Protestantism* (New York: Routledge, 2002), p. 21.

8. Taylor, *Sources of the Self*, pp. 217–18.

9. Collison, *The Reformation*, p. 8.

10. Ibid., p. 55.

11. Thomas Hobbes, *Leviathan*, trans. Edwin Curley (Indianapolis: Hackett Publishing, 1994), p. 3.

12. In *Terror and Liberalism* (New York: W. W. Norton, 2003), Paul Berman calls this "absolute freedom," contrasting it with the freedom to which liberalism aspires:

> . . . the recognition that all of life is not government by a single, all-knowing and all-powerful authority—by a divine force. It was the tolerant idea that every sphere of human activity—science, technology, politics, religion, and private life—should operate independently of the others, without trying to yoke everything together under a single guiding hand. It was a belief in the many, instead of the one. It was an insistence on freedom of thought and freedom of action— not on absolute freedom, but on something truer, stronger, and more reliable than absolute freedom, which is relative freedom: a freedom that recognizes the existence of other freedoms, too. (pp. 37–38)

For another perspective on absolute freedom, see Frithjof Bergmann, *On Being Free* (Notre Dame, IN: Notre Dame University Press, 1977).

13. Critics of the secularization thesis point out that the modern world looks more religious than ever. The explosive growth of the neo-pentecostal movement in Africa and Latin America suggests the coming a new, subequatorial Christendom, while Hindu nationalism and Buddhist revivalism thrive in India and Southeast Asia. Islamic cultures capitalize on modern technology without absorbing the secular ethos of science. The latest cell phones employ GPS technology to point prayers precisely Mecca-ward. (See Pervez

Hoodbhoy, "Science and the Islamic World: The Quest for Rapprochement," *Muslim World Today* [August 24, 2007]). Recent academic books herald an emerging "postsecular" era in higher education (C. John Sommerville, *The Decline of the Secular University* [New York: Oxford University Press, 2006]). A Centre for Post-Secular Studies has been established at London Metropolitan University.

However, as observed by Ronald Inglehart, chairman of the World Values Survey, the secularization thesis is compatible with the worldwide religion boom. This is because secularization "tends to bring, in the long run, dramatically declining fertility rates."

> That is the reason that empirically, although virtually all advanced industrial societies have been moving toward secular orientations, it is also true that the world as a whole has more people with traditional religious beliefs than ever before. The biggest single reason is that secularization leads to cultural changes that bring a huge decrease in fertility rates, from five or six children per woman to, in the average advanced industrial society, 1.6; and in some countries, Spain and Italy, for example, the rate is 1.2. children. ("Is There a Global Resurgence of Religion?" lecture at the National Press Club, Monday, May 8, 2006. Transcript prepared by Pew Forum on Religion and Public Life.)

14. George J. Holyoake, *English Secularism* (Chicago: Open Court, 1896), p. 60. Some liberals might worry that the concept of secularism implicitly accepts without question the dichotomy between the secular and the sacred or transcendent, and in that way affirms the idea of a sacred or transcendent realm. If *secular* means "not pertaining to the divine," then it presumes only that some things (like scriptures and prayers) *pertain to* the divine. That is not to place any particular value on the divine or even to assume that there is such a thing. Comic books can pertain to superheroes who don't exist. Perhaps this second objection is motivated by more general worries about dualistic oppositions. Jacques Derrida was right (or rather, some of his followers are right, since he always denied that deconstruction is "a method") that it is generally a good idea to question dualisms. But it doesn't follow that every dualism will turn out to be spurious. While "homosexual" and "heterosexual" might be problematic categories, "homogenized" and "nonhomogenized" are not.

15. Julian Baggini, "Toward a More Mannerly Secularism," *Free Inquiry* 27, no. 2 (February/March 2007): 41.

16. Nathalie Caron, "Läicité and Secular Attitudes in France," in *Secularism & Secularity: Contemporary International Perspectives*, ed. Barry A. Kosmin and Ariela Keysar (Hartford, CT: Institute for the Study of Secularism in Society and Culture, 2007), p. 114. Caron is quoting Henri Rena-Ruiz, *Qu'est-ce que Läicité?* (Paris: Gallimand, 2003), p. 21.

17. Ibid., p. 21.

18. Adam Smith, *An Inquiry into the Nature and Causes of the Wealth of Nations*, bk. 5, chap. 1, part 3, article III (New York: Modern Library, 1965); quoted in Barry A. Kosmin and Ariela Keysar, *Religion in a Free Market* (Ithaca, NY: Paramount Market Publications, 2006), p. 3.

19. "Uplifted," *Boston Globe*, July 10, 2005, http://www.boston.com/ae/tv/articles/2005/07/10/uplifted/?page=1 (accessed February 4, 2007).

20. Alan Wolfe, *The Transformation of American Religion: How We Actually Live Our Faith* (New York: Simon and Schuster, 2003), p. 3.

21. Michael J. Sandel, *Public Philosophy: Essays on Morality in Politics* (Cambridge, MA: Harvard University Press, 2005), p. 126.

22. Ibid., p. 129.

23. *Roe v. Wade* 410 US 113 (1973).

24. In fact, the decision is not entirely consistent on this point. The justices go on to say that in addition to the rights of women, the state "has still *another* important and legitimate interest in protecting the potentiality of human life. These interests are separate and distinct. Each grows in substantiality as the woman approaches term and, at a point during pregnancy, each becomes 'compelling.'" This remark seems to suggest that the Court does have a "theory of life." According to this theory, the life of the fetus generates increasingly weightier moral claims as it advances through its development, beginning very early in the pregnancy with no moral claims whatsoever and ending at the end of the pregnancy with moral claims that rival the claims of the mother.

25. Michael J. Sandel, *Democracy's Discontent: America in Search of a Public Philosophy* (Cambridge, MA: Belknap Press, 1996), pp. 20–21.

26. John Rawls, *A Theory of Justice* (Cambridge, MA: Belknap Press of Harvard University Press, 1971).

27. John Rawls, *Political Liberalism* (New York: Columbia University Press, 1996).

28. Kant, "What Is Enlightenment," in *Political Writings* (Cambridge: Cambridge University Press, 1995), p. 54.

29. Ibid., p. 55.

30. Ibid., p. 57.

31. Ibid., p. 55.

2. WHY BELIEF BELONGS IN PUBLIC LIFE (AND UNBELIEVERS SHOULD BE GLAD)

1. Fred Clarkson, "Will Roy Moore Crack the Bush Base?" *Salon*, May 4, 2004, http://dir.salon.com/story/news/feature/2004/05/04/roy_moore/?pn=1 (accessed July 24, 2007).

2. Rick Santorum, "Judges & Beliefs," letter to the editor, *New York Times*, August 11, 2003.

3. Some claim that private reasons are to be precluded from political discourse because of the equal respect that we owe all persons. The argument is roughly this: to respect others we must take them into consideration as thinking, perceiving beings who have a view of the world that may differ from our own. This implies that when we act in ways that have consequences for their lives, as we do in politics, we must explain and justify our actions to them in ways that make sense to them. Therefore, equal respect demands that political actions be publicly justified.

The liberal political theorist Charles Larmore puts it like this: "However much we may disagree with others and repudiate what they stand for, we cannot treat them merely as objects of our will, but owe them an explanation for those actions of ours that affect them" (Charles Larmore, *Patterns of Moral Complexity* [Cambridge: Cambridge University Press, 1987], p. 62). When a person demands that we justify our action to him, "he is recognizing that we, too, have a perspective on the world in which presumably our action makes sense, and indicating his willingness to discuss it rationally with us. . . . The obligation of equal respect consists in our being obligated to treat another as he is treating us—to use his having a perspective on the world as a reason for discussing the merits of our action rationally with him." Larmore, *Patterns of Moral Complexity*, p. 64.

The problem with this line of thought is that even if it were correct it would only establish an obligation to present to others the reasons that motivate us. It would not establish an obligation to present reasons that are motivating for us *and* acceptable to them. We can discuss the merits of our action rationally with others without invoking reasons that they find acceptable.

Suppose I oppose the death penalty on the grounds that only God may give and take a human life. Even if you do not share these grounds, we can discuss the merits of my opposition to the death penalty. I may fail to persuade you, but that would not show that I have failed to respect you. I could have demonstrated my respect, for example, by (1) recognizing the importance of explaining my reasons to you as best I can; (2) regarding you as basically rational and capable of grasping these reasons; (3) acknowledging that you may nevertheless honestly disagree; and (4) remaining civil toward you.

Political liberals might insist that respect makes the further demand that we offer to each citizen reasons that are compelling to him or her. Call this the strong conception of respect. The strong conception of respect, however, places liberals in a dilemma. The principle of public reason would have us construct our political arguments out of public reasons. But especially for the devout, public reasons sometimes will not be among the most important or relevant with respect to a political decision. For example, a Christian opponent to capital punishment might regard the Ten Commandments as a reason more important than some "public" considerations, like fairness or racial justice. This might be the case even if he endorses the public considerations as well. If respect demands that one offer each citizen reasons that are compelling to him, then arguably one ought to offer religious considerations to such an abolitionist. By offering public reasons to all, one fails to offer to some the reasons that they find most compelling. In this vein, Christian philosopher Nicholas Wolterstorff asks:

> Is there not something about the person who embraces, say, the Jewish religion, that I, a Christian, should honor? Should I not honor her not only as someone who is free and equal, but as someone who embraces the Jewish religion? Is she not worth honoring not only in her similarity to me, as free and equal, but in her particular difference from me—in her embrace of Judaism? (Robert Audi and Nicholas Wolterstorff, *Religion in the Public Square* [Lanham, MD: Rowman & Littlefield Publishers Inc., 1997], p. 111)

Under the strong conception of respect, a norm of public reason actually conflicts with respect. Secular liberals cannot have both a strong conception of respect and a strict principle of public reason.

Perhaps the thought underlying the argument from respect is that I am disrespectful of you whenever I am prepared to defend a political decision with reasons that you don't accept. I am disrespectful because I am implicating you in something that you do not endorse. This is a version of the argument from the principle of legitimacy, which was considered previously. Recall the limitations of that argument. It may be that I should only advocate those policies that you also have a reason to favor, but that doesn't show that you and I both must have *the same reason* to favor it. Our converging reasons might be reasons of conscience that we do not share. Respect demands of citizens that we strive for a polity in which important decisions are justifiable to all. But, contrary to the Privacy Fallacy, in such a polity citizens are free to assert and debate their competing claims of conscience.

4. James Rachels argued that the kinds of relationships we have with others are defined in part by the type and degree of their knowledge about us. As a consequence, exercising control over the type and degree of others' knowledge about us constitutes (at least partially) being autonomous with regard to our relationships. Exercising this control means restricting access to ourselves and our lives as we choose; in other words, determining the privacy and publicity of our behavior. Therefore, to determine the privacy and publicity of our behavior is at least in part to be autonomous with respect to our relationships. Insofar as others act contrary to our wishes concerning access to our lives, they fail to respect our autonomy. See James Rachels, "Why Privacy Is Important," *Philosophy & Public Affairs* 4, no. 4 (Summer 1975): 323–33.

5. See Stanley Benn, "Privacy, Freedom, and Respect for Persons," in *Philosophical Dimensions of Privacy: An Anthology*, ed. Ferdinand David Shoeman (Cambridge: Cambridge University Press, 1984), pp. 272–89.

6. See Joseph Kupfer, "Privacy, Autonomy, and Self-Concept," *American Philosophical Quarterly* 24, no. 1 (January 1987): 81–89.

7. David Dudley Field, "American Progress," in *Jurisprudence* (New York: Martin B. Brown, 1893), p. 6. Cited in Leo Pfeffer, *Church, State, Freedom* (Boston: Beacon Press, 1953), p. 1.

8. Granted, there will be cases in which political speech actually will violate individuals' privacy and so could be precluded on such grounds. For

example, in a debate taking place in the 2000 Kentucky legislative session over the public display of the Ten Commandments, Christian legislators began interrogating a dissenting legislator of Jewish heritage about her faith. Among other things, they asked her whether she believed in Jesus. If the assemblywoman could have justifiably denied others access to this information, then it is private, and the privacy of her religious beliefs would have made her colleagues' use of religion in politics inappropriate.

However, this kind appeal to religion is fairly uncommon. Much more common is the use of religion for rhetorical purposes or as a source of reasons for or against political decisions; for example, the use of a religious commitment to the truth and sacredness of the Ten Commandments as a reason for their public display. The privacy of conscience would not challenge this kind of use of religion, since it does not violate anyone's privacy in the way that the Kentucky legislators' questions do. So the privacy of conscience, in the sense of the personal, would not constitute adequate grounds for the exclusion of conscience from political discourse.

9. John Rawls, *Political Liberalism* (New York: Columbia University Press, 1996), p. 217.

10. An ideal or principle of public reason states that a certain class of political decisions must be explicitly discussed and supported by appeal to adequate public reasons. "Publicity" is often characterized in terms of some sort of mutual acceptance. Can anything more precise be said? We can begin with the most basic understanding of public reasons, as

PR1. Reasons that are or will be accepted by all citizens.

PR1 is too narrow. A theory of public reason must have a principled way of excluding some citizens from the class of individuals to whom a reason must be acceptable in order for it to be a public reason. Absent this, the rejection of a reason by a citizen would suffice to make that reason nonpublic, no matter how wrong or unfounded the rejection might be. For example, I might claim that a candidate's reason is unacceptable to me because I was experiencing a toothache when I first came to understand it. A theory of public reason that allowed objections such as this to disqualify a reason from publicity would lose all hope of finding any public reasons in practice. Since a theory of public reason presupposes that there are at least some public reasons, it must be able to exclude some objections from consideration. Many theories of public reason attempt to do this by way of a doctrine of "reasonableness." Thus, it is asserted that public reasons are

PR2. Reasons that are or will be accepted by all reasonable citizens.

According to PR2, only those rejections that are reasonable can disqualify a reason from being public. But what makes a rejection unreasonable? Rawls claims that reasonableness is an attitude that lies between rational self-interest and altruism. It includes rationality but also a certain commitment to social cooperation. Reasonableness among citizens, in his view, is like the relations among acquaintances who share an apartment building. They are bound to interact with one another under conditions of limited scarcity (peace and quiet, hot water, and so on) and they mutually and openly seek cooperative arrangements to govern these interactions. In these arrangements, tenants are not expected to sacrifice themselves altruistically to satisfy the preferences of their neighbors. Yet neither are they expected to simply aim at maximizing their self-interest but instead to genuinely seek and follow rules for the collective that are generally regarded as fair.

The exact nature of fair terms is crucial. As Rawls describes reasonable citizens, they are "ready to propose principles and standards as fair terms of cooperation and to abide by them willingly, given the assurance that others will likewise do so" (Rawls, *Political Liberalism*, p. 49). They "desire for its own sake a social world in which they, as free and equal, can cooperate with others on terms all can accept" (p. 50). Fair terms of cooperation are terms that "specify the reasons we are to share and publicly recognize before one another as grounding our social relations" (p. 53). In other words, fair terms of cooperation are expressed in public reasons. For Rawls, then, the idea of the reasonable "includes the idea of public reason" (p. 62).

However, it cannot be that an unwillingness to propose and abide by public reasons alone makes a rejection unreasonable. The citizen who rejects a reason cannot be accused of unwillingness to propose and abide by public reasons, since the reason in question is not acceptable to all (since it is not acceptable to him). Notice that this possibility cannot be avoided by claiming that the citizen's acceptance is not relevant to determining the publicity of the reason. The relevance of any citizen is supposed to be determined by an account of reasonableness, not presupposed by it.

It might be protested that the reason would be public were it not for this citizen's rejection, and that therefore he is displaying an unwillingness to propose and abide by public reasons. However, this protest assumes that it is unreasonable for one to reject any reason that would be mutually acceptable if not for one's rejection. But this understanding of reasonableness is surely too demanding. Suppose that there is a reason proposed that diminishes your moral significance and thereby opens the door for your victimization by others. Suppose further that all other citizens accept this reason or are prepared to accept it on the condition that you accept it. Clearly you could reject the reason without being unreasonable. Nevertheless, the reason would be public were it not for your rejection.

It follows that in the context of public reason, reasonableness cannot be understood as rationality plus the willingness to propose and abide by public reasons for a cooperative scheme. The problem with this understanding is that it ties fair terms too closely together with public reasons. A more minimal understanding of fair terms would characterize them as terms that specify a cooperative arrangement that is mutually acceptable. Note that mutual acceptance is distinct from mutual acceptance on the basis of shared reasons. People may accept the same arrangement for different reasons. On this account, reasonableness is rationality plus the willingness to propose and abide by terms specifying cooperative arrangements that are mutually acceptable. This seems to satisfy the pretheoretical sense, invoked by Rawls, that reasonableness is a motivation toward rational cooperation that lies between altruism and self-interest.

Still, PR2 is too narrow. It encompasses only reasons that citizens actually accept or will accept. Yet there may be reasons that reasonable citizens would accept although they are simply unaware of or unclear about them. A reason that is acceptable to all but not accepted by all is still a public reason. Suppose some reason is logically entailed by other public considerations. The fact that some people fail to recognize the entailment does not show that the reason is nonpublic. Rather it shows that some people are unaware of a public reason. To account for this, public reasons can be understood as

PR3. Reasons that are acceptable to all reasonable citizens.

But what does "acceptable to" mean? One option is to give it a modal sense:

PR4. Reasons that could be accepted by all reasonable citizens.

Note that when public reasons are understood in this way, at least some religious reasons are public reasons, for at least some religious reasons are reasons that could be accepted by all reasonable citizens. This is correct even in extremely religiously pluralistic societies such as the United States. For example, someone might claim that a political policy of recognizing a certain holy day is warranted because it is mandated in infallible sacred scripture. This reason *could be* accepted by all reasonable citizens, even though many in fact do not accept it. Therefore, it is public, according to PR4.

It might be thought that reasonableness is incompatible with such an argument, since the argument violates the notion of proposing mutually agreeable terms for social cooperation. How could a political decision based on a particular scriptural tradition be mutually agreeable, as reasonableness requires? One answer is that the decision could be supported by a convergence of views, only some of which are scriptural or religious. Another answer is that, for all PR4 tells us, it *could be* that all citizens embrace the scriptural tradition in question. This result dramatizes the weakness of PR4.

It might be objected that such a reason could not be accepted by nonreligious citizens, given the positions they actually hold. To do so would commit them to inconsistent beliefs. Since it is irrational to be committed to inconsistent beliefs, it is also unreasonable to be committed to inconsistent beliefs because reasonableness entails rationality. Therefore, such religious reasons could not be accepted by many reasonable citizens and so are not public reasons. Public reasons are

PR5. Reasons that could be accepted by all reasonable citizens, given their present positions.

Strictly speaking, PR5 overlooks the difference between the rationality or reasonableness of beliefs and the rationality or reasonableness of persons. We do not consider someone irrational just because there is a belief to which he is irrationally committed. Whether or not a person is rational depends on general patterns among his beliefs or the character of his general dispositions to believe. So someone could be irrationally committed to a belief without thereby being an irrational person. By implication, someone could be irrationally committed to a belief without thereby being an unreasonable citizen. The objection assumes that reasonable nonreligious citizens cannot accept religious reasons that are inconsistent with their other positions. But the mere acceptance of an inconsistent position does not make a person unreasonable.

In light of this qualification, public reasons could be characterized as

PR6. Reasons that could be reasonably accepted by all reasonable citizens, given their present positions.

At this point it is necessary to distinguish between two different sorts of acceptance. When considering what it means for a reason to be acceptable, one can take a *conditional* or an *unconditional* approach. In the broadest sense, this means that for a given reason R that is in question, a political agent A, and a set {P} of additional political reasons that are accepted by reasonable citizens, one can ask whether R is acceptable to A taking {P} into account or whether R is acceptable to A without taking {P} into account. Should public reasons be understood according to the conditional interpretation or the unconditional interpretation?

Unconditional public reason asks whether R is acceptable to all reasonable citizens without asking how they regard R in light of the additional reasons that other reasonable citizens accept. However, some citizens may accept R only if {P} has a particular content. This feature of collective decision making is familiar in simple interpersonal contexts.

Imagine that you and two friends are attempting to decide how to spend the day together. Some of you have clear ideas about where to go and what to do. Others do not. Still others have ideas that depend on the ideas of the rest of the group. You are agreeable to most anything to which the group is agreeable, and so you will adapt to the preferences of the group. For example, if your two friends wish to go to the museum, you will gladly go along. Or suppose one friend leans toward taking a trapeze class, but she will be resolved only after discussing the idea with others and perhaps revising it in light of their ideas. If the conversation reveals that someone in the group is afraid of heights, she may withdraw her suggestion of trapeze. So for each member of the group, acceptance of reasons for particular destinations and activities is conditional on the reasons accepted by others.

The same dynamic can be found in public deliberation and political decision making. There are citizens and organizations whose political reasons are conditional on the reasons advanced by others, and legitimately so. For example, in charitable or religious organizations, professional societies, and labor unions, many individuals wish to take into account the views of their colleagues and peers when forming political opinions. Some will even trust the group's leaders to the extent that on certain issues they will accept whatever political reasons the leaders accept, unless given grounds to do otherwise. For such citizens, acceptance of some politically relevant reasons is clearly conditional on acceptance by other citizens.

More generally, as defenders of "deliberative democracy" have pointed out, the process of political discourse and argumentation sometimes has the effect of transforming citizens' views on the issues. Engaging with other citizens and being confronted with the political reasons they accept can sometimes lead one to change the reasons one accepts. In this way the acceptance or rejection of certain reasons by one citizen can influence the acceptance or rejection of certain reasons by another. No doubt there are citizens who welcome and seek this influence. They consider it an appropriate and important contribution to their thinking about politics and, hence, to their overt political reasoning.

It is obvious that these forms of conditionality of one's political reasons are not uncommon. And from the point of view of the ideal of public reason, it is hard to see what could be objectionable about them. This point can be made apparent by appreciating the fact that the conditional interpretation merely permits the conditionality of some citizens' political reasons. It does not require the conditionality of any. Reasons that are held unconditionally in the present sense are not barred from publicity under such an interpretation. In this way, the conditional interpretation is theoretically modest.

Although the admission of the conditionality of some political reasoning is a modest one, its implications for the theory of public reason are far-reaching. If the acceptability of at least some political reasons depends on whether and how they are introduced into politics, then apart from a particular political discourse and the reasons that are introduced therein, there is no general fact of the matter about whether some reasons are acceptable to all reasonable citizens. It follows that there can be no defensible principle that would preclude from political discourse all of those reasons that are not acceptable to reasonable citizens. The question "May R be advanced in political discourse?" cannot be addressed by asking "Is R acceptable to all reasonable citizens?" for whether R is acceptable to all reasonable citizens depends on whether and how R is advanced in political discourse. Since this result holds for reasons of all sorts, it holds for reasons of conscience.

In summary, given an adequate characterization of public reasons in terms of reasonable acceptance or rejection, there can be no constraint on the introduction of reasons into political discourse. Another way to put this is to say that such reasons cannot be *precluded* from discourse, or ruled out prior to their introduction. However, it is another question whether or not they may be *excluded*, or ruled out subsequent to their introduction.

11. See Stephen L. Carter, *The Culture of Disbelief: How American Law and Politics Trivialize Religious Devotion* (New York: Anchor Books, 1994); Noah Feldman, *Divided by God: America's Church-State Problem and What Should Be Done about It* (New York: Farrar, Straus & Girous, 2005); Philip L. Quinn, "Political Liberalisms and Their Exclusion of the Religious," *Proceedings and Addresses of the American Philosophical Association* 69, no. 2 (1995): 35–56; Richard John Neuhaus, *The Naked Public Square* (Grand Rapids, MI: W. B. Eerdmans Publishing Co., 1986); Paul Weithman, ed., *Religion and Contemporary Liberalism* (Notre Dame, IN: University of Notre Dame Press, 1997).

12. Silver, "The Clash of Biotechnology and Post-Christian Spirituality," *Skeptical Inquirer* 31, no. 2 (March/April 2007): 31–37.

13. Thomas Nagel, "Moral Conflict and Political Legitimacy," *Philosophy & Public Affairs* 16 (1987): 230–32.

14. Benjamin Radford, "Psychic's False Bomb Tip Cancels Flight," *Skeptical Inquirer* 28, no. 4 (July/August 2004): 6.

15. Ibid.

16. Carter, *The Culture of Disbelief*, pp. 21–22.

17. In America, God is always on the ballot. This is an American tradition that did not begin with Bush, or even Jimmy Carter. Woodrow Wilson's internationalism was rooted in a Presbyterian belief that America should "exemplify that devotion of the elements of righteousness which are derived from the revelations of Holy Scripture." (Elizabeth Edwards Spalding, "True Believers," *Wilson Quarterly* [Spring 2006], p. 41). Harry Truman worked to enlist Catholic, Anglican, Lutheran, and Greek Orthodox churches in the cold war, to "mobilize the people who believe in a moral world against the Bolshevik materialists" (Spalding, "True Believers," p. 44). In his 1949 inaugural address, after taking the oath of office on a Bible laid open to the Ten Commandments, Truman intoned that "human freedom is born of the belief that man is created equal in the image of God and therefore capable of governing himself."

In 2003, 64 percent of Americans reported that the religion or irreligion of a candidate for president could determine their vote, even when the candidate is an otherwise well-qualified member of their own party. What's a secular liberal to do, besides insisting (to no avail) that religion be divorced from American electoral politics? While it would be illegal and unconstitutional to impose religious tests for public office, there is nothing illegal or unconstitutional about religious preferences on the part of voters. However, it usually doesn't make much sense to pick candidates by religion. Religious identification is not a good guide to selecting the best public official. Furthermore, it is bad citizenship to support a candidate who makes religion central to his public identity.

The US Constitution forbids religious tests for office. For instance, it cannot be part of the formal eligibility requirements that a candidate is a Christian or a theist. However, most legal scholars agree that voter preferences for candidates of faith do not constitute a religious test, even though they might have the effect of barring an atheist or a Muslim from holding public office, at least at this point in the nation's history. Nevertheless, such preferences are a bad idea. Why?

First, a candidate's religion is often a poor predictor of how he will behave in office and what policies he will pursue. The religion of the 2004 presidential hopefuls was a perfect example. George W. Bush was forthcoming about his Christianity, but it was a highly idiosyncratic, nondoctrinal, and individualistic variety. He told journalist Bob Woodward: "I was praying for strength to do the Lord's will. . . . I pray that I will be as good a messenger of His will as possible" (Bob Woodward, *Plan of Attack* [New York: Simon and Schuster, 2004], p. 379). Bush would simply aim to do God's will, but rely on his own intuitions and judgment—rather than church dogma or clerical leaders—to indicate what God wills. Bush's prophetic management style was unconstrained by any principled religious ethics that voters could have endorsed or rejected in advance.

The result? Policy decisions that would have been difficult to predict on the basis of his denominational background. For instance, Bush disappointed many religious conservatives by constructing a compromise on stem cell research that permitted the destruction of embryos by private researchers. (Is a privately funded murder less criminal than a publicly funded one?) On abortion, Bush spoke up for a "culture of life" but stopped well short of condemning all abortion as murder. And then there was his highly controversial justification of preemptive war, which most denominations opposed. On each of these issues, Christians might well feel that Bush strayed from important teachings of their faith.

A responsible citizen will want to know what a candidate stands for, what he will do in office. To that end, it is better to look at the candidate's record in politics, his party platform, the political philosophy of his advisors, his campaign promises, and so on. In other words, a candidate's values in action are a better predictor of his behavior in office than his religion.

It would be interesting to find out whether American voters care about religion per se when they go to the polls or whether they care about religion as indicator of "moral values," or the kind of person they would like to have dinner with. Some suggestive statistics: The Interfaith Alliance found in 2007 that 68 percent of Americans believe that presidential candidates should not use their religion to influence voters. The Pew Foundation found that 42 percent of Americans said politicians should be guided by religious principles, and 46 percent said "religion and politics don't mix." A 2000 survey by Public Agenda indicated that among those who want religion and politics to mix more, three-quarters don't care which religion it is, only that it's sincere. Meanwhile, Pew showed 64 percent of likely voters saying "moral values" are very important to their vote. Sociologically, the American preference for religious candidates is not necessarily a preference for religious politics.

18. "House Passes Bill for Stem Cell Research," Associated Press, January 11, 2007, http://abcnews.go.com/Politics/wireStory?id=2786588 (accessed July 24, 2007).

19. From a statement by Representative James Langevin. Transcript available at http://www.house.gov/list/speech/ri02_langevin/stmtstemcell veto71906.html (accessed July 24, 2007).

20. Louis Guenin, "Morals and Primordials," *Science* 292, no. 5522 (June 1, 2001), http://www.sciencemag.org/cgi/content/full/292/5522/1659 (accessed July 24, 2007).

3. SPINOZA'S GUIDE TO THEOCRACY

1. Richard Hofstadter, *Anti-Intellectualism in American Life* (New York: Vintage Books, 1962), p. 59.

2. Moses Coit Tyler, quoted in Hofstadter, *Anti-Intellectualism in American Life*, p. 59.

3. In his reporting from Iran, Foucault commented that industrial capitalism was "the harshest, most savage, most selfish, most dishonest, oppressive society one could possibly imagine." Quoted in Kevin Anderson and Janet Afary, *Foucault and the Iranian Revolution* (Chicago: University of Chicago, 2005), p. 75.

4. Plato, *Complete Works*, ed. John M. Cooper (Indianapolis: Hackett Publishing, 1997), pp. 871, 885, 909, 950.

5. Ibid., pp. 716, 728–34.

6. Benedictus de Spinoza, *Theological-Political Treatise*, trans. Samuel Shirley (Indianapolis: Hackett Publishing, 1998), pp. 231–32.

7. Ibid., p. 167.

8. Ibid., p. 157.

9. Ibid., p. 164.

10. Ibid., p. 158.

11. Ibid., p. 164.

12. Ibid., p. 158.

13. Ibid., p. 164.

14. Ibid., pp. 166–67.

15. Ibid., p. 191.

16. Ibid., p. 106.

17. Ibid., pp. 234–35.

18. *Hier stehe ich; ich kann nicht anders.* Scholars dispute whether Luther actually uttered these words or a less pithy but similar comment.

19. Roger Scruton, *Spinoza* (New York: Routledge, 1999), p. 2.

20. Quoted in Henry Kamen, *The Rise of Toleration* (London: Weidenfeld & Nicolson, 1967), pp. 60–61.

21. See Edmund Morgan, *Roger Williams: The Church and the State*, chap. 4 (Fort Worth, TX: Harcourt, 1967).

22. Nancy F. Cott, Jeanne Boydston, Ann Braude, Lori Ginzber, Molly Ladd-Taylor, eds., *Roots of Bitterness: Documents on the Social History of American Women*, 2nd ed. (Lebanon, NH: University Press of New England, 1996), pp. 8–9.

23. John Locke, *A Letter concerning Toleration* (Indianapolis: Hackett Publishing, 1983), p. 36.

24. Nevertheless, Locke insisted that atheists should not be tolerated

because "promises, covenants, and oaths, which are the bonds of human society, can have no hold upon an atheist. The taking away of God, though but even in thought, dissolves all." Locke, *A Letter concerning Toleration*, p. 51.

25. Marsilius, *Defensor Pacis*, trans. Alan Gewirth (New York: Columbia University Press, 1956), p. 164.

26. Quoted by Roland Bainton in his edition of Sebastian Castellio, *Concerning Heretics* (New York: Columbia University Press, 1935), p. 33.

27. Edward Bean Underhill, ed., *Tracts on Liberty of Conscience and Persecution: 1614–1661* (London: Adamant Media Corporation, 2005), p. 17.

28. Locke, *A Letter concerning Toleration*, p. 27.

29. Ibid., pp. 26–27.

30. James Madison, *Memorial and Remonstrance*, ed. Donald L. Drakeman and John Wilson (Westview Press, 2003), p. 64.

31. Ibid., p. 65.

32. Ibid.

33. W. W. Hening, ed., *Statutes at Large of Virginia*, vol. 12 (1823), p. 84.

34. Locke, *A Letter concerning Toleration*, p. 27.

35. In James Harvey Robinson, ed., *Readings in European History: A Collection of Extracts from the Sources Chosen with the Purpose of Illustrating the Progress of Culture in Western Europe since the German Invasions* (Cambridge, MA: Harvard University Press, 1904), pp. 72–73.

36. Salman Rushdie, "Yes, This Is about Islam," *New York Times*, November 2, 2001.

37. The terms are Irshad Manji's. Moderate Muslims "denounce terror that's committed in the name of Islam *but* they deny that religion has anything to do with it," whereas reform-minded Muslims "denounce terror that's committed in the name of Islam *and* acknowledge that our religion is used to inspire it." See Bret Stephens, "Islam's Other Radicals," *Wall Street Journal*, March 6, 2007.

38. Thomas Friedman, "Dinner with the Sayyids," *New York Times*, August 10, 2003.

39. *Kitah al-Zumurrud*, or *The Book of the Emerald*. Discussed in Jennifer Michael Hecht, *Doubt: A History* (San Francisco: HarperCollins, 2004), p. 225.

40. This strategy is taken up in the following chapter.

41. At a meeting sponsored by the Pew Forum on Religion and Public Life, the American Academy of Religion, and the Library of Congress's Kluge Center at the Library of Congress, Washington, DC, November 20, 2006.

42. Michael Ledeen, "Adventuresome Men of Peace," *National Review Online*, June 29, 2007, http://article.nationalreview.com/?q=MTI0MGE3 NWRjZDJlYzBiNWQ1OTQ5MGU5ZDVhOGE1N2M= (accessed July 22, 2007).

43. Jean-Jacques Rousseau, *The Social Contract* (New York: Hafner Publishing Company, 1947), p. viii.

44. Ibid., pp. 123–24.

45. Ibid., p. 124.

46. The most stark example is found in the writings of Machiavelli. A central problem in Machiavelli's political philosophy is the freedom of the city-state from coercion or assault by hostile, external political powers. Machiavelli holds that although revealed religions have no special claim to political authority, religion in general is the best means for inducing citizens to abide by the city's laws. Machiavelli held that "no make of extraordinary laws who did not have recourse to God has ever existed in any society, because these laws would not otherwise be accepted, and because although the good things known to a prudent man are many, these things in themselves lack the self-evident qualities that can persuade others. Wise men who wish, therefore, to avoid this difficulty have recourse to God" (Niccolo Machiavelli, *Discourses on Livy*, trans. Julia Conaway Bondanella and Peter Bondanella [New York: Oxford University Press, 2003], p. 52). The Machiavellian statesman uses religious morality to inculcate civil obedience. Yet he also knows that this morality is strictly false, since Christianity, with its theology of punishments and rewards in the afterworld and its morality of cosmopolitan benevolence, has made Christian nations idle and poor at defending their earthly welfare. The good of the city demands that the conduct of its rulers not be held to the same moral standards as the conduct of citizens. Christianity enjoins universal benevolence and honesty. But the effective statesman is malevolent and deceitful whenever necessary in public affairs. This contradicts the universalism of Christian ethics. So, in order to protect itself, the Machiavellian city-state may have to engineer or reengineer the religious morality of its population.

47. It makes a declaration about what is good or true, and "whether what it takes or declares to be good is actually so, is ascertainable only from the

content of the good it seeks to realize," Hegel observed. "Conscience is therefore subject to the judgment of its truth or falsity, and when it appeals only to itself for a decision, it is directly at variance with what it wishes to be, namely the rule for a mode of conduct which is rational, absolutely valid, and universal." G. W. F. Hegel, *Philosophy of Right*, trans. T. M. Knox (London: Oxford University Press, 1953), pp. 90–91.

48.   I am not here defending the view, rightly attacked by communitarian critics of liberalism, that a person's choices are only worthy of respect when they issue from a self "unencumbered" by any nonnegotiable commitments (of ethnic or religious identity, for example) that in part constitute her as the particular person she is. Indeed, this model of choice is connected to the fallacious understanding of freedom I have been arguing against. By contrast, a coherent liberal account of freedom of conscience, like Spinoza's account, will attach value to judgments that are legally and socially free because such judgments are bound by the intellectual and moral standards that properly govern the conscience. Understood correctly, then, the liberal conscience is free but not unconstrained. Furthermore, liberalism need not suppose that once a religious framework has been adopted freely, the duties entailed by that framework are somehow voluntary in the sense of optional. Neither are the duties entailed by a liberal moral framework experienced as optional by the liberal. Finally, the liberal ideal of freedom of conscience should not be narrowly construed to imply that for your commitment to have been freely adopted there must have been some discrete moment in which a deliberate act of will took place, before which you lacked the commitment and after which you possessed it. Often times we simply find ourselves with a particular commitment. In such cases, being free with respect to that commitment will be a matter of critically reflecting on whether you have reason to retain it, all things considered.

4. WHY THERE ARE NO RELIGIONS OF THE BOOK

1. John Milton, *A Treatise of Civil Power in Ecclesiastical Causes; Showing That It Is Not Lawful for Any Power on Earth to Compel in Matters of Religion*, in *John Milton: Selected Prose*, ed. C. A. Patrides (Columbia: University of Missouri Press, 1985), p. 314.

2. Ibn Warraq, *Which Koran?* (Amherst, NY: Prometheus Books, forthcoming).

3. Michael Cook, *The Qur'an: A Very Short Introduction* (Oxford: Oxford University Press, 2000), p. 88.

4. Patrick Collison, *The Reformation: A History* (New York: Random House, 2004), p. 34.

5. We would experience God directly, just as we experience the world with our ordinary senses. Atheists may not like it, but they cannot deny the possibility of a divine sense without denying the existence of a creator (and that would mean presupposing atheism rather than arguing for it).

6. Some essential reading in reformed epistemology: Alvin Plantinga and Nicholas Wolterstorff, eds., *Faith and Rationality* (Notre Dame, IN: University of Notre Dame Press, 1983); Alvin Plantinga, *Warrant: The Current Debate* (New York: Oxford University Press, 1993); *Warrant and Proper Function* (New York: Oxford University Press, 1993); *Warranted Christian Belief* (New York: Oxford University Press, 2000); Nicholas Wolterstorff, *John Locke and the Ethics of Belief* (Cambridge: Cambridge University Press, 1996); William Alston, *Perceiving God: The Epistemology of Religious Experience* (Ithaca, NY: Cornell University Press, 1991).

7. Richard Gale, "Alvin Plantinga's *Warranted Christian Belief*," *Philo* 4, no. 2 (Fall/Winter 2001): 138–47; "Response to My Critics," *Philo* 6, no. 1 (Summer 2003): 132–65.

8. Robert McKim, *Religious Ambiguity and Religious Diversity* (New York: Oxford University Press, 2001), p. 89.

5. HAS GOD FOUND SCIENCE?

1. Martin M. Hanczyc, Shelly M. Fujikawa, and Jack W. Szostak, "Experimental Models of Primitive Cellular Compartments: Encapsulation, Growth, and Division," *Science* 302 (October 23, 2003): 618.

2. Isaiah 45:9.

3. See *The Blind Watchmaker* (New York: W. W. Norton, 1986).

4. As the research of Russell Doolittle has demonstrated.

5. Kenneth R. Miller, "The Flagellum Unspun: The Collapse of 'Irreducible Complexity,'" in *Debating Design: From Darwin to DNA*, ed.

William A. Dembski and Michael Ruse (Cambridge: Cambridge University Press, 2004), pp. 81–97.

6. Brian Greene, *The Fabric of the Cosmos* (New York: Random House, 2004), p. 272.

7. In John Polkinghorne, *Science and Creation: The Search for Understanding* (Boston: New Science Library; New York: Random House, 1989), p. 22.

8. For additional responses, see Victor Stenger, *God: The Failed Hypothesis* (Amherst, NY: Prometheus Books, 2007).

9. Martin Rees, *Before the Beginning: Our Universe and Others* (New York: Perseus Books, 1997), pp. 253–55.

10. Charles Taylor makes a related point in *A Secular Age*. For Taylor, the advent of the secular age "takes us from a society in which it was virtually impossible not to believe in God, to one in which faith, even for the staunchest believer, is one human possibility among others. . . . Belief in God is no longer axiomatic. There are alternatives. And this will also likely mean that at least in certain milieux, it may be hard to sustain one's faith." (*A Secular Age* [Cambridge, MA: Harvard University Press, 2007], p. 3.)

11. Stephen J. Gould, *Rock of Ages: Science and Religion in the Fullness of Life* (New York: Ballantine Publishing Group, 1999).

12. Ibid., p. 175.

13. Sometimes science hits upon unanticipated methods of inquiry. A recent colorful example comes from the field of hyperbolic geometry. Hyperbolic geometry, created in the 1820s and '30s, studies certain kinds of spaces and objects that don't obey Euclidian assumptions. A hyperbolic plane, for example, is a counterintuitive surface in which the space curves away from itself at every point. Since the 1950s, geometers had been trying to construct models of hyperbolic spaces but with limited success. Many believed it impossible, until Daina Taimina came along. Taimina, then a mathematician at Cornell University, made a discovery in the handicraft she had learned as a girl in her native Latvia: crocheting. In 1997, she crocheted the first usable model of a hyperbolic space. Together with her Cornell colleague and husband, David Henderson, she wrote up the results and submitted them to the journal *Mathematical Intelligencer*. According to Taimina, the editors' response was something like, "You want us to publish *what*? A sewing pattern?" Of course, it was the first time that crocheting directions had been submitted to a peer-reviewed math journal. But after some correspondence with

the authors, the editors became convinced that this method of modeling could lead to new developments in the field. In fact, Taimina's technique has already proved useful to some research in cosmology.

14. As Paul Draper puts it in "Comments on *World without Design*," *Philo* 7, no. 2 (Fall/Winter 2007):

> The tendency to favor naturalistic explanations emerged gradually over a long period of time. . . . In very many cases, a little investigation reveals natural causes for natural events, even unusual ones. Thus, it follows inductively that, prior to investigation, the probability that the proximate causes of any given natural event are themselves natural is high. . . . Science, however, has added greatly to the strength of this presumption of naturalism. In many cases in which no naturalistic explanation seemed particularly promising, sufficient effort in searching for one turned out to bear fruit.

> The reason scientists should not look for supernatural causes is that natural causes are much more likely to be found. A methodological naturalism justified in this way is "modest" because it implies that scientists should look *first* for naturalistic explanations, and (depending on how strong the presumption of naturalism is) maybe second, third, and fourth too, but it does not absolutely rule out appeals to the supernatural. We can state this more modest methodological naturalism in the form of the principle that scientific explanations may appeal to the supernatural only as a last resort.

> It does not imply that an appeal to the supernatural is justified simply because scientists fail after much effort to find a naturalistic explanation for some phenomenon. Very strong reasons to believe there is no *hidden* naturalistic explanation would be required as well. In other words, the search for natural causes should continue until the best explanation of the failure to find one is that there is none.

15. What if theism were true and there is a supernatural person who created and sustains the cosmos? If this being has acted at all in the history of the cosmos, then our best efforts to understand that history (why the actual universe exists rather than another kind of universe, or rather than "nothing,"

or why humans possess consciousness, for instance) would have to make reference to its actions. If the sciences were barred in principle from invoking the behavior of supernatural persons, then they would be incapable of explaining these important features of the cosmos. But surely we should want a science that can help us to understand such interesting things, *even in case theism is true.*

16. Something similar has been suggested by Alvin Plantinga.

17. To put the argument succinctly: Suppose it were true, and known to theology, that God created humans; and suppose it were also true, and known to science, that humans are mildly polygamous primates. It would follow logically that God created mildly polygamous primates. The statement *God created mildly polygamous primates* is every bit as theological in character than the statement *God created humans.* In fact, it may have theological implications that *God created humans* does not have. Clearly, the claim postulates a supernatural entity. Nevertheless, it would be a theological statement that we have a scientific reason to adopt (relative to a background belief that God created humans). This is so despite the fact that *humans are mildly polygamous primates* postulates only natural things and processes. Scientific knowledge can have theological implications even if scientific knowledge neither affirms nor denies anything supernatural.

18. This marvelous metaphor was introduced by Harry M. Collins and Trevor Pinch, *The Golem: What You Should Know about Science* (Cambridge: Cambridge University Press, 1998).

6. DARWIN MADE ME DO IT

1. Charles Darwin, *The Descent of Man and Selection in Relation to Sex,* 2nd ed. (New York: D. Appleton and Company, 1909), p. 623.

2. Adrian Desmond and James Moore, *Darwin: The Life of a Tormented Evolutionist* (New York: W. W. Norton, 1991), p. 581.

3. Jon H. Roberts, *Darwinism and the Divine in America: Protestant Intellectuals and Organic Evolution: 1859–1900* (Notre Dame, IN: Notre Dame University Press, 1998), p. 115. These arguments remain especially popular among Protestant intellectuals. William Lane Craig, a philosopher and influential Christian apologist, argues:

If atheism is true, objective moral values do not exist. If God does not exist, then what is the foundation for moral values? More particularly, what is the basis for the value of human beings? If God does not exist, then it is difficult to see any reason to think that human beings are special or that their morality is objectively true. Moreover, why think that we have any moral obligations to do anything? Who or what imposes any moral duties upon us? . . . If there is no God, then any ground for regarding the herd morality evolved by homo sapiens as objectively true seems to have been removed. After all, what is so special about human beings? They are just accidental by-products of nature which have evolved relatively recently on an infinitesimal speck of dust lost somewhere in a hostile and mindless universe and which are doomed to perish individually and collectively in a relatively short time. Some action, say, incest, may not be biologically or socially advantageous and so in the course of human evolution has become taboo; but there is on the atheistic view nothing really wrong about committing incest. (William Lane Craig, "The Indispensibility of Theological Meta-ethical Foundations for Morality," http://www.leaderu.com/offices/billcraig/docs/meta-eth .html, [accessed January 9, 2007])

4. Charles Darwin, *The Autobiography of Charles Darwin, 1809– 1882: With Original Omissions Restored* (New York: W. W. Norton, 1993), p. 90. Maybe such suffering is permitted by God for good reasons that we finite, imperfect beings cannot know. Then again, one can just as easily imagine that there is a being who permits the good things that occasionally happen in our world because they ultimately serve a higher evil, which we cannot know. Maybe every silver lining has a cloud, and every success is necessary to bring about failure on a grander scale. We have no reason to believe that there are any such unknowable evils, but we have no less reason to believe in them than to believe in unknowable goods. The insistence that there must be such goods is merely an attempt to save the hypothesis of a perfectly good God from refutation at all costs, not a rational response to any independent reasons.

5. Darwin, *The Descent of Man*, p. 625.

6. Michael Ruse, "Evolutionary Theory and Christian Ethics," in *The Darwinian Paradigm* (London: Routledge, 1989), pp. 262–69.

7. Elliott Sober, *From a Biological Point of View: Essays in Evolutionary Philosophy* (Cambridge: Cambridge University Press, 1994), pp. 18–19.

8. Elliott Sober and David Sloan Wilson, *Unto Others: The Evolution and Psychology of Unselfish Behavior* (Cambridge, MA: Harvard University Press, 1998).

9. I believe Michael McKean once put it that way.

10. Cara Buckley, "A Man Down, a Train Arriving, and a Stranger Makes a Choice," *New York Times*, January 3, 2007.

11. See Robert Axelrod, *The Evolution of Cooperation*, rev. ed. (New York: Perseus Books, 2006); Matt Ridley, *The Origins of Virtue: Human Instincts and the Evolution of Cooperation* (New York: Viking, 1997); Brian Skyrms, *Evolution of the Social Contract* (Cambridge: Cambridge University Press, 1996); Robert Wright, *Nonzero: The Logic of Human Destiny* (New York: Pantheon, 2000).

12. See Frans de Waal, *Primates and Philosophers: How Morality Evolved* (Princeton, NJ: Princeton University Press, 2006); *Good Natured: The Origins of Right and Wrong in Humans and Other Animals* (Cambridge, MA: Harvard University Press, 1996).

13. See Jerome H. Barkow, Leda Cosmides, John Tooby, eds., *The Adapted Mind: Evolutionary Psychology and the Generation of Culture* (New York: Oxford University Press, 1992). For critical discussion, see Dan Sperber and Vittorio Girotto, "Does the Selection Task Detect Cheater-Detection?" in *From Mating to Mentality: Evaluating Evolutionary Psychology*, ed. Kim Sterelny and Julie Fitness (New York: Psychology Press, 2003), pp. 197–226.

14. M. Iacoboni, I. Molnar-Szakacs, V. Gallese, G. Buccino, J. C. Mazziotta et al., "Grasping the Intentions of Others with One's Own Mirror Neuron System," *Public Library of Science Biology* 3, no. 3 (2005), http://dx.doi.org/10.1371/journal.pbio.0030079 (accessed July 25, 2007).

15. Daniel Dennett, *Freedom Evolves* (New York: Penguin, 2003), p. 247.

16. Ibid.

17. Ibid., p. 248.

18. Daniel M. Wegner, *The Illusion of Conscious Will* (Cambridge, MA: MIT Press, 2002), p. 326.

19. Ibid., p. 325.

20. Dennett, *Freedom Evolves*, p. 251.

21. David Hume, *Dialogues concerning Natural Religion* (New York: Penguin Classics, 1990), p. 105. The passage reaches its climax with this: "The whole presents nothing but the idea of a blind Nature, impregnated by a great vivifying principle, and pouring forth from her lap, without discernment or parental care, her maimed and abortive children!" (p. 121).

22. Desmond and Moore, *Darwin*, p. 329.

23. Thomas Henry Huxley, *Evolution & Ethics and Other Essays* (London: Macmillan and Co., 1894), pp. 81–82.

24. Sometimes in order to make the case for specific ethical claims, the evolutionary ethicist abruptly stops citing scientific literature and starts invoking moral principles. Consider Michael Shermer's discussion of the abortion controversy, which he encapsulates like this: "Pro-lifers want to make it a political moral issue in which the rights of the fetus take precedence over the rights of the mother so that society determines what a woman can or cannot do with her body and her fetus. Can science help settle this dispute?" (*The Science of Good and Evil: Why People Cheat, Gossip, Care, Share, and Follow the Golden Rule* [New York: Henry Holt, 2003], p. 203). He begins by suggesting that science can settle the dispute because the dispute is, in the end, a factual one: "Pro-lifers and pro-choicers all agree that murder is immoral. What they disagree about is whether aborting a fetus constitutes murder." The apparently moral question is actually a factual question because abortion constitutes murder only if it involves killing a human being:

> Of all the characteristics used to define what it means to be human, the capacity to think is provisionally agreed upon by most scientists to be the most important. By this criterion, since virtually no abortions are performed after the second trimester, and before then there is no scientific evidence that the fetus is a thinking human individual, it is reasonable for us to provisionally agree that abortion is not murder and to offer our provisional assent that abortions within the first two trimesters are not immoral because the evidence confirms that during this time the fetus is not a fully functioning human being. (p. 205)

Of course, as Shermer realizes, no sane antiabortionists assert that an early fetus is a fully functioning human being. What they argue is that as a member of the human species, or as a potential human person, a fetus ought to be accorded the same moral status and consideration as a human person. Now it becomes necessary to turn to moral principles.

> I believe that we can discern the difference between right and wrong through three principles. (1) The ask first principle: to find out whether an action is right or wrong, ask first. (2) The happiness principle: it is a higher moral principle to always seek happiness with someone else's happiness in mind, and never seek happiness when it leads to someone else's unhappiness. (3) The liberty principle: it is a higher moral principle to always seek liberty with someone else's liberty in mind, and never seek liberty when it leads to someone else's loss of liberty. To implement social change, the moderation principle states that when innocent people die, extremism in the defense of anything is no virtue, and moderation in the protection of everything is no vice. (p. 252)

The first thing to note about these principles is that they have nothing whatever to do with evolutionary science. The second thing to note is that it is altogether unclear how they are to be applied to this case. Who do we "ask first" about the permissibility of abortion?

> We cannot first ask a fetus if it would like to be aborted or not; we can, however, run that thought experiment by imagining ourselves in the position of an unborn potential human who would be granted personhood rights and dignity value upon birth. Presumably, most of us would choose life. By the ask first principle, we would have to conclude that abortion is immoral. However, although asking the unborn can never be more than a thought experiment, there is someone we can ask first, and that is the pregnant woman. . . . Given the choice between asking the fetus in a thought experiment and actually asking the woman what she thinks should be done, it is logical to give the moral nod to the woman. (p. 207)

Is it just a matter of logic that the interests of those we can ask take precedence over those we cannot ask? Certainly we are under no obligation whatever to first ask an abusive pet owner about the moral permissibility of his abuse, just because his victim can't speak for itself. Shermer also deploys the Liberty Principle in support of the permissibility of abortion:

> One of the most important sources of freedom and autonomy for women has been control over their bodies, especially in relation to reproduction. . . . To take away an important source of reproductive control from women by outlawing abortion would be a significant step backward in the historical trajectory of liberty. Thus, given the choice between increasing the liberty of an adult person and the liberty of an unborn fetus, it makes more sense—historically, legally, logically, and morally—to grant that liberty to the adult person, the woman. (p. 208)

Increasing the liberty of woman makes more sense than increasing the liberty of the unborn because there is already a *trend* of increasing liberty among women? That principle would not have served well those whose moral claims for liberty didn't take place against a backdrop of an existing trend toward liberty—enslaved peoples, for example.

More to the point, why should anyone accept Shermer's Ask First Principle or Liberty Principle? Whatever can be said about the reasons, strictly scientific they are not. The Moderation Principle seems only "reasonable," but that is because it asserts nothing of substance: "When innocent people die, extremism in the defense of anything is no virtue, and moderation in the protection of everything is no vice" (p. 208). In the end, Shermer concludes that "abortion remains a personal moral choice" (p. 208).

25. See the work of Michael McCloskey and his colleagues (e.g., Caramazza et al., 1981; McCloskey and Kohl, 1983; McCloskey et al., 1980).

26. Marc Hauser, "Basic Instinct" *Science & Spirit* 17, no. 4 (July/August 2006), http://www.science-spirit.org/printerfriendly.php?article _id=645 (accessed July 25, 2007). See also *Moral Minds: How Nature Designed Our Universal Sense of Right and Wrong* (San Francisco: Ecco/ HarperCollins, 2007).

27. Hauser, "Basic Instinct."

28. Marc Hauser and Peter Singer, "Morality without Religion," *Free Inquiry* 26, no. 1 (December/January 2006): 18–19.

29. Desmond and Moore, *Darwin*, p. 662.

7. ORIGINAL VIRTUE

1. Gabriel Kahn and Alessandra Galloni, "In Choosing Pope, Church Stakes Future on Its Base: German Cardinal Ratzinger, Now Benedict XVI, Is a Champion of Doctrine: A Life Combating Secularism," *Wall Street Journal*, April 20, 2005. Adapted from my op-ed "Believing in Doubt," *New York Times*, February 3, 2006.

2. The expression is Ibn Warraq's.

3. "On the Priesthood and Those with Homosexual Tendencies," http://www.catholicculture.org/library/view.cfm?recnum=6717 (accessed July 22, 2007).

4. John Allen, *Cardinal Ratzinger: The Vatican's Enforcer of the Faith* (New York: Continuum, 2000).

5. Sam Harris, in *The End of Faith: Religion, Terror, and the Future of Reason* (New York: W. W. Norton, 2004), calls for a stance toward religious faith he terms "conversational intolerance": we should not pass over in silence the irrational utterances of others just because they are religious utterances. Harris's conversational intolerance is an attempt to change others' minds, animated by a sense of the moral urgency of diminishing the social impact of religious unreason.

6. Timothy O'Connell explains in "An Understanding of Conscience," in *Conscience: Readings in Moral Theology*, vol. 14, ed. Charles E. Curran (Mahwah, NJ: Paulist Press, 2004), pp. 25–26:

> Traditional moral theology distinguished between *synderesis* and *syneidesis*, claiming that these two terms and ideas were to be found in Scripture itself. By *synderesis* they understood the habit of conscience, the basic sense of responsibility that characterizes the human person. And by *syneidesis* they understood the act of conscience, the judgement by which we evaluate a particular action. . . . The term *syneidesis* is clearly present in Scripture. But what of *synderesis*? The simple and embarrassing fact is that this term does not appear in Scripture. Indeed, there is no such word in the Greek language. Rather, it appears that this entire theological tradition is the result of a massive error.
>
> As nearly as we can tell, it was St. Jerome who first alleged the existence of these two different words for conscience. In preparing

the first Latin text of the Bible, Jerome was apparently working from a Greek manuscript that was not altogether legible. He had to deal with selections where the topic was clearly conscience but the word did not appear to be "*syneidesis*" but rather "*synderisis*." Jerome studied the text and thought he detected differing nuances when one or the other word was used. Thus he concluded that the latter must simply be a Greek word with which he was unfamiliar, a word being used to make a very specific point. But recent scholarship has made clear that Jerome was wrong. There are not two words in Greek for conscience, but only one.

7. Søren Kierkegaard, *Fear and Trembling*, trans. Walter Lowrie (New York: Doubleday, 1955), p. 67.

8. Ibid., p. 69.

9. Wing-Tsit Chan, trans. and ed., *A Source Book in Chinese Philosophy* (Princeton, NJ: Princeton University Press, 1963), pp. 75–77.

10. *Gaudium Et Spes* (Pastoral Constitution on the Church in the Modern World), Promulgated By His Holiness, Pope Paul VI, December 7, 1965, chap. 1, no. 16, http://www.vatican.va/archive/hist_councils/ii _vatican_council/documents/vat-ii_cons_19651207_gaudium-et-spes_en .html (accessed July 22, 2007).

11. Outspoken secularists are often asked why they don't run amok, cheating, stealing, or murdering to maximize their own self-interest in what they take to be a godless universe. Historian Susan Jacoby likes to answer, "You know, it honestly never occurred to me to murder anyone!" Personal communication.

12. Walter Isaacson, "In Search of the Real Bill Gates," *Time*, January 13, 1997, p. 44.

13. The most generous is the Netherlands. This according to the Commitment to Development Index 2006, an annual ranking produced by the Center for Global Development and published in *Foreign Affairs*. The finding that Denmark is the happiest country comes from a global survey of eighty thousand by Adrian White at the University of Leicester. See "Denmark 'Happiest Place on Earth,'" BBC News Online, July 28, 2006, http:// news.bbc.co.uk/2/hi/health/5224306.stm (accessed June 30, 2007). As Sam Harris points out, the least religious societies in the world "are also the healthiest, as indicated by life expectancy, adult literacy, per capita income,

educational attainment, gender equality, homicide rate, and infant mortality"
(*Letter to a Christian Nation* [New York: Knopf, 2006], p. 43). Harris notes
that there is no easy way to infer cause-and-effect relationships from the correlations in such a broad sea of data: "Leaving aside the issue of cause and
effect, however, these statistics prove that atheism is compatible with the
basic aspirations of a civil society; they also prove, conclusively, that widespread belief in God does not ensure a society's health" (p. 45).

14. From the Barna Research Group, part of a larger organization committed to facilitating "spiritual transformation in America," http://www
.barna.org/FlexPage.aspx?Page=BarnaUpdateNarrowPreview&Barna
UpdateID=273 (accessed June 30, 2007).

15. Consider the well-known "bystander effect": the more bystanders
observing a person in distress, the less likely any one of them will be to help.
But bystanders consistently report that the number of bystanders has no
effect on their decision not to help.

16. See Stephen Law, *The War for Children's Minds* (New York: Routledge, 2006).

17. See Dierdre N. McCloskey, *The Bourgeois Virtues: Ethics for an
Age of Commerce* (Chicago: University of Chicago Press, 2006).

8. THE SEARCH FOR THE THEORY OF EVERYONE

1. David Hume, *An Enquiry concerning the Principles of Morals: A
Critical Edition*, ed. Tom Beauchamp (New York: Oxford University, 2006),
p. 75:

> When a man denominates another his enemy, his rival, his antago-
> nist, his adversary, he is understood to speak the language of self-
> love, and to express sentiments, peculiar to himself, and arising from
> his particular circumstances and situation. But when he bestows on
> any man the epithets of vicious or odious or depraved, he then
> speaks another language, and expresses sentiments, in which, he
> expects, all his audience are to concur with him. He must here, there-
> fore, depart from his private and particular situation, and must
> choose a point of view, common to him with others: He must move

some universal principle of the human frame, and touch a string, to which all mankind have an accord and symphony.

2. Peter Railton, *Facts, Values, and Norms* (Cambridge, MA: Cambridge University Press, 2003), p. 21.

3. J. L. Mackie, *Ethics: Inventing Right and Wrong* (New York: Penguin, 1977), p. 40.

4. Ibid., p. 38.

5. Neo-Kantian philosopher Christine Korsgaard had this to say about Mackie's argument from queerness: "Of course there are entities that meet these criteria. It's true that they are queer sorts of entities and that knowing them isn't like anything else. But that doesn't mean that they don't exist. . . . For it is the most familiar fact of human life that the world contains entities that can tell us what to do and make us do it. They are people, and the other animals." Christine Korsgaard, *The Sources of Normativity* (Cambridge, MA: Cambridge University Press, 1996), p. 166.

6. Philip Pettit and Michael Smith, "Freedom in Belief and Desire," *Journal of Philosophy* 93, no. 9 (September 1996): 429–49.

7. Simon Blackburn, *Being Good: A Short Introduction to Ethics* (New York: Oxford University Press, 2001), p. 129.

8. Ibid., p. 130.

9. German philosopher and social theorist Jürgen Habermas captures the practice of reasoning together in his "theory of communicative action." Habermas says we engage in communicative action when we use language to coordinate our interaction by rationally bringing about an agreement regarding a course of action, a belief, an evaluation, or an expression of an attitude or feeling. Agreement is rationally brought about in the sense that it is brought about by the recognition of claims or implicit claims that would rationally warrant the action, belief, evaluation, or expression. Habermas calls these "validity claims" and divides them into three sorts. There are claims to truth, which concern matters of fact; claims to rightness, which concern norms; and claims to truthfulness or sincerity, which concern expressions of one's attitude or feeling. Insofar as people "wish to coordinate their action through understanding rather than force or manipulation, they implicitly take on the burden of redeeming claims they raise to others regarding the truth of what they say, its normative rightness, and its sincerity" (quoted in Stephen K. White, "Reason, Modernity, and Democracy," in *The Cambridge*

Companion to Habermas, ed. Stephen K. White [Cambridge: Cambridge University Press, 1995], p. 7).

Habermas contrasts communicative action with "strategic action." He says that whereas in strategic action "one actor seeks to *influence* the behavior of another by means of the threat of sanction or the prospect of gratification in order to *cause* the interaction to continue as the first actor desires, in communicative action one actor seeks *rationally* to *motivate* another." *Moral Consciousness and Communicative Action*, trans. Shierry Weber Nicholsen and Christian Lenhardt (Cambridge, MA: MIT Press, 1992), p. 58.

Imagine that you and I are planning to meet for breakfast tomorrow morning. We each sincerely express our preferences concerning the restaurant at which we would like to meet. I advise you, as I believe to be true, that the restaurant you have selected will be closed tomorrow morning. In light of this, you sincerely opt for the restaurant I have selected and we sincerely agree to meet there. This is a (noncontroversial) instance of communicative action because (1) we coordinate our interaction by the mutual use of language; (2) we each forego deceit, manipulation, and coercion; but instead (3) seek to rationally motivate the other by offering redeemable validity claims, in this case claims to truth about the restaurants in question and claims to truthfulness or sincerity about our preferences and intentions.

Habermas stresses that communicative actions are not limited to cases where the claims are actually valid: "The fact that a speaker can rationally motivate a hearer to accept such an offer is due not to the validity of what he says but to the speaker's guarantee that he will, if necessary, make efforts to redeem the claim that the hearer has accepted" (*Moral Consciousness and Communicative Action*, p. 58). It is this guarantee of redeemability, and not redeemability itself, that effects the coordination between speaker and hearer. My claim that a certain restaurant will be closed tomorrow may or may not be correct, but it can rationally motivate you because of our mutual assumption that I would attempt to redeem the claim if necessary.

The theory of the conversational stance defended above is not the theory of the "ideal speech situation" defended by Habermas, and "discourse ethics" more broadly. This is so, first because the conversational stance need not presuppose the substantial moral ideals that characterize Habermas's ideal speech situation. By engaging in conversation, one does not necessarily endorse the moral equality of one's conversation partners. Second, the publicity condition of the conversational stance is much weaker, and therefore, far more attainable in actual discourse. There is no assumption that all the reasons advanced in conversation will be acceptable to all conversation partners, but only that they are open to the evaluation of all. Finally, discourse ethics is often put forward as a foundational theory of morality. The conversational stance, as I am using it, is not a moral theory but an account of the norms that people implicitly accept when they converse in public.

10. Blackburn, *Being Good*, p. 131.

11. David Brink, "Moral Realism and the Sceptical Arguments from Disagreement and Queerness," *Australasian Journal of Philosophy* 62 (1984): 111–25.

9. ETHICS FROM BELOW

1. J. S. Mill, *On Liberty and Other Writings*, ed. Stefan Collini (Cambridge, MA: Cambridge University Press, 1989), p. 13.

2. It is a subject of scholarly controversy whether Mill is best interpreted as a subjectivist or an objectivist. Although I think he is best interpreted as a kind of objectivist, I won't enter into that controversy here. For present purposes, it is enough to show that in Mill's philosophy of liberalism one can find resources for objectivity about ethics.

3. Mill, *On Liberty*, p. 76.

4. Ibid., p. 13 (emphasis mine).

5. Ibid., p. 62.

6. Ibid., p. 68.

7. Ronald Dworkin, *Is Democracy Possible Here?* (Princeton, NJ: Princeton University Press, 2006), p. 12.

8. Ibid., p. 13.

9. This discussion comes from Peter Railton, *Facts, Values, and Norms* (Cambridge, MA: Cambridge University Press, 2003).

10. Ibid., p. 11.

11. Notice that Railton is not putting forward a definition of the meaning of the word *goodness* in a way that would run afoul of the so-called naturalistic fallacy. According to G. E. Moore's famous "Open Question Argument" in his *Principia Ethica* (1903), for any natural property we attempt to equate with *goodness*, we can ask, "Is that property really good?" For example, if I

claim that pleasure is the highest intrinsic good, the question can be asked, "But, is pleasure actually good?" The fact that this question makes sense shows that *pleasure* and *goodness* are not identical concepts. Compare the question: "But, is this bachelor really an unmarried man of marriageable age?" This question is nonsensical because *bachelor* and *unmarried man of marriageable age* mean the same thing.

Railton and other contemporary metaethical naturalists respond that their naturalism is synthetic rather than analytic, where analytic naturalism aims show that a moral term *means* the same thing as a natural term, and synthetic naturalism aims to show that a moral property *is in fact* the same thing as a natural property. In the same way, *the morning star* and *the evening star* have different meanings although they refer to the same object, the planet Venus, which is visible in the morning and the evening. See also Geoffrey Sayre-McCord, "Introduction: The Many Moral Realisms," in *Essays in Moral Realism*, ed. Geoffrey Sayre-McCord (Ithaca, NY: Cornell University Press, 1988), pp. 1–23; Richard N. Boyd, "How to Be a Moral Realist," in *Essays in Moral Realism*, ed. Geoffrey Sayre-McCord, pp. 181–228.

12. Adam Smith, *The Glasgow Edition of the Works and Correspondence of Adam Smith* (Oxford: Oxford University Press, 1976), pp. 571–72.

13. Smith held the chair of moral philosophy at the University of Glasgow beginning in 1752.

14. Adam Smith, *The Theory of Moral Sentiments*, ed. D. D. Raphael and A. L. Macfie (Indianapolis: Liberty Fund, Inc., 1982), pp. 134–35.

15. Ibid., p. 135.

16. Ibid., p. 137.

17. I do not mean to suggest that Smith was a utilitarian. Smith writes that the deliverances of conscience are such that they will tend to produce the most happiness, but it is not clear that promoting happiness is meant to serve as a criterion of rightness, and if so, what its relation would be to the judgments of the spectator: "By acting according to the dictates of our moral faculties, we necessarily pursue the most effectual means for promoting the happiness of mankind" (Ibid., p. 166).

18. In characterizing consequentialism, I mean to remain neutral between so-called "maximizing" and "satisficing" versions, which continue to be debated in the literature. Satisficing consequentialism holds that an option can be best even if it doesn't maximize the good, so long as it produces enough good. There are many forms of consequentialism, but the most

famous example is called utilitarianism, the theory of ethics developed by Jeremy Bentham, John Stuart Mill, and Henry Sidgwick. Classical utilitarianism holds that an action is right when it maximizes pleasure; that is, when the value of happiness for all minus the unhappiness for all resulting from the action is greater than the value of any other action available to the actor. Mill spoke not only of the "lower" forms of physical pleasure but also the "higher" pleasures of conversation, art, and professional attainment. The utilitarian doctrine was a potentially radically egalitarian one ("everyone counts for one, and no one more than one") and it spurred early nineteenth-century British social reforms aimed at raising the conditions of the dispossessed, women, the poor, and animals. Although it is the best known, utilitarianism is only one species of consequentialism in ethics.

Consequentialism's account of moral normativity coheres well with the dominant view of rational or prudential normativity, or so-called instrumental rationality. This is noteworthy because many leading moral theories claim that there is some kind of intimate link between rationality and morality. According to instrumentalism about rationality, the prudent thing to do is choose the best means to one's ends; that is, efficiently to promote one's own good. Nonconsequentialist accounts must explain why this extremely attractive approach to prudential goods—promoting them— cannot be extended to moral goods.

Despite the irresistability of consequentialism's basic insight (or perhaps because of it), it has many critics. According to its critics, consequentialism has counterintuitive, even incredible, implications. For it cannot prevent justice and individual rights from being trammeled and lost in the pursuit of the good. Consider any two actions, A and B, that are exactly equal in their potential to promote the good. Suppose A involves causing a significant injustice, such as punishing someone for a crime he didn't commit. In spite of this, it seems, consequentialism must hold that A and B are morally equivalent, since the consequences of each are—by hypothesis—equally good. Surely something is wrong here. Our reflective moral judgments, and the accumulated ethical wisdom of humanity, tell us that there are certain things that we may not do to others even if doing them would bring about a desirable result. People have rights, and we have corresponding duties to respect those rights. These duties are not to be weighed against other values that we could promote by violating them. Torture, on this view, is abhorrent because it violates individual rights and dignity, not because on balance it produces undesirable consequences. Our duty not to torture is not balanced against anything. It acts as a constraint on what may or may not be balanced. Consequentialism, it seems, fails to capture this dimension of our ordinary moral experience.

Another objection against consequentialism is that it is *impracticable*. The consequences of our actions are often highly unpredictable, so how can they serve as the criterion by which we morally evaluate our options? More troubling is a problem Daniel Dennett has called the Three Mile Island Effect. Events have causal repercussions extending indefinitely into the future, so whether they promote the consequentialist's favorite goods may be dependent on the future point at which one surveys those effects (consider the possibility that the Three Mile Island disaster eventually had the effect of improving the safety of America's energy supply and preventing similar disasters). How far into the future does consequentialism count, and why?

Similarly, consequentialism has also been indicted as being *too demanding*. By treating everyone's good as equal, it asks the moral agents to overlook their special obligations to those with whom they have special relationships, such as children or spouses. Although one of two people caught in a burning building might be your daughter and the other might be a stranger to you, the consequentialist analysis appears incapable of accommodating the intuition that you have more reason to save your daughter than the stranger. Also, as philosophers such as Peter Singer, Peter Unger, and Tom Regan have argued, consequentialist ethics go much further than traditional ethics in obligating us to act on behalf of others' good; for example, by assisting faraway people suffering from famine or preventable disease, or foregoing the unnecessary consumption of animals for food or research. A common reaction to such suggestions is that morality simply cannot require that much of us.

Consequentialists have pursued two different general strategies in response to these objections. One strategy is to "bite the bullet" and insist that the counterintuitive results of consequentialism, in view of its various theoretical advantages, do not give us reasons to reject the theory, but instead give us reasons to revise our conventional moral outlooks. If the most plausible moral theory offered turns out to be "too demanding" or "unjust" by the lights of conventional ethics, so much the worse for conventional ethics.

The other strategy is to distinguish between *direct* and *indirect* consequentialism, which can be appreciated by grasping the difference between a decision procedure and a criterion of rightness. A decision procedure is a pattern of reasoning or psychological disposition that tends to result in right action. A criterion of rightness states what makes it the case that an action is right. Consequentialisms contain an account of *what a right action consists in*—bringing about more good than any of the available options (or on "satisficing" versions, bringing about enough good). But consequentialisms can also contain accounts of *how to decide which action is right* (for a particular kind of agent in a particular situation). Given the cognitive and affective constraints of human nature and circumstance (such as highly imperfect knowledge of the probable results of our actions or certain kinds of emotional bias), there may be many situations in which we will be worse at promoting the good to the extent that we deliberately attempt to promote the good. By analogy, although the criterion for promoting a financial asset might be net investment returns over time, the best decision procedure might be selecting an annuity with a diverse portfolio.

One of the remarkable things about consequentialism is its theoretical flexibility with respect to decision procedures, which, like everything else in a consequentialist universe, are subject to evaluation in terms of their overall effect. This flexibility is exploited in defenses against the above objections. For example, it can be argued that we can best promote certain goods indirectly by recognizing some constraining rights or according special weight to the interests of one's friends and relatives. Indirect consequentialism is not the same as so-called rule consequentialism. Rule consequentialism is an alternative criterion of rightness: it says that right actions are those that comply with general rules whose adoption promotes the good. Therefore rule consequentialism generates conflicts with consequentialism as such, which looks at whether each action maximizes. Indirect consequentialism likewise evaluates any given action on whether it maximizes. It just denies that the action will be successful only by aiming at maximizing. Considerable work in ethics is now being devoted to articulating a defensible indirect consequentialism. (This material is reprinted from Austin Dacey, "Consequentialism," *Encyclopedia of Unbelief* [Amherst, NY: Prometheus Books, 2007]).

19. "It is thus that the general rules of morality are formed. They are ultimately founded upon experience of what, in particular instances, our moral faculties, our natural sense of merit and propriety, approve, or disapprove of." Smith, *The Theory of Moral Sentiments*, p. 159.

10. THE UMMA AND THE COMMUNITY OF CONSCIENCE

1. The speech was delivered in Persian. The translation provided by the Iranian delegation appears in the official records of the United Nations General Assembly, Fifty-third Session, document no. A/53/PV.8, p. 6, http://www.un.org/documents/a53pv8.pdf (accessed July 25, 2007).

2. "Annex to the Letter Dated 15 October 2001 from the Permanent Representative of China to the United Nations Addressed to Secretary General: Summary of the 'Twenty-first Century Forum—Symposium on Dialogue among Civilizations,' Hosted by the External Committee of the Chinese People's Political Consultative Conference," http://www.un.org/documents/a56471.pdf (accessed July 25, 2007).

3. Amir Taheri, "Lies They Loved at Harvard," *New York Post*, September 13, 2006, http://www.nypost.com/seven/09132006/postopinion/opedcolumnists/lies_they_loved_at_harvard_opedcolumnists_amir_taheri.htm (accessed September 13, 2006).

4. Shawn Macomber, "Show Me the Money (Quote), Khatami!" *American Spectator*, September 11, 2006, http://www.spectator.org/dsp_article.asp?art_id=10339 (accessed September 13, 2006).

5. From a United Nations press release online at http://www.un.org/Dialogue/background.html (accessed July 25, 2007).

6. "Van Gogh Killer Jailed for Life," BBC News, July 26, 2005, http://news.bbc.co.uk/2/hi/europe/4716909.stm (accessed July 26, 2005).

7. Bruce Bower, *While Europe Slept: How Radical Islam Is Destroying the West from Within* (New York: Doubleday, 2006), p. 205. The following section draws heavily on Bower's research.

8. Ibid., p. 5.

9. Ibid., p. 195.

10. Ibid., p. 196.

11. Ibid., p. 201.

12. Rowan Atkinson, "Religion as a Fit Subject for Comedy," *Times of London*, October 17, 2001.

13. Bower, *While Europe Slept*, p. 197.

14. Ibid., p. 215.

15. Ibid., p. 204.

16. Ibid., p. 212.

17. From a speech by Mohammad Khatami at the UN-sponsored Conference of Dialogue among Civilizations in New York, September 5, 2000. Translated by the US Federal Broadcasting Information Service (FBIS), as reported in the *Iranian*, September 8, 2000, http://www.iranian.com/Opinion/2000/September/Khatami/ (accessed July 25, 2007).

18. English translation published by *Le Monde*. See "La lettre de Mahmoud Ahmadinejad à George W. Bush," http://www.lemonde.fr/web/article/0,1-0@2-727571,36-769886@51-677013@45-1,0.html (accessed July 25, 2007).

19. The statistics come from the RAND Corporation. See Kim Cragin and Andrew Curiel, "Prime Numbers: 9/11 + 5," *Foreign Policy* (September/October 2006): 34–35.

20. Some summit delegates, including Irshad Manji, Mona Abousenna, and Mourad Wahba, declined to endorse the declaration.

21. Writing in the *New Republic*. Quoted in Christina Hoff Sommers, "The Subjection of Islamic Women and the Fecklessness of American Feminism," *Weekly Standard* 12, no. 34 (May 21, 2007).

22. Sommers, "The Subjection of Muslim Women."

23. Natasha Walter, "Religion and Righteousness," review of *The Caged Virgin* by Ayaan Hirsi Ali and *Murder in Amsterdam* by Ian Buruma, *Guardian Unlimited*, December 2, 2006, http://books.guardian.co.uk/review/story/0,,1961714,00.html (accessed July 25, 2007).

24. See Paul Berman, *Terror and Liberalism* (New York: W. W. Norton, 2003) and Peter Beinart, *The Good Fight: Why Liberals and Only Liberals Can Win the War on Terror and Make America Great Again* (New York: HarperCollins, 2006).

25. Christopher Hitchens has been relentless in trying to awaken his fellow secularists to a "very deep and frightening cultural crisis":

> We are in fact menaced, in my opinion, by all forms of monotheism, but at this present moment, almost certainly most by the ideology, the theory, and the practice of Islamic jihad. By which I mean, the attempt by Muslim fundamentalists to impose Islamic law first on the Muslim world, and then on the rest of the world. And to spread this idea by terrifying force and violence. . . . I have noticed, to my great depression and despair, that many of those who are willing to recognize their enemy, and indeed to combat it, are themselves

people of faith. Whereas those who are people of reason and secularism are tepid, if not worse, about the necessity to fight and to win this war. And as long as this fatal ambiguity persists, as long as the best lack all conviction, you can count on the worst being full of passionate intensity. And I tremble to think what the outcome of that will be.

From remarks to the Institute for the Study of Secularism in Society and Culture, Trinity College, Hartford, Connecticut, on November 2, 2005. Published in "The View from the Beltway," *Religion in the News* 8, no. 3 (Winter 2006), http://www.trincoll.edu/depts/csrpl/RINVol8no3/secularism%20 insert/View%20FromThe%20Beltway.htm (accessed July 25, 2007).

26. "Opening Up Islam," *New York Post*, February 18, 2006, http:// www.benadorassociates.com/article/19336 (accessed July 25, 2007).

27. Ibn Warraq, personal communication.

28. This section is adapted from Austin Dacey, "Reading Madison in Tehran," *Free Inquiry* 25, no. 4 (June/July 2005): 26–27.

29. Soroush Danesh, "A Secular Student in Tehran," *Free Inquiry* 25, no. 4 (June/July 2005): 35.

30. Transcript by Iran Press Service, http://www.iran-press-service .com/ips/articles-2006/june2006/ganji_awarded_6606.shtml (accessed July 25, 2007).

11. THE FUTURE IS OPENNESS

1. Geoff Mulgan, Tom Steinberg, and Omar Salem, *Wide Open: Open Source Methods and Their Future Potential* (London: Demos, 2005), p. 7.

2. Ibid., pp. 17–22.

3. Actually, it was not that easy to look through Galileo's telescope. At the time he invited colleagues to use the telescope to corroborate his own observations, it was a new instrument that brought with it a set of unfamiliar techniques that had to be learned. Before the instrument could be accepted by all as a source of incontrovertible observational evidence, Galileo had to spent considerable time explaining and justifying the optics of the device (which he had invented) and accounting for various visual distortions that the

novice users were experiencing. See Thomas Kuhn, *The Copernican Revolution* (Cambridge, MA: Harvard University Press, 1957). Still, the democratic lesson is there, with the addendum that the citizens of the republic of science must be informed enough to be competent. But there is nothing barring anyone in particular from becoming informed and competent.

4. John Dewey, *The Moral Writings of John Dewey*, ed. James Gouinlock (Amherst, NY: Prometheus Books, 1994), p. 256; reprinted from *The Problems of Men* (New York: Philosophical Library, 1946).

5. Ibid., p. 256.

6. Joel Mokyr, *The Gifts of Athena: Historical Origins of the Knowledge Economy* (Princeton, NJ: Princeton University Press, 2002).

7. Doron S. Ben-Atar, *Trade Secrets: Intellectual Piracy and the Origins of American Industrial Power* (New Haven, CT: Yale University Press, 2004).

8. David A. Shaywitz and Dennis A. Ausiello, "The 15% Solution for Majority Health Concerns," *Nature* 415 (February 7, 2002): 575.

9. J. S. Mill, *On Liberty*, in *On Liberty and Other Writings*, ed. Stefan Collini (Cambridge: Cambridge University Press, 1992), p. 21.

10. J. S. Mill, *On Liberty and Other Writings*, ed. Stefan Collini (Cambridge: Cambridge University Press, 1989), p. 54.

11. Ibid., p. 24.

12. *Collected Works of John Stuart Mill*, vol. 8, John M. Robson, general editor (London: Routledge, 1963–91), p. 833.

Index